"Startups are one of the most important forces for change. But far too many regions have fixated on the Silicon Valley model as the only way to build a startup ecosystem. *Out-Innovate* takes you on a tour of innovative entrepreneurs and companies around the globe, to provide a guidebook on how to successfully start and scale world-changing businesses wherever you might be."

—**CHRIS YEH**, coauthor, *Blitzscaling* and *The Alliance*

"*Out-Innovate* is replete with inspiring and instructive stories of innovation from around the world. Whether in middle America or middle Africa, it's a go-to book for anyone with an idea for starting and scaling a business."

—**DIANA FARRELL**, president and CEO, JPMorgan Chase Institute

"In *Out-Innovate*, Alex Lazarow has perfectly captured Silicon Valley's 'Detroit Moment'—the realization that Asia and other emerging markets aren't simply generating local clones of American startups, but raising the bar for innovation and product quality on a global basis. Brilliant."

—**NICK NASH**, co-founder and managing partner, Asia Partners; retired Group President, Sea Limited

"Silicon Valley is a source of inspiration for many tech entrepreneurs around the world, but innovation coming from emerging countries, Africa, and other locales beyond the Valley is now raising the game. In his captivating book, Alex Lazarow vividly describes this changing context and the strategies required to succeed within it."

—**SACHA POIGNONNEC**, co-founder and co-CEO, Jumia

"The wide world of innovation does not always look and act like Silicon Valley. In fact, among rising markets in particular, there is a shared experience entrepreneurs and investors navigate—regardless of history, culture, language, or geography—where the Silicon Valley model is only part of the story. This important book articulates rich new models for local and global entrepreneurs looking to engage on those markets' terms. This book could not be more timely."

—**CHRISTOPHER M. SCHROEDER**, co-founder, Next Billion Ventures; advisor and venture investor; and author, *Startup Rising*

"We need to move beyond the Silicon Valley 'playbook' for startup innovation. In this trenchant work, Alex Lazarow shows that there are new principles and practices that apply in quickly changing conditions of scarcity and adversity. In other words, wherever you are."

—**VIJAY SHEKHAR SHARMA**, founder and CEO, Paytm

"Lazarow's book will not only inspire you with its global stories of innovation, it will give you real models to follow. Wherever you are, if you have an entrepreneurial idea, you need to read *Out-Innovate*."

—**MUDASSIR SHEIKHA**, co-founder and CEO, Careem

"If disruption is about moving fast and breaking things, Lazarow zooms us out of the Valley, beyond borders and buzzwords. *Out-Innovate* is the new global playbook for how to observe different and create different."

—**SCOTT HORTLEY**, author, *The Fuzzy and the Techie*

"Alex Lazarow draws on his vast global experience to shed light on the models and practices of startups all over the world. In doing so, he articulates one of the great promises of today's high-tech world: that access to innovation is no longer the exclusive right of a select few locations. Anyone, anywhere, who is interested in innovation will benefit from reading this book."

—**YOSSI VARDI**, one of Israel's early entrepreneurs

Out-Innovate

Out-Innovate

How Global Entrepreneurs from Delhi to Detroit Are Rewriting the Rules of Silicon Valley

Inno-vate

ALEXANDRE LAZAROW

HARVARD BUSINESS REVIEW PRESS • BOSTON, MA

The web addresses referenced in this book were live and correct at the time of the book's publication but may be subject to change.

Library of Congress Cataloging-in-Publication Data

Names: Lazarow, Alexandre, author.
Title: Out-innovate : how global entrepreneurs—from Delhi to Detroit—are rewriting
   the rules of Silicon Valley / Alexandre Lazarow.
Description: Boston, MA : Harvard Business Review Press, [2020] | Includes index. |
Identifiers: LCCN 2019046745 | ISBN 9781633697584 (hardcover) | ISBN
   9781633697591 (ebook)
Subjects: LCSH: New business enterprises. | Entrepreneurship. | Success in business. |
   Globalization—Economic aspects. | Creative ability in business.
Classification: LCC HD62.5 .L39 2020 | DDC 658.1/1—dc23
LC record available at https://lccn.loc.gov/2019046745

ISBN:978-1-63369-758-4
eISBN: 978-1-63369-759-1

The paper used in this publication meets the requirements of the American National Standard for Permanence of Paper for Publications and Documents in Libraries and Archives Z39.48-1992.

To the men and women in the arena

It is not the critic who counts; not the man who points out how the strong man stumbles, or where the doer of deeds could have done them better. The credit belongs to the man who is actually in the arena, whose face is marred by dust and sweat and blood; who strives valiantly; who errs, who comes short again and again, because there is no effort without error and shortcoming; but who does actually strive to do the deeds; who knows great enthusiasms, the great devotions; who spends himself in a worthy cause; who at the best knows in the end the triumph of high achievement, and who at the worst, if he fails, at least fails while daring greatly, so that his place shall never be with those cold and timid souls who neither know victory nor defeat.

—THEODORE ROOSEVELT

We need to out-innovate, out-educate, and out-build the rest of the world.

—BARACK OBAMA

Contents

Introduction

Beyond Silicon Valley

Xavier Helgesen was troubled. He had just returned to his home base of
Arusha, Tanzania, after weeks spent pitching Zola, his startup, to Silicon
Valley investors. It was 2014, two years into the journey, and Zola already
had thousands of paying customers and a large potential market. But
Xavier had secured only a fraction of the capital that a pedestrian San
Francisco startup might expect to raise in months.

Xavier had co-founded Zola with Erica Mackey and Joshua Pierce to
tackle a seemingly intractable problem: eight hundred million people in
Africa live "offgrid" and are vulnerable to systematic disadvantages resulting from a lack of electricity.[1] These hardships include respiratory
health problems from kerosene smoke inhalation, lower educational at-
tainment due to limited light sources, and the inability to plug in mobile
phones and thereby access the opportunities of the digital world.

Xavier was raising funds for a $7 million Series A round of financ-
ing, one of the first large rounds in the burgeoning market for offgrid
energy in developing countries. The check he needed was well beyond
what could be raised locally in Tanzania—or, for that matter, across the
African continent—and so Xavier had looked to Silicon Valley.

But he had received mixed feedback. "You're building a technology startup—why do you have so much overhead? A training academy for the sales force, *and* an in-house payments platform? Can't you be leaner?" "The Tanzanian shilling was devalued precipitously last year. What is your hedging strategy?" "You're raising a Series A now. Who could lead your Series B, and what stock market do you think you'll eventually list on?"

On their face, these questions are not necessarily misguided. But they are deeply rooted in a set of beliefs unique to Silicon Valley and its conception of how to build a startup. Unsurprisingly, these beliefs do not always translate well to the Tanzanian marketplace.

As Xavier patiently explained to his potential investors, it's hard to be lean when you need to provide basic business training to your new recruits or manage collections in a predominantly cash-based economy. The Tanzanian shilling, unlike the US dollar, fluctuates wildly, and hedging is prohibitively expensive. Budgeting for capital commitments and enjoying the necessary certainty of business forecasts are both distant dreams for local startups. And all this is complicated by the limited availability of follow-on funders and a lack of viable exit options in Tanzania.

Many of the investors could not get behind the notion that a company could break the Silicon Valley paradigm so extensively and still succeed. They turned their backs on Xavier.

Instead of telling him how things should be, those potential investors should have listened to how things are.

I first met Xavier in 2014. At that time, I had recently moved to San Francisco and joined a venture capital firm. I had one foot firmly planted in Silicon Valley, and the other investing thousands of miles away—in Asia, Africa, Europe, and Latin America.

The world of technology and emerging markets was not new to me. My maternal grandfather was a computer engineer, in the most literal sense. He replaced vacuum tubes for IBM's early supercomputers and later helped set up one of IBM's early offices in Africa. His stories of attempting to install computers in the steamy Congo are family legend. My own journey to the innovation industry was less technical, and perhaps less exotic. I have spent the majority of my career—be it as an investor, a regulator, a consultant, or an investment banker—advising CEOs and entrepreneurs around the world and teaching future entrepreneurs in my MBA classes.

Xavier's paradox resonated with me. For my own investing, I was trying to make sense of similar questions about innovation in emerging ecosystems. My venture firm took the plunge and invested in Zola, and I accompanied Xavier and his colleagues on an eye-opening journey through the unique challenges and opportunities of scaling a business outside Silicon Valley.

"Startups Can Change the World!"

This mantra has become a global rallying cry, preached with religious fervor.

The optimism is not unfounded. In the United States, startups—companies founded by entrepreneurs and often supported by venture capital—include household names like Apple, Amazon, Facebook, and Genentech. Indeed, more than 40 percent of publicly traded US companies listed after 1979 were once startups.[2]

Entrepreneurship is a driving force for employment. In the United States, entrepreneurship is responsible for all net new jobs created in the past decade, and in all but seven years since 1977.[3]

Startups are also a key driver of national innovation, including everything from the creation of the iPhone to the commercialization of drones and driverless cars. Studies have demonstrated that one dollar invested in startups funds three to four times the amount of innovation as a similar dollar in corporate research and development.[4]

The economic value of startups has doubled as a percentage of global gross domestic product (GDP) since 1992 and is projected to double again in the next fifteen years. It is no wonder that our time is referred to as the "age of innovation."[5]

If we are in the age of innovation, then its economic, philosophical, and spiritual center is Silicon Valley.

Certainly, Silicon Valley's track record is undeniable. If Silicon Valley were a country, its $750 billion GDP would be in the top twenty globally, larger than the GDP of Switzerland, Argentina, or Taiwan.[6] Three of the world's five largest companies, all of which were once startups—Alphabet (Google), Apple, and Facebook—call the San Francisco Bay Area home. There are about forty thousand startups, nearly a thousand venture capital firms, and more than 320,000 people in the technology industry in the Bay Area.[7] Silicon Valley even has its own ambassadors.[8]

Silicon Valley used to have a monopoly on innovation. Only twenty-five years ago, 95 percent of the world's venture activity occurred in the United States, the vast majority concentrated in the two hundred square miles spanning San Francisco and San Jose.[9]

No longer.

Advances in technology mean innovation can now take root everywhere. Cloud computing has brought down the cost of starting companies, allowing anyone to rent Google's enormous computing power by the hour rather than having to purchase and maintain dedicated servers. The plunging cost of telecommunications infrastructure, combined with the advent of collaboration software, has given rise to frictionless remote work. Global markets themselves are looking more attractive for startups. The proliferation of mobile phones provides a way to reach more than five billion users worldwide.[10] More than two billion people have online identities and interconnect and establish digital footprints through social media.[11] These trends have had a tremendous global impact and will only continue to evolve.

The historical near-absolute US monopoly on venture investing has fallen to less than half the global share.[12] Over the past few decades, a number of more-developed, major economic centers have made up the remainder. Cities like London, Berlin, Tallinn, and Tel Aviv are becoming global startup powerhouses.

China in particular has propelled itself to the forefront of the global innovation landscape, with more than one hundred thousand startups (more than double those in Silicon Valley) and more than nine thousand venture capital firms (ten times the number in Silicon Valley) concentrated in Shenzhen, Beijing, and Shanghai.[13] China is now home to 35 percent of the world's *unicorns* (a universally used colloquial reference to companies valued at more than $1 billion), up from a mere 4 percent in 2014.[14]

The most exciting story, however, is what's happening in the rest of the world, outside these economic powerhouses. Innovators are increasingly taking root everywhere. There are currently more than 1.3 million technology startups globally.[15] Startup ecosystems are popping up all over the world to support them, with more than 480 hubs worldwide, from Detroit to Bangalore to Puerto Rico to Nairobi to São Paulo.[16] In emerging ecosystems, the incidence of entrepreneurship is double that of the developed world.[17]

Already about 10 percent of all unicorns are located outside Silicon Valley, and outside the traditional major developed economic centers in Europe and Asia.[18] International entrepreneurs are quickly eclipsing their Silicon Valley counterparts. Uber has 75 million users worldwide, and China's DiDi has 550 million users, but emerging market leaders like Grab, Gojek, 99, and Cabify are not far behind across Latin America and Southeast Asia, with 36, 25, 14, and 13 million users, respectively.[19] Similarly, PayPal, founded in 1998, has 267 million users, while Paytm, founded over ten years later in India, boasts 300 million users.[20]

However, despite the globalization of technology, our knowledge of the way startups are built remains stagnant and myopic, centered in a specific time and place and a particular type of company: the Silicon Valley software business.

Questioning the Silicon Valley Gospel

Silicon Valley has codified what a startup should look like, dictated how it should be built, and defined what its culture should be. Via a panoply of channels, including books, blogs, podcasts, graduation speeches, tweets, and Reddit recommendations, the Valley has successfully spread its vision around the world.

Although Silicon Valley entrepreneurs did not intentionally or collaboratively craft a theory of success, their opinions did eventually morph into a cohesive philosophy on how to build a startup. The gospel according to Silicon Valley covers everything from a startup's raison d'être (to "disrupt" existing industries with new technology, more-efficient processes, and a fresh attitude), to the yardsticks of success (to grow as rapidly as possible, with the hope of becoming a unicorn), to an entrepreneur's comfort with risk (to "move fast and break things" in hopes of scaling rapidly).

Silicon Valley's rule book has been the only proven paradigm we have had to work with so far. What has risen in the Valley is considered the authority on innovation best practices everywhere.

As a result, the global innovation community is inextricably tied to Silicon Valley's principles for building a startup. Would-be innovators from around the world look to the Valley for guidance on how to drive their own innovations. Politicians regularly make pilgrimages to meet San Francisco's leading players and thought leaders, hoping to glean their secrets. Corporations the world over install innovation outposts in San Francisco. Venture capitalists from international ecosystems pursue executive education from Stanford or local fellowships. And universally, they voraciously read what the leading luminaries are sharing.

In many ways, the Silicon Valley phenomenon is reminiscent of the global economic development complex and the Washington Consensus, an economic model exported from America in the 1960s for the development and democratization of countries all over the world. The Washington Consensus was the best system we had, and America sought to transplant it, sometimes for self-serving purposes but also because many well-meaning people in the West honestly believed that the unique US cocktail of liberal democracy and capitalism would solve the world's problems. Yet, as the past century has taught us, America's model cannot simply be exported, and various other systems work in their own local contexts— from Scandinavia's democratic socialism to China's communism.

In a similar way, Silicon Valley has exported its model globally—and, like the Washington Consensus, it doesn't work everywhere. In markets where there is a venture capital shortage, macroeconomic uncertainty, a lower tolerance for risk, less acceptance of entrepreneurship as a career, or limited enabling infrastructure, how could it?

The Silicon Valley model is also starting to show cracks at home. The year 2017 was ignominiously referred to as the "year the world turned on Silicon Valley," as people reacted to the high cost of living, questionable ethical practices at startups like Uber, the impact on neighborhoods by platforms like Airbnb, the revelations of pervasive discrimination and harassment, and the growing frustration with social media platforms and their controversial roles in the 2016 US elections.[21] Since then, these trends have only accelerated. There is a mounting backlash against the industry, and a growing demand to reexamine the status quo.[22]

Furthermore, Silicon Valley is no longer generating the innovation we're looking for. As Peter Thiel, investor and entrepreneur, once quipped, "We wanted flying cars, [but] instead we got 140 characters."[23] Many argue that even though Silicon Valley continues to deliver technological advancement and richly valued companies, recent innovation has been incremental rather than world changing. Major news outlets accuse Silicon Valley of catering to "tech bros" who are building products and services to match their own lifestyles, often providing basic services they are unaccustomed or unequipped to provide for themselves. On-demand laundry, food, or home cleaning, anyone?[24]

Lessons from Detroit

Silicon Valley may be about to have a Detroit moment. In the 1950s, the technology of the day was automobiles, not computers. At the time, Detroit was on top of the world. The top three global car companies were headquartered there. The world's leading entrepreneurs flocked there for access to talent, capital, and culture. Detroit was leading the way in automotive technology, which promised to reinvent the ways we built our cities, organized our society, and lived our lives. Every engineer dreamed of moving there. It was also where the majority of car startups emerged. At its peak, there were more than a hundred emerging car companies in Detroit, and many more innovators were building companies to serve the burgeoning industry.[25] Famously, Charles Wilson, secretary of defense to President Eisenhower, told a House committee, "What is good for General Motors is good for the country."[26]

But now Detroit is a shadow of its former self. General Motors, the largest of the Detroit-based car manufacturers, is no longer in the top three globally. The leaders are Japanese (Toyota), German (Volkswagen), and Korean (Hyundai). Even among General Motors' nearly two hundred thousand cars and trucks produced, only 40 percent are built in the United States.[27]

What happened?

Innovation started to take root all over the world. Car companies emerged in France, Italy, Germany, Poland, Sweden, and Japan. Over time, certain regions specialized, and others surpassed Detroit. Italy became the home of the best and fastest sports cars, and Germany the home of raw engineering. The playbook on car making was also rewritten abroad. Toyota, for instance, pioneered the transformative approach of "just in time" manufacturing.

If it fails to look beyond its insular bubble, the same thing may happen to Silicon Valley. These days, it is more expensive to rent a U-Haul to drive out of the San Francisco Bay Area than to drive it in.[28] Many people are fleeing to more-affordable centers of innovation.

The world of innovation needs a refresh. And that refresh is already well under way at what I call the *Frontier*, which collectively refers to innovation centers located outside Silicon Valley and its closest counterparts. At the Frontier, operating in tough, underresourced, and often underregulated environments, these outside-the-Valley entrepreneurs are out-innovating their Silicon Valley counterparts. To succeed, they are making their own rules and charting their own paths. Along the way, they are challenging us to rethink what the model for innovation should be, both globally and in Silicon Valley. Born at the Frontier, outside Silicon Valley, they are developing a framework for the next generation of innovation, along with the economic and social transformation that the world is looking for.

So what exactly is the Frontier, and who are its innovators?

Frontier Innovators: The Heroes of Our Tale

By "Frontier," I mean the nascent urban and rural startup ecosystems in developed countries like the United States and Europe as well as in emerging markets.[29]

These latter areas present an entirely different context from Silicon Valley and other economic powerhouses, and obviously are themselves heterogeneous. Many parts of the Frontier are in developing countries. Innovators at the Frontier must deal with unique constraints that range from the potential for political or macroeconomic instability and dysfunctional or nonexistent infrastructure or government services, to customers that simply cannot afford, or are too risk averse, to purchase newfangled products. Even Frontier regions in developed countries often lack indispensable resources such as angel investors, incubators, venture capitalists, an experienced employee pool, cultural support for risk and failure, interested acquirers, and public markets.

In other words, the world cannot simply be divided into categories of "Silicon Valley" and "Not Silicon Valley." The reality is that the Frontier is much more nuanced. For simplicity, I focus on two particular dimensions.

The first is economic—factors unrelated to the startup ecosystem that reflect the general level and stability of the environment. Is the currency stable? Does the government provide stability? Are there high corruption rates? How high is GDP per capita? The effect of each factor may differ but collectively will impact the level of the ecosystem's development. Ultimately, low ecosystem development makes the operating environment that much more challenging.

The second dimension is the strength of the local startup ecosystem. Is there sufficient capital available? Is there experienced technical talent (e.g., software engineers) or digital talent (e.g., online marketing

FIGURE I-1

The many faces of the Frontier

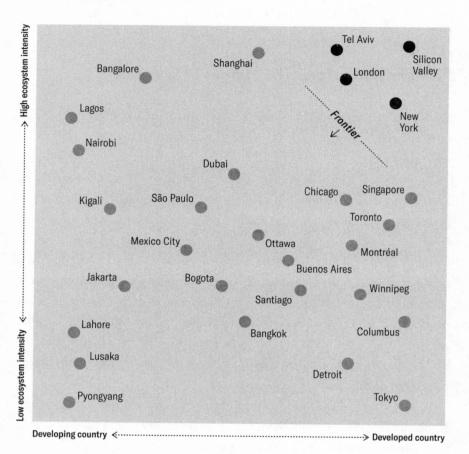

Note: Location placements are approximate and indicative only.

executives) present? Do corporate laws support startups (e.g., is bankruptcy legal)?[30] I refer to this dimension as *ecosystem intensity*; the higher the intensity, the stronger the local ecosystem.

By mapping these two dimensions, a simple heuristic model emerges, as shown in figure I-1. Markets that look like Silicon Valley tend to cluster in the upper-right, with both macroeconomic stability and ecosystem intensity. While Silicon Valley is not alone in the upper-right—places like Tel Aviv, New York, and London sit nearby as well—these ecosystems are the exception rather than the rule.[31]

This book covers geographies as expansive as the Frontier itself. You will meet innovators in Chicago, Dubai, Jakarta, Mexico City, Mumbai, Nairobi, São Paolo, Winnipeg, and even North Korea. Each of these locations has both its own unique political, economic, and social contexts and its own distinct ecosystem intensity. Still, entrepreneurs operating at the Frontier have much more in common with each other than they do with their counterparts in Silicon Valley.

To juxtapose extreme differences between Silicon Valley and the Frontier, you will visit some of the toughest ecosystems in the lower-left quadrant, where you will observe acute challenges. In addition, to explore particular nuances of the Frontier, you will visit ecosystems in the other two quadrants, having either stronger macroeconomic contexts or relatively higher ecosystem intensities (or both).

Our characters are the innovators—admittedly, also a nebulous term. Some studies loftily suggest there are more than 400 million entrepreneurs worldwide, or about 6 percent of the population of every woman, man, and child on the planet.[32] You will zoom in on a key subset of the 400 million.

For the purposes of this book, *Frontier Innovators* embody three specific qualities:

1. They are entrepreneurs of opportunity. In many markets, people become entrepreneurs as a last resort. These are the *entrepreneurs of necessity*—the roadside fruit vendors, beachside masseuses, and street hawkers. In Silicon Valley, news outlets optimistically claim that half of millennials start new businesses. Yet these numbers are misleading; many of them are 1099 contract workers in the gig economy, such as Uber drivers and on-demand delivery providers. Their efforts are significant and their challenges serious, but their situation is outside the scope

of my focus. I define *entrepreneurs of opportunity* as those who identify a market failure and proactively choose to leave gainful employment to solve it.

2. Frontier Innovators leverage some sort of innovation. To be clear, this book is not only about using software. I focus on leveraging any combination of business model and technological innovation that underpins the opportunity-capturing approach of these entrepreneurs.

3. I focus on entrepreneurs who aspire to scale their businesses. There are millions of entrepreneurs of opportunity who start a business voluntarily and innovate on the model, thereby meeting the first and second criteria, but do not have scale in mind. Picture an individual who starts a single-location restaurant with a modern design and menu, or a hair salon with unique style options. Of course, this phenomenon also exists in technology companies. An analysis of more than six hundred entrepreneurial software companies in Nairobi determined that more than half, which on the surface might appear as startups, were in fact "low-productivity microbusinesses" (e.g., small technology consulting services).[33]

When I started this book, my natural conception of innovators was of traditional entrepreneurs, laboring in small teams, building their own companies. In my exploration, I discovered a range of unconventional Frontier Innovators, including venture capitalists starting new investment models, ecosystem developers building startups to serve their geographies, and "intrapreneurs" who operate within family businesses or large corporations but leverage similar methodologies. Many of them were challenging Silicon Valley's rule book in related ways. This book explores their work as well.

Using this lens, I define Frontier Innovators as *entrepreneurs of opportunity who operate outside the most-developed startup ecosystems, leverage technological or business model innovation, and seek to scale their businesses.*

Ultimately, as you will see, Frontier Innovators' mindsets, principles, and practices represent a striking departure from and an alternative to the Silicon Valley gospel.

A New Model for Innovation at the Frontier

Frontier Innovators are writing their own innovation playbook. Their methods, while derived from practical necessity, are not only reinventing the rules but also redefining what it means to innovate. This book explores ten elements of this new model for innovation.

First, Frontier Innovators are *Creators*. Silicon Valley is focused on disrupting established industries, but at the Frontier, innovators must create new industries because often there are no established industries to disrupt. They must build entirely new sectors that offer customers a range of products and services that Silicon Valley takes for granted, such as education, health care, financial services, energy, and even infrastructure.

Silicon Valley's obsession with asset-light, highly focused startups is not practical when enabling infrastructure does not exist, as is often the case when industries are being created. Frontier Innovators must often build the "full stack"—including the enabling infrastructure that their businesses and products require.

Where Silicon Valley strives to breed unicorns, the Frontier raises *Camels*—organizations that can capitalize on opportunity but also can survive in a drought. Frontier Innovators do not focus on growth at any cost; they focus on sustainability and resilience.

Frontier Innovators also cross-pollinate. They leverage diverse lived experiences, often across multiple geographies, industries, and sectors, to build their businesses. They tap global networks for capital and resources.

Silicon Valley may teach its startups to be based in the Bay Area, build their teams there, and focus on the $18 trillion US domestic market, but Frontier startups have no such obvious path. In fact, many are born global; they strategically target multiple global markets from day one.

Frontier Innovators don't just sell to the world. They also build the fabric and machine of the organization in a distributed way. They recruit the best talent, regardless of where they are from, and foster an integrated culture through technology and organizational design.

With Silicon Valley's rich talent pool, entrepreneurs have the luxury of recruiting A-players as needed. Companies tolerate high turnover because employees are replaceable from Silicon Valley's sea of talent. At the Frontier, innovators build A-teams with a growth mindset toward employees and a long-term outlook.

Frontier Innovators are also Multi-Mission Athletes who interweave both profit and impact-based goals into the core fabric of their business models.

Silicon Valley's blasé approach to risk—of moving fast and breaking things—is not tolerable when acceptance of risk is lower and the consequences of failure are higher.[34] Frontier Innovators manage risk, build customer trust, and formalize their industries.

Venture capital and technology startups exist in a symbiotic relationship; neither can survive without the other. Yet, while the venture capital model serves Silicon Valley's unicorns, it is not adapted to the rest of the world's capital needs. Venture capitalists at the Frontier are themselves innovators in their own right, because they are adapting the model for challenging environments.

Silicon Valley has a rich mosaic of support systems: corporations with innovation departments, venture capitalists who offer support teams, accelerators who specialize in myriad topics, and even regulators who are increasingly looking to engage with innovators. Frontier Innovators often feel isolated by comparison. By necessity, Frontier Innovators don't just scale their startups; they take an active role in building their ecosystems by laying the cornerstones of entrepreneurial culture, creating a community of mentors and supporters, and building the requisite infrastructure for the ecosystem.

Of course, Frontier Innovators are not alone in building their ecosystems. Governments, regulators, investors, large corporations, charities, foundations, and other interested parties can have a disproportionate impact on Frontier ecosystems—not by copying Silicon Valley but by leveraging the lessons from the Frontier.

Each chapter of this book explores one of these thematic lessons. The book is rooted in the lived realities of Frontier Innovators and shares practical advice for all participants in the ecosystem. Chapters also draw on my own data, more than two hundred interviews, industry publications, and, where it exists, leading academic research in the field.

Who This Book Is for and Why It Is Crucial

This book seeks to answer four basic questions: What unique strategies do Frontier Innovators employ to successfully develop their innovations? How can these strategies be replicated by others at the Frontier? What can Silicon Valley learn from these emerging approaches? How should we use these lessons to promote vibrant and successful innovation ecosystems around the world?

Out-Innovate is relevant to a number of key audiences. The first are Frontier Innovators themselves. Silicon Valley has been the sole fount of innovation wisdom for too long. My hope is that this book will start a conversation about what it means to innovate in the rest of the world. Of course, these lessons are equally important for Silicon Valley, if it hopes to stay on top. The Valley must begin to challenge its own conventional wisdom and accepted philosophies and learn from the hard-fought lessons at the Frontier.

This book is also designed to be interesting and accessible for people in the public and social sectors. Supporting entrepreneurs and their innovation ecosystems is increasingly at the top of national agendas worldwide. Policy makers are looking to entrepreneurship for job creation. Nonprofits are looking to innovation to promote and foster social, environmental, and economic change. The lessons in *Out-Innovate* should prove instructive for these players.

At the same time, leaders of large, global, publicly traded companies, ranging from Boeing and Bank of America to General Electric and

General Motors, know their industries are evolving rapidly and want to update their business models. Through innovation departments, corporate acquisition strategies, and investment firms, they are more proximate to innovation than ever. Global corporations must adopt a global view on how innovation works, where, and why. *Out-Innovate* may be a good starting place.

At the other end of the spectrum, the social enterprise movement continues to gain momentum. One study estimated that more than 3 percent of the world's population is involved in social ventures (it is nearly double in the United States, at 5.8 percent), and 90 percent of these organizations were created in the past decade.[35] Startup approaches are foundational as social enterprises look to the next phase of their evolutions.

Excitingly, the first wave of entrepreneurial activity in many Frontier ecosystems is only beginning to crest. The ranks of innovators across the globe increase daily. In the United States alone, by some counts more than half a million people become entrepreneurs every month. Most are not building Silicon Valley–style software startups.[36]

Uncritically following Silicon Valley's principles and applying them to different local contexts is a recipe for failure. Learning the lessons of successful Frontier Innovators is crucial for new entrepreneurs, technology workers, and students looking to join their ranks.

When I ask my friends which current Silicon Valley entrepreneurs they see as a positive force on humanity, they often mention Elon Musk. But when I ask for a few more names, they struggle. At the Frontier, I can point to dozens of Elons. They are building various types of companies, in various ways, and they are driving world-changing innovation. This book shares their stories and hopefully will inspire my friends in Silicon Valley to learn from their practices.

William Gibson once said, "The future is already here, it's just not evenly distributed." In this case, Frontier Innovators across the world are leading the charge and providing a glimpse of the future of innovation and entrepreneurship worldwide and, per Gibson, a future that is more evenly distributed. And maybe their lessons hold the key for innovation and startups to change the world after all.

1.

Create

Create Rather Than Disrupt

Beads of sweat ran down Timbo Drayson's forehead, stinging his eyes. It was his fourth consecutive day spent in the hot Nairobi sun, methodically taking photos, tying them to GPS coordinates, and building an early testable dataset. Timbo, CEO of a startup called OkHi, was gathering data to create uniquely identifiable locations—what the rest of the world calls street addresses—for downtown Nairobi. To that end, he was gathering coordinates, visual cues, and other familiar markers that Nairobi residents use when giving directions.

In developed Western countries, street addresses are provided by governments and are considered table stakes for a variety of public and private services.

Registering for a driver's license? *What's your address?*

Want your Amazon package? *What's your address?*

Need an ambulance? *What's your address?*

So when I first met Timbo in 2014, I was shocked to find out that more than half the world does not have street addresses. In Kenya, where Timbo is based, only 2 percent of all buildings have them.[1]

A city without street addresses doesn't mean a city without directions. It just means that current systems are highly inefficient. In Nairobi, if you're getting a delivery, you might say, "When you get to Jogoo and First Avenue, please turn left at the red house. You go down the road to the green shanty, up the road where the three dogs sleep, and down the dirt path for thirty seconds. I'm the fourth house on the right. It is blue."

This seems difficult in the daytime. It is often impossible at night.

More than half the world lives in slums, favelas, shantytowns, or other areas with tenuous property rights and where the government has yet to designate official street names or numbers for residents. Globally, some four billion people don't have addresses, a figure expected to double by 2050.[2]

Addresses are a massive public good that powers an array of services. Consider that the average ambulance response time in Nairobi is more than two hours, versus six minutes and ten seconds in New York.[3] A large part of this problem is improper location and addressing, causing ambulances to circulate for critical minutes to find an exact location. Similarly, a lack of addresses stalls commerce. It takes 3.1 phone calls for a KFC delivery, and 1.4 phone calls per ride for an Uber pickup.[4]

To solve this problem, Timbo founded OkHi, a technology-driven startup that creates addresses where there are none. OkHi's mission statement is "Be Included."[5]

Timbo no longer collects the needed information manually in the hot sun. Instead, OkHi's crowdsourced digital addresses—a unique combination of a GPS point, a location's photo, and additional descriptors—are ever-evolving and growing. OkHi lets its partners access the database for a small fee. When partners look up an address, they are given turn-by-turn directions to the GPS point and oriented to the proper building based on the qualitative descriptors and the pictures.

Since its early days, OkHi has made groundbreaking progress. By partnering with the ubiquitous Uber and Jumia (a leading e-commerce player), OkHi acquired the GPS coordinates necessary for building an extensive database. Since then, Timbo has partnered with players ranging from restaurant chains to appliance retailers to public services.[6]

What Does a Startup Look Like?

To most, OkHi's story does not seem like a typical startup. When people think of addresses, they might think of boring government infrastructure or twee street names, if they think about the subject at all. Where is the hooded techie, slurping Soylent, writing code into the night and disrupting an industry?[7]

This last phrase deserves a moment of pause. Most Silicon Valley startups are focused on *disruption*, a word that has taken on near-mythical qualities. It refers to a startup's raison d'être: upending stodgy and inefficient industries by adopting new technologies, new processes, and new attitudes. The mandate to disrupt has become a clarion call to the technology industry, and in particular to Silicon Valley. Everyone is disrupting everything in Silicon Valley, from health care to driverless cars to education, and even to politics.[8] The most famous pitch competition in Silicon Valley is TechCrunch Disrupt, the Olympics of the startup community. And disruption isn't only for entrepreneurs. There are disruptors in venture capital, angel investing, and accelerators.[9]

A scene from the HBO satire *Silicon Valley* perhaps best reveals the absurdity of the industry's fixation on the concept. In an early episode of the first season, Pied Piper, the hero's fledgling startup, is pitching at TechCrunch Disrupt. His competitors are a set of startups, including Immeadabug, set to "revolutionize the way you report bugs on your mobile platform"; Tappen, which will "revolutionize location-based mobile news aggregation as you know it"; and Systobase, which will "make the world a better place through paxos algorithms for consensus protocols."[10]

These satirical startups are all-too realistic. If this is disruption, perhaps we have forgotten what the word means.

The Origins of Disruption

Our modern conception of disruption stems from research at Harvard Business School conducted by Clayton Christensen, professor of strategy. Christensen pioneered this thinking in his book *The Innovator's Dilemma* and his ensuing research on disruptive innovation. In an article, Christensen and colleagues write as follows:

> "Disruption" describes a process whereby a smaller company with fewer resources is able to successfully challenge established incumbent businesses . . . [Entrants start by gaining a toehold in overlooked segments] by delivering more-suitable functionality—frequently at a lower price. Incumbents, chasing higher profitability in more-demanding segments, tend not to respond vigorously. Entrants then move upmarket, delivering the performance that incumbents' mainstream customers require, while preserving the advantages that drove their early success. When mainstream customers start adopting the entrants' offerings in volume, disruption has occurred.[11]

Despite the centrality of Christensen's theory in Silicon Valley, his classic example wasn't about digital technology startups at all. His theory originated instead in the steel industry. Large, integrated steel mills saw competition on the low end of the market from minimills. The integrated mills ceded the low end of the market, allowing the minimills to get a foothold and over time develop better infrastructure to drive efficiencies and process flexibility, eventually overtaking the large mills altogether.[12]

Disruptive innovation is an emotionally attractive concept. It is a modern version of the story of David and Goliath, where the small player, eating scraps at the periphery, rises to become the victor, not only of the market but also for righteousness, because the larger player ignored parts of the market, did not innovate, and ultimately did not serve people's needs.

And thus Christensen's theory of innovation became the philosophical underpinning of Silicon Valley and the technology industry more broadly. As Jill Lepore wrote for the *New Yorker,* "Ever since *The Innovator's Dilemma,* everyone is either disrupting or being disrupted. There are disruption consultants, disruption conferences, and disruption seminars . . . You live in the shadow of *The Innovator's Dilemma.*"[13] If disruption became the anthem, startups became the marching band. Startups bring lower-cost solutions or more efficient processes enabled by technology and couple it with an outsider's attitude. They promise to remake industries in their own image.

The Creators

Of course, this doesn't sound much like the OkHi story. Where is the inefficient industrial incumbent thrown by the wayside? Where is the relentless march upmarket from an inferior product? OkHi does not fit the definition of a disruptor, because there is no industry that is being disrupted—unless of course it's the three sleeping dogs you met earlier.

Timbo Drayson is a *Creator* working in a *Frontier* ecosystem, which I define as those innovation centers located outside Silicon Valley and its closest counterparts. *Frontier Innovators,* often by necessity, are creating new industries, new business models, and ultimately new products and services for their markets.

Creators do three fundamental things simultaneously. First, they offer a product or service that solves an unserved, acute pain point in the formal economy. Where there are existing informal, unlicensed, or unofficial alternatives, Creators bring legitimacy and formality to their industries.

Second, Creators offer a solution for the mass market. While certainly new product categories can be created for the top of the market (think Virgin Galactic space travel), the Creators in this book focus on innovation that serves everyone and not only the rich.

Finally, Creators are focused on game-changing innovations that fundamentally rethink a market and a sector. Technology is often a key enabler, but it is accompanied by new ways of structuring the business, working with customers, or operating. In this way, many Creators share an important point of similarity with their cousins, the disruptors.

The difference in the number of Creators between the Frontier and Silicon Valley is striking. Within a sample of leading emerging-market startups, 63 percent are creating new industries. This includes companies like Rivigo, which is formalizing and expanding the trucking industry in India; Dr. Consulta, which is developing a nationwide chain of affordable medical clinics in Brazil; and M-KOPA Solar, which is providing solar energy home systems in Africa. By comparison, using the same definition and looking at a sample of the most successful Silicon Valley startups, only 33 percent are Creators.[14]

However, things are rarely black or white, and neither these bright-line definitions nor the ensuing analysis is, or can be, perfect.[15] While we may disagree about categorizing specific companies, the overall trend is clear: the Frontier is spawning many more Creators than Silicon Valley is.

Of course, this dynamic is often the natural result of necessity. Frontier Innovators, particularly those operating in developing ecosystems, are Creators because that's where the largest unmet opportunities exist. They offer platforms in education, health care, transportation, and financial services to the mass market, where technological and business model innovations promise to successfully bridge historical gaps.

In an interview, I asked Timbo who he thought was the most significant Creator in Sub-Saharan Africa. Without hesitation, he said M-PESA.

From Physical to Digital Cash Transfers

In emerging markets, nearly two billion people are "financially excluded," meaning they have no access to formal financial services.[16] They don't have bank accounts, checks, debit cards, access to formal loans, a stock trading account, insurance—or any way to transfer money other than physically handing over a stack of cash. A further two to three billion are underbanked, with insufficient access to these essential services.[17] Nearly half of our planet's population is either unbanked or underbanked.

It isn't that the banking industry doesn't want to provide bank accounts for everyone. It's that it can't. The traditional banking model, with physical branches, tellers, and outdated technology infrastructure, just doesn't work when trying to serve customers living in remote parts of emerging markets, with tiny bank balances and highly infrequent use.[18] The business case does not make sense.

Enter M-PESA, Kenya's largest mobile money platform and the leading example of this business model globally. M-PESA created a network of stores—think of a massive human ATM network across Kenya—where anyone can deposit money into their phone's account or send money to any other phone or store. The difference is that this system does not rely on a bank card, a voice call, or a smart-phone-enabled app like WhatsApp. Instead, it's all done on a simple mobile phone via the texting capability built in to even the simplest low-cost phones. This innovation was transformational in a country where the average GDP per capita was $840 in 2007.[19]

M-PESA was an audacious project. It was also not a traditional startup. M-PESA was incubated inside the leading Kenyan telecom, Safaricom (an entity jointly owned by the Kenyan government and the global telecom Vodacom).[20] The company formed an entrepreneurial team to develop the project and received external seed funding. But again, this wasn't typical early-stage funding: it was a grant from Department for International Development (DFID), the UK international development agency.[21]

M-PESA's new SMS-based banking tool did not disrupt a traditional inefficient payment network. There were no broadly accepted payment networks in the country. M-PESA's biggest competitor was the local *hawala* system, where people gave envelopes full of cash to bus drivers and asked them to give it to a specific friend or relative a few stops away. The driver would receive a commission for driving the cash to the village. You can imagine that beyond being inefficient, this system presented a high risk of loss, theft, and fraud.

Today, M-PESA reaches eighteen million people in Kenya, with more than one hundred thousand agents processing more than one hundred million transactions, which some estimates put at equivalent to 40 percent of Kenya's GDP.[22] M-PESA was also foundational in creating the mobile banking industry globally. Studies have indicated it has been the primary driver of lifting nearly two hundred thousand households out of poverty (2 percent of Kenyan households).[23]

As a former member of the steering committee of the Mobile Money group of the GSMA (the global telecom industry association), whose mission is to help scale mobile banking across the world, I have enjoyed a front-row seat to the staggering growth of this ecosystem. On the back of M-PESA's example, the industry has exploded, with replicators around the world. There are now more than 250 mobile money deployments serving more than 850 million people across the world.[24]

The First-Mover Disadvantage

The story of M-PESA is inspiring. But the company was by no means an overnight success and encountered many roadblocks along the way. Nick Hughes, one of the founders of M-PESA, explains:

> The project faced formidable financial, social, cultural, political, technological, and regulatory hurdles . . . To implement, Vodafone had to marry the incredibly divergent cultures of global telecommunications companies, banks, and microfinance institutions—and cope with their massive and often contradictory regulatory requirements. Finally, the project had to quickly train, support, and accommodate the needs of customers who were unbanked, unconnected, often semi-literate, and who faced routine challenges to their physical and financial security. We had no roadmap.[25]

There is a name for this: the first-mover disadvantage.[26] Contrary to conventional wisdom, research indicates that not every first mover will have an advantage. There is a tug-of-war between the situation when technology is disrupting an industry (likely first-mover advantage) and the situation when technology is creating an industry or leading a market change (unlikely first-mover advantage).[27] Creators like Timbo and Nick faced a long, arduous path to scale that necessarily began with not only the creation of an entirely new industry but also the need to shape a new mindset for their prospective customers.

For M-PESA's customers, the concept of having money stored in a format other than cash was a complete novelty. Thus, the idea of giving cash to a stranger with the promise it would be sent via mobile phone to its intended recipient was unthinkable. To overcome this, M-PESA had to educate its customers at length. As one of the early product managers reflects, "The first obstacle we encountered was the agents' hesitation to pay out cash withdrawals . . . It was a brave shop assistant who opened the employer's till and handed out cash because they had been sent a text message telling them to do so."[28]

Similarly, regulators had never overseen a mobile banking platform. Would they be comfortable with having a parallel financial system operating outside the banks? Which regulator would be in charge—the telecom regulator or the central bank? In M-PESA's case, as noted by one of the regulators in charge, "M-PESA was a gamble . . . Clearly, M-PESA is a classic case in which innovation preceded policy. In such cases, policymakers take the risk and, through system wide consultations, push for supportive policies."[29]

For all these reasons and more, being a first mover to create an industry often takes much longer, and requires more endurance, than undertaking any disruption-type endeavor. But despite the first-mover disadvantage, Frontier Innovators succeed in building successful businesses. They enjoy the Creator's advantage, as you'll see next.

Capturing the Creator's Advantage

Being a Creator is difficult, but it has unique advantages as well. Let's explore four in turn.

Creating a Huge Market

First, creating new industries has the potential to create immense markets. This is one of the first questions a venture capitalist will ask: How large is the market? For many Creators, the market can be nearly unlimited. M-PESA is targeting a financially underserved market of two billion people. OkHi could one day serve the billions of people who lack street addresses.

Peter Thiel makes a similar argument in his book *Zero to One*, arguing that the best companies are creating new industries rather than playing in an existing sandbox. Going from "zero to one" requires enabling something that has never been done before.[30] It is different from horizontal progress, where we see something that is already working and grow it or replicate it, resulting in incremental, "one to n" progress.[31]

Often Creators instinctively know they're developing an important market. But they rarely know how it will evolve. When Alexander Graham Bell was awarded a patent for sending voice signals over an electric wire, could he possibly have foreseen the mobile phone revolution?

Benefiting from Competition

For Creators, competition is not always a bad thing. Here, Thiel would disagree. He often proclaims, "Competition is for losers," meaning that by targeting new markets, Creators can build a monopoly and thus have the potential to capture a greater share of the opportunity.[32] This can be the case; however, simultaneously, in large, created markets there is often an advantage to competition.

Seeing M-PESA's success in Kenya, Vodacom (Safaricom's parent company) launched a similar product next door in Tanzania. In Kenya, Safaricom had a monopoly, but in Tanzania, two other telecom operators had significant presences, and each launched similar products. It took more than six years for Kenya to reach eighteen million users, but, in much less populous Tanzania, it took less than five years.[33] Growth in other markets in West Africa has taken even less time. With more players, the large investments in customer education and infrastructure development are shared, and multiple brands in the same space can bring greater legitimacy in the public eye.

Gaining Ecosystem Support

Creators are often supported by the ecosystem around them. In the United States, Uber is probably best characterized as a disruptor of the existing taxi industry, but in emerging markets, Uber (like its ride-hailing cousins) is a Creator, legitimizing an informal economy. Its reception there was in line with the different ecosystem: by and large, the existing informal taxi drivers eagerly welcomed and participated in Uber's platform. Regulators, too, often took a friendlier stance in emerging markets: of the locations where Uber is banned, all twelve are in more-developed markets across Europe, Australia, China, Japan, and the United States.[34]

This ecosystem support can take many forms, including a diversity of funding sources. In mobile money, for example, providers have received investments from impact investors, foundations, development institutions, and corporate social responsibility investment vehicles. The same is true in other created industries.

Expanding the Pool of Talent

Creators can draw on a larger pool of talent. Startups live and die by the quality of their teams, and it can be difficult to attract top talent. Startups pay less, involve higher risk, and require longer hours. But the most ambitious startups—the Creators—offer a higher calling: a real opportunity to change the world. Employees are often willing to work for less, stay longer, and work harder than in comparable noncreating roles. Startups can often attract candidates from other sectors like nonprofits or government. You will explore the nuances of human capital in chapters 6 and 7 and the social impact of Frontier Innovators in chapter 8.

Standing on the Shoulders of Giants

Creators don't just build companies. They create industries. They are the giants upon whose shoulders their successors stand.

Not only did M-PESA become one of Safaricom's largest and fastest-growing revenue streams (representing more than one-third of total revenues), but also it kick-started a range of industries.[35] Nick Hughes has lived this himself. His next venture, M-KOPA, is an energy access startup (similar to Zola). With M-PESA as the payment platform, homes that use M-KOPA's solar-powered lighting system can pay for daily or weekly use.

M-KOPA's business model would never have been possible without M-PESA, because the collection of a large volume of daily or monthly subscription payments by cash is too costly. And as a bonus, creating an application that relies on M-PESA forged a symbiotic relationship. M-KOPA customers become better M-PESA customers—using the platform regularly, teaching others in their community, and trying yet other products that have sprung up on the platform.

Another industry that has been reimagined thanks to mobile money is microfinance. In its early days, a key insight was that the poor were creditworthy borrowers. By placing borrowers into groups with a sense of strong social accountability and shared responsibility on the loans' repayment, microfinance lenders found that repayment rates were high.

But this insight was also the biggest challenge: the in-person nature of putting people in groups, making regular visits to collect money, and maintaining deep customer engagement is expensive. Companies like Tala, Branch International, and Safaricom's own M-Shwari now offer consumer loans, relying entirely on the mobile money platform. These next-generation digital lenders, much like those in microfinance, also look for social signals to identify creditworthy borrowers. But they do this entirely digitally. By leveraging big data like phone-calling patterns, a customer's social graph, and spending patterns, digital lenders can determine creditworthiness without the overhead of a field staff, physical cash collection, and antiquated technology. This revolution is predicated on M-PESA and its fellow mobile money Creators.[36]

As for OkHi, even though Timbo is much earlier in his journey, he is already enabling other industries. He interviewed ambulance drivers, and that inspired him to push for a solution to slow response times. He recently got his wish: a startup called Flare launched an ambulance platform in Nairobi whose rapid service is predicated on accurate addressing—enabled by OkHi.[37]

Where Are My Flying Cars?

I teach an MBA class on emerging-market entrepreneurship. My students often ask for my feedback on the direction of their business ideas. I am asked questions like, "Will this even be possible?" "Am I making things too hard on myself by trying to build this new idea that has never been done?"

I ask them, "Why are you doing this?" Almost exclusively, they tell me they want to make the world a better place. The reality is that building a startup, any startup, is extremely hard and takes a long time. If you're going to work that hard, for a large portion of your life, you might as well build something meaningful. Or at least try to.

What's exciting is that the Frontier affords us many examples of entrepreneurs creating new industries. Timbo and Nick are not alone. There are many more like them.

I tell my students they should be Creators. I tell them that others have forged ahead, and they should look to them for inspiration. Perhaps the rest of the Valley should look to them as well for inspiration for their next businesses and remember why they got into this game in the first place.

Foster the Full Stack

Don't Just Rely Only on Software

In Silicon Valley's classic model, startups are "asset light." They focus on one piece of the value chain and solve a customer's problem using an innovative product or solution—one whose launch ideally requires limited capital, hardware, or complexity.

If you want to build an audacious, world-changing photo-sharing platform, then this strategy works effectively. The existing technology and infrastructure ecosystem allow you to focus on the user interface and partner with others for storage, user authentication, and social media integration. Similarly, even for complicated ventures like on-demand delivery, many parts of the value chain—such as street addresses, local maps, route optimization software, and logistics support—can be obtained from existing technology or ecosystem providers.

Silicon Valley's asset-light modus operandi is enabled by a rich tapestry of companies that provide the necessary infrastructure for disruptors. Other dogmatic startup principles—such as the imperative to create a lean startup—further encourage entrepreneurs to focus narrowly on one part of the value chain and one product. The idea is to build excellence in one area and get the rest from the ecosystem.

Yet for most of the world, and particularly for Creators no matter where they are located, this model is simply impractical. Because the rich ecosystem of enabling technologies is typically nonexistent or is severely lacking for the type of business they are building, Frontier Innovators often need to construct the "vertical" full stack themselves—developing both the ultimate product or service and the enabling infrastructure that underpins it.

The full stack isn't always a vertical one. Often startups build the "horizontal" full stack—offering a wider range of products and services than their Silicon Valley equivalents in order to create an ecosystem.

Building the Vertical Stack

Two men who exemplify building the vertical stack are Ben Gleason and Thiago Alvarez. In 2012, they decided to tackle the critical need for financial inclusion in Brazil. This South American country has some of the highest interest rates and balances in the world: the average bank lending rate is greater than 50 percent (compared with 5.5 percent in the United States and 1.75 percent in the United Kingdom).[1] At the same time, Brazilians have high levels of short-term credit card debt.[2] Many customers do not understand their financial situation holistically, and they lack the tools that would empower them to take concrete steps to improve it.

In the United States, Mint created a digital personal finance manager (PFM) to address a similar challenge. The product quickly attracted more than 1.5 million users and was ultimately sold to Intuit.[3] Now US customers have their choice of a panoply of PFMs, ranging from apps to free products provided by banks. Specialized service companies like Credit Karma, which helps customers improve their credit scores, focus on improving key aspects of the customer's financial life.

Brazil had no such plethora of options. To solve this challenge, in 2012 Ben and Thiago launched Guiabolso, Brazil's first PFM. Below the surface, Guiabolso looked very different from its rapidly scaling US counterparts (Mint and Credit Karma).

At first blush, Guiabolso appeared to be a budgeting tool. It allowed consumers to enter their spending habits to track how much money they had used and how much would remain at the end of the month. But like many apps where customers self-reported spending, Guiabolso faced the GIGO challenge: garbage in, garbage out. The app's insights were based on what customers input. Unless customers reported information accurately and consistently to the app, the insights the app provided would be worthless.

For Silicon Valley PFMs, resolving this was an easy challenge. Mint gets actual financial data straight from customer bank accounts, bypassing the customer-input phase. Mint can do this because preexisting platforms like Yodlee connect the PFM to banks.

These platforms did not exist in Brazil in 2012. Ben and Thiago had to decide: would they continue with the imperfect budgeting tool, or bet the fragile startup's future on building the bank connection layer themselves?

They decided to bet. Developing the platform was no easy feat. Brazil's banks have excruciatingly variable security features. It took more than a year to create a stable platform that could reliably access banking data. And that was on top of the need to make sense of the complex data, create insights from the information, build an engaging customer front end, and develop a strategy to reliably find users and get them to join the platform.

As soon as Guiabolso had solved that issue, the next problem emerged.

To engage users around their biggest pain point—credit card debt— the app needed to give customers insights into their creditworthiness and their ability to access lower-priced credit. Brazil did not have an all-encompassing FICO score equivalent. For most Brazilians, the credit score is binary: you are either in default or you're not.[4] That is not very insightful for most customers. Nor is it helpful for banks that make credit decisions on customers who are not their clients.

So Guiabolso built a proprietary Financial Health Index. In addition to informing customers whether or not they are on the blacklist, the app proactively gives them an impartial view of their financial health and sets them up with the tools to improve it.

Guiabolso's customers now understood their current financial health and learned ways to improve their creditworthiness. Naturally, next they wanted to benefit from these insights. In the United States, Mint and Credit Karma helped customers secure more-affordable loans by matching them with providers across the country. Guiabolso thought it might be able to do something similar.

Again, however, the company was stymied. The traditional lenders in Brazil were reticent to provide targeted offers through the platform. Many were uncomfortable with this new method of acquiring and serving customers online, particularly because they were unaccustomed to issuing fairly priced loans on the basis of a credit score to customers with whom they had no direct relationship. Unlike the United States, with its rich ecosystem of financial technology (fintech) lenders, Brazil had none.

Guiabolso had to build the infrastructure itself. It launched a de novo financial lender in Brazil that would lend through Guiabolso's platform. It opened the platform to up-and-coming lenders and banks that wanted to increase their loan book and were eager to reach new customers, and yet weren't equipped to sell loans in a rapidly moving digital format. In this way, Guiabolso's product is transformative, offering users access to credit at lower rates than rates Brazilian consumers can otherwise obtain in the market.

Guiabolso has more than five million users on the PFM and has distributed more than $200 million in loans. It has also raised more than $80 million in venture capital funding (including from me when I worked at Omidyar Network).[5]

To achieve this traction, Guiabolso had to create four separate businesses in order to provide a single product: an interconnection layer to connect to banks digitally; a consumer app with valuable insights for customers; the Financial Health Index and credit-scoring platform; and a lending product to jumpstart the marketplace. It was no easy feat in any market but particularly challenging in Brazil.[6]

Guiabolso may seem to be an exceptional case. Yet many of the Frontier Innovators you've met so far have faced a similar challenge. If anything,

Guiabolso had it easy. Many Frontier Innovators must build physical enabling infrastructure, rather than only software. To offer their home energy systems, for example, Zola (see the introduction) built an R&D facility to design low-cost appliances, a rural sales force and centralized call-center operations, a customized software solution for its sales force, and an in-house financing business to offer customers a pay-as-you-go service. Similarly, M-PESA could not build a fully digital payment network. Instead, it had to cultivate a network of mom-and-pop stores across the country to allow customers to deposit and withdraw cash from the system.

Inanc Balci, a co-founder of Lazada Group, a leading Southeast Asia e-commerce platform, summarized the dynamic: "It is absolutely counter-intuitive that to launch an e-commerce business, we had to create an entire logistics business. But for us, it was consequential for survival."[7]

The stories of Guiabolso, Zola, and Lazada naturally raise questions about when it makes sense to build the full stack and how entrepreneurs should prioritize precious resources.

When to Build the Full Stack

The decision to build more pieces of the stack should not be made lightly. It requires capital and time—both critical resources for startups. It also increases interdependencies and risk, because the pieces of the stack must work together seamlessly.

To decide when and what to integrate, an innovator should begin by considering a series of questions.

Does the Ecosystem Have the Infrastructure You Need?

The process begins by understanding what is required for your business model to function and whether others in the ecosystem provide the requisite pieces at a sufficiently high level of service.

Guiabolso required two linchpins. The first was a front-end customer application or web experience that provided insights about how customers used their money and where they could improve. This was core to the business, and something that the company would build. The second key ingredient was the bank interconnections to enable customer data to be fed automatically to the app. Guiabolso would have preferred not to build this layer. It conducted a market study before determining that no suitable solution existed.

Some businesses decide to vertically integrate more parts of the value chain than strictly necessary (e.g., Apple and Tesla, which vertically integrate the product design, distribution, and large parts of the supply chain of their products), deeming this model core to their competitive advantage. But innovators in developing ecosystems often find that the vertical full stack is a matter of necessity, building essential infrastructure just to make the core model work.

Frontier Innovators should evaluate any alternatives that exist in the market. The available infrastructure will differ in various regions and industries. Startups located in the United States but outside Silicon Valley—say, in Detroit or Milwaukee—will still benefit from the rich US technological infrastructure. An entrepreneur building Lazada in Detroit could tap in to the established US payment and shipping ecosystems. Similarly, it would be redundant for a PFM startup in Europe to build a new credit-scoring infrastructure.

Ultimately, if innovators can borrow a stack, or if it is available in a commoditized manner at a sufficient quality level, they do not need to build it and should not waste resources. If they cannot use an existing stack, then they must explore the next question.

Can Others Provide the Stack?

Sometimes, just because the stack is not available doesn't mean it can't be accessed. Frontier Innovators can enable others to provide the stack for them, often through technology. Sacha Poignonnec is the co-CEO of Jumia, a leading pan-Africa e-commerce platform and the first technology company in Africa to go public on the New York Stock Exchange. Sacha emphasizes that certain elements can be outsourced if the right enabling tools are provided. When Jumia started scaling its e-commerce platform, no one provided deliveries with the requisite level of service in Jumia's markets. To offer end-to-end logistics in rural African markets—with item tracking, delivery time estimates, and other features now standard in the West—Jumia offered technology tools for local entrepreneurs to track delivery, optimize routes, and collect payments. Jumia created these enablement tools internally but empowered others to fill the gaps. Now Jumia has more than eighty-one thousand partners on its system in fourteen African markets, including Egypt, Morocco, Uganda, and Nigeria.[8]

An important reflection is whether partners can scale with you. David Vélez, CEO of Nubank, learned this the hard way. Nubank is a credit card company for the mass market, operating in Argentina, Brazil, and Mexico. David explains:

> When we started, we worked with a third-party credit card processor, but realized rapidly their technology was not strong enough to scale. We also worked with a banking partner because we didn't have a license initially. However, there was too much risk depending on them, so we had to get our own. We faced the same problem with customer service. We decided to build it in house from the beginning, rather than depend on a third party. It was the only way we could guarantee quality.[9]

For Nubank, local solutions existed but were not strong enough to scale with the business. David had to build each in turn. Nubank has raised more than $800 million and now is a leading Latin American fintech worth more than $10 billion.[10]

Can You Stage the Full Stack Over Time?

Building a startup is extremely challenging. Having to build a vertical stack—the equivalent of building multiple startups at the same time—often proves impossible. Some pieces of the vertical stack must be built in tandem, but often not everything. Staging is key.

For Guiabolso, the PFM was the first crucial product. This meant the company had to build the bank interconnections immediately. The rest, however, could wait. If customers didn't care about the PFM insights or if the bank interconnections didn't work, it wouldn't matter if the company could build a lending platform. That's why Ben and Thiago decided to wait a few years before providing the credit-scoring and lending products.

Deferring might mean others will build instead. Markets are dynamic, and others are constantly filling out pieces of the stack. Companies like OkHi are building different pieces of the infrastructure in their areas, including street addresses and logistics. Similarly, platforms like M-PESA and its many replicators around the world are creating the payment ecosystem. Before investing in vertical infrastructure, you will find it worth investigating whether other pieces of the stack may get filled out with time.

Ultimately, for Frontier Innovators, having to build the full(er) stack is not a strategic choice; it's a practical reality. Indeed, building the full stack is one of many examples in this book where Frontier Innovators have to do more with less. If at all possible, finding partners or enabling others to support you are valuable options to explore.

This may sound daunting. However, there is a bright side. Building the full(er) stack confers competitive advantages as well.

The Full-Stack Moats

Building the full stack is a double-edged sword. Although at first it makes the mountain that much higher to climb, it also makes it that much harder for anyone else to imitate the model afterward. Frontier Innovators often enjoy three types of full-stack *moats* (a natural defense that allows a company to maintain its advantage over time): competitive, capital, and technical.

The Competitive Moat

The competitive moat is clearest. In Brazil, for a competitor to create a competitive PFM and a credit-scoring lending product would require rebuilding much of Guiabolso's infrastructure. It's no wonder Guiabolso doesn't have much competition, even after five years. Those that move first and get a head start in launching gain significant advantage, because once competitors notice the opportunity, they are still years away from being able to replicate the model.

The Capital Moat

This same phenomenon drives a capital moat. Guiabolso has raised more than $80 million.[11] For other companies looking at the space, the knowledge that even replicating the existing offering would take a similar amount of capital is daunting. Funding such a competitor is unappealing to investors. Venture capitalists would consider it a losing proposition to invest in the number two player that is a number of years behind (particularly in markets that are dominated by network effects and where one winner will emerge). Saed Nashef, co-founder of Sadara Ventures, which invests in capital-starved Palestine, explains: "Capital can be a powerful advantage. When companies raise large rounds ahead of competitors, it becomes a driver to become a winner."[12]

This capital moat plays out in another, more nuanced way. In Brazil, for example, there are limited investors who lead large rounds. By its third funding round, Guiabolso had already received capital from many of the leaders: Kaszek Ventures (one of Latin America's leading early-stage funds, which is covered in chapter 11); the International Finance Corporation (IFC; the private investment arm of the World Bank); Omidyar Network (my former employer, a global philanthropic investment firm); Ribbit Capital (a global fintech investor); and Valor Capital (a cross-border Brazil venture capital fund). Guiabolso was able to do this before another competitor emerged in a meaningful way.[13]

Investors are often reluctant to support two competing companies in the same market. Because being full stack often requires more capital, it is an opportunity to lock up more of the leading investors in the space, thus making it more challenging for an up-and-coming competitor to thrive.

The Technical Moat

Being full stack also confers a technical advantage. As Guiabolso built its interconnection capabilities with banks, many of them were opposed to the company's central idea. It is within a customer's rights to share their read-only internet banking credentials and allow Guiabolso to access their account information. However, many banks resisted, rightly believing it would decrease their relationship with the customer. Banks developed increasingly sophisticated ways of thwarting Guiabolso's attempts at reading customer data, but Guiabolso became increasingly proficient at getting through. New competitors coming in would have to repeat the technical and strategic iterations that Guiabolso went through.

Similarly, Fetchr, which you will get to know in chapter 4 and which offers last-mile deliveries in the Middle East, had to integrate into a range of e-commerce platforms; in doing so, it learned what it takes to fix bugs rapidly to provide customers a seamless experience. Developing this kind of expertise takes many iterations and discourages online vendors from experimenting with other providers.

This is the full-stack moat. Frontier Innovators often endure significantly more organizational complexity upfront than their Silicon Valley counterparts. However, this yields a better position for them to endure and succeed over the longer term.

Building the Horizontal Stack

So far, we have focused primarily on the vertical stack—the infrastructure required to enable primary business functions. Often, entrepreneurs need to go one step further. To bring customers into the system, they have to offer a wider range of products than their Silicon Valley equivalents, either directly or via partnerships. Frontier Innovators do this much earlier in their journeys than conventional wisdom recommends. This is the horizontal stack.

Gojek: The Full Ride

The traffic in Jakarta is among the worst in the world. It often takes well over two hours to get from one end of the city to the other. And it's only getting worse. Over the past decade, the city grew to more than thirty million people, and five million cars and fifteen million motorbikes clog the streets.[14] Car ownership is increasing nearly 9 percent every year.[15] Fewer than 25 percent of Indonesians use public transport.[16]

Ojeks, low-cost motorbike taxis, represent one way around this problem. While these motorbikes are less comfortable than cars—subjecting riders to frequent rain, pollution, road noise, and higher accident risk— they do something cars can't. They weave through traffic during the frequent congestion. If you want to arrive in style, you take a car. But if you'd like to arrive on time (and affordably), you take an ojek.

In 2010, the ojek market was informal and unregulated. Many ojek drivers operated with little documentation, few safety standards, and little tracking. Drivers had difficulty locating would-be passengers. They often took home fewer than three or four fares a day, spending hours driving around (or waiting in traffic), hoping to get a passenger.[17] Demand couldn't find the supply, something that consistently limited the market.

Nadiem Makarim wanted to do something about it. After graduating from Harvard Business School in 2011, he started a centralized ojek taxi service: a physical call center that identified drivers and directed them to customers. Nadiem started with six personal phones, twenty drivers, and customers from his personal network. The business solved a personal problem for him and his family but did not expand beyond sustainable subscale operation for a few years.[18]

In January 2015, Nadiem finally secured the funding to infuse technology into his small call center, and he launched Gojek. His vision was to formalize the entire informal ojek economy through a centralized technology platform. Gojek operates similarly to the Uber app, allowing users to call an ojek wherever and whenever.

For drivers, Gojek's value proposition was clear. Historically, they worked long hours but completed only a few rides every day. With Gojek, they could easily double their orders. Although prices are lower, drivers make more money (and with more consistency) due to the reliable order flow. Furthermore, Gojek gives every driver on the platform a helmet (often for the first time), a uniform, and access to a high-quality motorbike.

Gojek also proved valuable for customers, allowing them to secure an ojek when they needed one (it's important to avoid waiting in the rainy season) and quickly travel to any location in the city. Customers also found a safer alternative to the informal system in Gojek. Nadiem says it's one of the reasons the majority of Gojek's riders are women.[19] Much like other ride-hailing businesses, Gojek offers a fixed price, eliminating the need to haggle with the driver.[20]

By the end of Gojek's first month, there were one thousand motorcyclists on the app. By the end of the year, the company had two hundred thousand drivers in five cities and more than four hundred thousand downloads. Gojek's popularity skyrocketed, its brand aided by the suddenly ubiquitous green helmets and jackets peppering the city.[21]

More Products, More Services

Yet to truly scale, Nadiem knew he'd have to offer more than transportation. Many of his customers were unbanked and did not have access to credit cards or other digital means of payment, so they needed to pay for rides in cash. In Indonesia, 48 percent of the population doesn't have a smart phone, and 33 percent have only a simple-feature phone.[22] Gojek was an early online experience for many customers, making the platform an ideal place to offer a range of services. Furthermore, many drivers had free time outside commuting hours, when demand for transport tended to spike. To bring more customers onto the platform (and often online for the first time), and to engage drivers throughout the day, Gojek created an entire ecosystem of products and services.

The first element was support for digital payments. Most Indonesians were unbanked or underbanked. Yet Nadiem knew that digital payment would facilitate product adoption and greatly improve the customer experience.[23] Furthermore, digital payments represented an opportunity to create a significantly wider ecosystem.

Inspired by the success of platforms like Tencent's WeChat and Alibaba's Alipay, which have 1.1 billion and 900 million users, respectively, Nadiem set out to make Gojek the leading payment platform in Indonesia. Gojek already had two critical elements: an agent network (drivers) to get cash into and out of the system, and a ready transaction ecosystem (rides).[24] The latter is particularly critical because it is habit-forming behavior and creates a repeatable use case. In 2017, Gojek acquired Mapan, a community savings network; Kartuku, an offline payment-processing company; and Midtrans, a payment gateway, to build the network further.[25]

Now Gojek drivers can also offer financial products and services—a huge step beyond traditional ride-sharing services. Drivers act as human ATMs: riders deposit and withdraw money from GoPay, Gojek's mobile payment ecosystem, directly through drivers. Customers can then use GoPay to make payments (e.g., paying bills or transferring money to other Gojek users) and accumulate savings (by keeping a balance in the account). Over time, a greater range of financial products will be offered, including insurance and loans.

Gojek went even further. To respond to customers' need for a wider selection of products in one destination, and to smooth demand for its drivers, the company's range of services now includes food delivery (GoFood), commerce (GoMart, GoShop), massages (GoMassage), shipping (GoSend), and cell phone airtime (GoPulsa). One day, Nadiem hopes customers will be able to get almost anything from Gojek's singular platform.

Nadiem aims to create a full ecosystem. As he explains it, "In the mornings, we drive people from home to work. At lunch, we deliver them meals to the office. In the late afternoon, we drive people back home. In the evenings, we deliver ingredients and meals. And in between all this, we deliver e-commerce, financial services, and other services."[26]

The strategy is working. By mid 2019, Gojek had two million drivers, three hundred thousand merchants, and one hundred million monthly transactions on its platform.[27] Major players like Tencent, JD.com, KKR, and Sequoia Capital back the company. In February 2018, Gojek closed a Series E financing round of $1.5 billion. Tencent led the round, with participation from investment firms across the United States, China, Europe, and Indonesia.[28]

Nadiem, however, is proudest of a different accomplishment. As he explained, Gojek has become the largest income source in Indonesia. Millions of people receive income through Gojek. Nadiem emphasizes that for him the most important part of this victory is that Gojek has "increased the opportunities of [its] drivers."[29]

Approaching the Horizontal Stack

Building the horizontal stack is a different manifestation of the full(er) stack approach. Whereas entrepreneurs like Ben Gleason and Thiago Alvarez had to build enabling infrastructure only to offer their ultimate product, Nadiem Makarim had to build horizontally, offering related business models that mutually reinforced the core offering.

For many Frontier Innovators, building an ecosystem of activities is a strategy to create a viable business. As with the vertical stack, the horizontal stack should start with an examination of which pieces of the ecosystem are required, and in what order. For Gojek, this started by creating a core ride offering and rapidly expanding to other product categories. Vijay Shekhar Sharma, the founder of Paytm, a venerable Indian technology company worth more than $15 billion, explains: "Eventually businesses become an ecosystem at scale. In emerging markets you have to do it earlier to monetize within your customer base. At Paytm, our ecosystem includes payments, of course, but online commerce, a digital travel agency, [and] wealth management, among others."[30]

In some cases, building the horizontal stack may not be strictly necessary. Rather, it offers an opportunity to leverage an existing customer base to capture more of a nascent market, building the profitability of the business and improving its competitive positioning at the same time. Gojek has an opportunity in Indonesia to go much further than ride-hailing apps in developed markets. Rather than being constrained to a narrow product category (e.g., Uber and Lyft for rides, Instacart for deliveries), Gojek has a viable chance to create a "super-app," which would allow it to dominate a number of sectors. WeChat has taken a similar strategy in China, in some ways becoming the de facto platform for consumers in China to access products and services on the internet.[31]

Often, Frontier Innovators can enable others to provide the horizontal stack with them. Gojek partners with others for most services (e.g., restaurants, merchants, and masseuses). Similarly, M-PESA enables anyone to leverage its payment platform, including financial institutions that offer services spanning insurance, savings, and loans.

Sometimes, however, an innovator needs to kick-start a nascent ecosystem by building the first pieces internally. Ctrip, the Chinese travel company, started as a travel community review service similar to TripAdvisor. The challenge was that even if the online portal existed, it was challenging to book hotels or purchase flights online. As a first step, Ctrip methodologically partnered with existing hotels and airlines in Shanghai and other major Chinese cities to add them to the platform. However, the inventory of flights to the interior of China was limited, and once tourists arrived, there were even fewer hotels and organized local tourist activities. Ctrip itself played a role in creating the Chinese travel ecosystem, launching vacation packages with charter flights to select destinations, building hotels, and organizing tours.[32] Over time, the ecosystem flourished. Now the company has a market cap of more than $24 billion, and more than 250 million users.[33]

Ecosystems often have powerful network effects. As others provide services within the ecosystem, the innovator's centrality to the model will only get stronger. As Gojek enables more service providers to sell through the Gojek platform, or as more businesses use M-PESA to offer financial products, Gojek becomes the de facto standard for customers. Innovators driving these network effects, like M-PESA, Gojek, and Ctrip, enjoy an enduring advantage.

Putting It All Together

In Silicon Valley, best practice suggests providing a software-based, asset-light product or service. Startups are told to focus on their "wedge"—the narrow segment in which they will compete and hopefully dominate. Providing a full end-to-end experience is a bold, expensive, and often foolhardy strategy.

Indeed, operating as a full stack seems intimidating. It confers more operational complexity and risk and increases the likely time to reach scale. However, the strategy also has distinct advantages, particularly since it offers competitive, capital, and technological moats. Similarly, by building a horizontal stack, Frontier Innovators can capture a greater share of the market, increase their relevance to customers, and improve their competitive long-term positioning.

Full-stack approaches are not new. They are reminiscent of Silicon Valley twenty years ago. To launch a business, many startups had to build their own servers in house. To create new products, they hard-coded—literally. Innovators were not only building their products or services but also creating enabling infrastructure and ecosystems.

Marc Andreessen, founder of Netscape and now a leading Silicon Valley venture capitalist, captured Silicon Valley's zeitgeist when he proclaimed, "Software is eating the world."[34] This does appear to be true in Silicon Valley. Yet for entrepreneurs operating in nascent ecosystems, and especially for Creators, software is rarely sufficient to solve complex problems or build new industries. Perhaps "Software-enabled technological solutions, incorporating a more expansive view of the stack, are eating the world" is a more accurate, if less catchy, slogan for the Frontier.

3.

Raise a Camel
Build for Sustainability and Resilience

Keith Davies, CFO of Zoona, was in a tricky spot.

Zoona's iconic lime green booths dotted many African cities. The company was identifying locations, installing its purpose-built booths, and recruiting local micro-entrepreneurs to serve their communities. Zoona's agent network offered its customers basic financial services, including money transfers, bill payments, savings, and loans. Keith, along with the three other founders, was committed to offering Zoona customers a high-quality, reliable service and driving financial inclusion along the way.

On the surface, the company was performing well. At the time, its agent network had just crossed more than one thousand booths and was serving more than one million customers.[1] Although Zambia was its primary operating market, the company was expanding to other markets, including Malawi and Mozambique. Zoona had international investors, including Quona Capital and Omidyar Network.[2] The previous month, it had even become profitable.

But that morning in August 2015, Keith knew Zoona was in trouble. Chinese stocks, on the back of macroeconomic uncertainty, had taken a turn for the worse. China's demand for industrial materials, including copper, was projected to crater.[3] As a consequence, Zambia, where copper sales to China represent 80 percent of exports, saw its currency, the kwacha, drop precipitously.[4]

This was calamitous for Zoona. Its revenues were in Zambian kwachas, but its costs were primarily denominated in South African rand and US dollars, and most of its investors (including debt holders) were looking for US dollar returns. With no effective means of hedging the currency risk at the scale of Zoona's requirements, Keith knew a decrease in the kwacha meant lower revenues. But with no corresponding decrease in costs, the company would no longer be profitable and investor returns would tumble.

The kwacha decreased to 5:1 and then broke through the previously inconceivable psychological barrier of 8:1. But it did not stop there. It plummeted further. The exchange rate hit 10:1, then 12:1, and finally 14:1—the largest depreciation in the country's history, and the world's worst-performing currency for the year. It ended at 15:1, depreciating nearly 80 percent in three months, and fell 115 percent by the end of 2015.[5]

Zoona's situation was extreme, but, at the Frontier, that's not unique.

My Other Investment Is a Unicorn

On my laptop cover, I have a sticker, handed out at some startup conference or another: "My other investment is a unicorn." So pervasive is the myth of the single-horned creature in Silicon Valley that venture capitalists have been spotted donning unicorn costumes at demo days (where startups pitch their ideas)—physical embodiments of this mythical animal.[6]

Why is the unicorn Silicon Valley's mascot, and what does it represent?

Coined in 2013 by Aileen Lee, a Silicon Valley venture capitalist, the unicorn represents an elusive objective—unique, pure, and perfect—

referring to the near-impossible milestone of being valued at more than $1 billion.[7]

Unicorns were once a rare breed. Between 2003 and 2013, only thirty-nine unicorns were started in Silicon Valley.[8] Historically, billion-dollar valuations were bestowed only on the few startups with the magic elixir of the right teams, business models, profitability, and timing.[9]

In recent years, the stable of thoroughbreds has become much larger. As of March 2019, there were 326 unicorns around the world. A new tier has been created, with 20 companies vaulting to "decacorn" status—companies that have reached more than $10 billion in valuation.[10]

Unicorns are not simply descriptors of an end result. Rather, they represent a philosophy, an ethos, and a process of building startups. Like the ceremonial haka dance performed by the All Blacks, New Zealand's rugby team, as a pregame ritual, achieving unicorn status serves as a rallying cry, uniting a company around a common objective and inciting fear in the incumbents it seeks to displace.[11]

When being a unicorn is the objective, very rapid growth is the method.

Silicon Valley luminaries have defined the objective and method explicitly. Paul Graham, founder and former leader of the venerable accelerator Y Combinator, famously defined a startup as "a company designed to grow fast."[12] He likens its mission to that of a mosquito: "A bear can absorb a hit and a crab is armored against one, but a mosquito is designed for one thing: to score. No energy is wasted on defense . . . Startups, like mosquitos, tend to be an all-or-nothing proposition"—one of growth.[13]

Reid Hoffman and Chris Yeh embody this approach fully in their hit book on Silicon Valley startup best practice, *Blitzscaling: The Lightning-Fast Path to Building Massively Valuable Companies*. Derived from the German word *blitzkrieg*, "blitzscaling is prioritizing speed over efficiency in the face of uncertainty."[14] Where blitzscaling is used, growth trumps sustainable unit economics (the associated revenue and costs for a business model, expressed on a per-unit basis) and profitability.

But for many startups operating in ecosystems where capital is less readily available and shocks are frequent, a growth-only mindset is not only impractical but also unjustifiable. Frontier Innovators are pioneering an alternative model.

At the Frontier, the Camel Survives

The growth-at-all-cost model simply does not translate to the realities of the Frontier. Instead of the unicorn, then, I propose the camel as the more appropriate mascot. Camels live in and adapt to multiple climates. They can survive without food or water for months. Their humps, primarily composed of fat, protect them from the desert's scorching heat. When they do find water, they can rehydrate faster than any other animal.[15] Camels are not imaginary creatures living in fictitious lands. They are resilient and can survive in the harshest places on earth.

In this chapter, I explain how Camels prioritize sustainability, and thus survival, from the get-go by balancing growth and cash flow. But first, it is important to understand Silicon Valley's perspective on how startups succeed.

Scaling through the Valley of Death

Startups are not companies. In the early days, they are developing a new product or service and don't yet have customers. Therefore, startups spend more money than they earn. Eventually, they begin to sell to customers. For some startups, this process takes a few months. For others, such as Magic Leap, which raised $1.9 billion over eight years before ever releasing a product, it can take years.[16]

Even after startups are successfully selling products to customers and are generating revenue, they continue to lose money. Fixed costs may be large, given the investment required to build technological infrastructure—the same investment whether there is one customer or thousands. Therefore, sales are too small at first to cover operating costs.

FIGURE 3-1

Classic valley of death

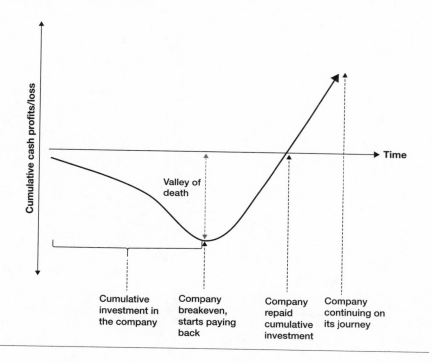

Compounding this, startups are spending capital to attract new custom-ers (often taking a few months to start generating revenue).

The classic "valley of death" model, pictured in figure 3-1, describes this phenomenon. Startups might have a good business model but have negative cash flow until they hit sufficient sales volume to support their operations. This is the irony of the valley of death; the company could be performing well, but it still requires capital to get out of the valley and to survive until it reaches profitability.

What distinguishes Silicon Valley's approach to building startups is its prioritization of growth over profitability. This deepens the valley of death into a chasm, heightening the absolute need for venture fund-ing for survival—and ensuring an increasingly binary outcome of either

FIGURE 3-2

Silicon valley of death

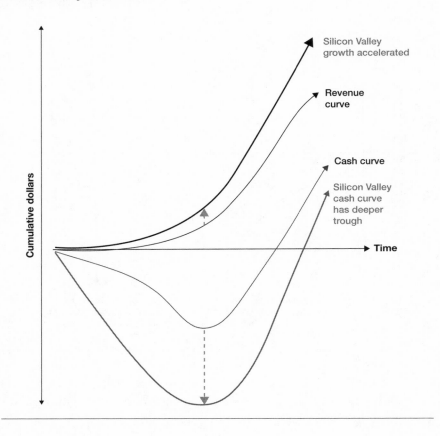

massive success or oblivion for the company. Figure 3-2 explains it succinctly.

Silicon Valley startups raise and invest huge amounts of capital (the curve at the bottom that dips very deep) to invest in growth, often subsidizing costs to drive usage. The hope is that the revenue line will shift upward and increase exponentially, mimicking a shape my fellow Canadians know intimately: a hockey stick.

As revenue scales, and assuming costs don't scale commensurately, profitability eventually sneaks past zero (the bottom of the cash curve) and grows rapidly beyond. This strategy works well for startups that successfully make it through to the other side: if rapid user growth takes off, they can indeed become very large, very fast.

To succeed in this construct relies on a relentless pursuit of growth. It is in some ways the forced march of Silicon Valley. Investment rounds are called Series A, B, C, and so on, sequentially taking on the next letter for the next stage in a company's growth.

As companies progress on growth, their capital needs (to fund the bottom of the curve) become even more dire. Funding rounds thus become ever larger. However, their capacity to raise future investment is predicated on ever-accelerating revenue and the promise of future profitability. If things continue as planned, valuations and companies continue to grow. But profits don't necessarily follow. Companies like Lyft and Uber have recently gone public. Neither is anywhere near profitability. In the first quarter after its IPO and after ten years in operation, Uber lost $1 billion.[17]

If growth is the objective, then venture capital is both its talisman and its servant. When companies raise venture capital, they turbocharge their growth. As First Round Capital's Josh Kopelman once explained, "I sell jet fuel."[18]

Venture capital can also be addictive. If companies get used to running on jet fuel, it becomes harder to switch to diesel. When a startup accelerates growth, it needs to hire people, invest in new infrastructure, expand offices, and spend more on marketing—all before new revenue materializes. The bottom curve, the valley of death, gets pushed ever deeper. If, at that point, the company wants to stop raising capital, it can't. Even though it has growing revenue, it will not be profitable. It will fail unless it stays on the venture capital merry-go-round and raises more capital.

Because growth is a key metric that determines a venture capitalist's enthusiasm, entrepreneurs in Silicon Valley are incentivized, once they've started using jet fuel, to spend even more aggressively. This practice both deepens the cash curve (bottom curve) and accelerates the revenue hockey stick.

Hopefully, the startup comes out the other side. If it does, it will be on the road to success, and possibly even become a unicorn. Unicorn founders are rewarded not only with riches but also with fame, adulation, and nearly guaranteed funding for their next venture. The same is true for venture capitalists. Because each individual investment is extremely high risk, venture capitalists look for opportunities that may individually provide outsized returns. A measly return of two times the investment doesn't move the needle when half of a portfolio's bets lose everything.

What's more, successes become notches on an investor's belt. The best venture capitalists are enshrined on the Midas List, the industry's ranking of top professionals (though perhaps the organizers forgot how that particular myth ends).[19] Employees are equally motivated by growth. Typically, employees are rewarded with stock options—a right to purchase stock for a particular price. These are valuable only if the company's value increases. They can be very valuable. When Facebook went public, it minted more than a thousand millionaires.[20] In Twitter's case, it was more than fifteen hundred.[21]

Yet, if success in Silicon Valley means rapid growth, then failing to hit these aggressive growth targets is considered failure. If no significant progress is made after an investment round and the traditional eighteen-month cash window it provides, startups will go for "extensions" or "bridge rounds"—code words for underachievement—to buy more time to hit the right milestones. Investor enthusiasm wanes, and future investment rounds are priced below previous rounds—something that heavily dilutes founders' and managers' shareholding and decreases their incentive to stay with the company. Ultimately, if a company continues to underperform—which in this case might still mean growth that most companies would be excited about, but more modest than the 100 percent or 200 percent increase projections on which the entrepreneurs raised capital—it will go under.

McKinsey & Company, the global consultancy, examined the life cycles of more than three thousand Silicon Valley–style software companies. Its report explains this Silicon Valley dynamic succinctly: "If a health-care company grew at 20 percent annually, its managers and investors would be happy. If a startup grows at that rate, it has a 92 percent chance of ceasing to exist within a few years."[22]

In a recent article about the downside of venture capital for startups, the *New York Times* put it this way:

> For every unicorn, there are countless other start-ups that grew too fast, burned through investors' money and died—possibly unnecessarily. Start-up business plans are designed for the rosiest possible outcome, and the money intensifies both successes and failures. Social media is littered with tales of companies that withered under the pressure of hypergrowth, were crushed by so-called "toxic V.C.s" or were forced to raise too much venture capital—something known as the "foie gras effect."[23]

Signing up for Silicon Valley's unicorn-hunting strategy is a bit like mortgaging your home to buy three new homes. If things go well and the market moves in the right direction, then the rewards are massive. Facebook's eye-watering returns for investors are a case in point. Yet this approach also increases the likelihood of losing everything.

In Silicon Valley, this is the strategy par excellence. The *burn* rate (an apt reference to the amount of cash that startups spend every month before profitability) at startups in Silicon Valley is the highest it has been since 1999. More people are working for money-losing companies now than in the past fifteen years. Attitudes seem to be changing as well. As the *Wall Street Journal* reports, "In '01 or '09, you just wouldn't go take a job at a company that's burning $4 million a month. Today everyone does it without thinking."[24]

Frontier Innovators remind us that a different model exists. While they still pursue and achieve rapid growth, Frontier Innovators balance it with other objectives.

Alone on an Island at the Frontier

Silicon Valley has an entire system to create and support unicorns. At the Frontier, things could not be more different.

Entrepreneurs are often alone on an island.

First and foremost, there is less capital. Brazil, which enjoys one of the larger startup ecosystems in emerging markets, received $575 million in venture investment capital in 2017.[25] To put that into context, it's a mere $2.75 per capita, versus Silicon Valley's whopping $1,809 per capita.[26]

Lack of capital is a problem not only for emerging markets. In the United States, the 60 percent of startup investments outside the West Coast received only 40 percent of the capital.[27] Regions like the Midwest and the South receive much less capital per capita. For example, in 2016, Chicago and Austin received $443 million and $583 million in capital, respectively, versus San Francisco's $6 billion.[28]

Fundraising timelines are also longer. Competitive Silicon Valley deals move from first meeting to term sheet (contract with venture capital firm to invest) in a matter of weeks, and to investment closure (after review of legal documents) in a couple of months. Rounds tend to follow a natural cadence, every twelve to eighteen months, as companies progress from Series A to Series D.[29] In emerging markets, most rounds take months to get to a term sheet and longer still to close—a reflection of the global nature of the businesses and the investors, and often a lack of urgency given a lack of competition for the deals.

This system leads to a perpetual cycle of fundraising. The dearth of capital at the Frontier means rounds are smaller and more frequent, and thus companies are regularly undercapitalized, something that leads to having to fundraise again sooner.[30] Research from Endeavor, a global entrepreneurship-focused nonprofit, indicates that among emerging-market entrepreneurs in its network, 69 percent had spent more than six months fundraising in the past year.[31]

At the same time, the cost of failure for founders is considerably greater at the Frontier. Starting a business in an emerging ecosystem tends to require an assumption of great personal risk. It can take many years for a company to gain access to venture capital funding, and, in the meantime, salaries don't come in and fees pile up. In many markets, debts are not forgiven in bankruptcy and can follow you for the rest of your life. In other places, bankruptcy can even be illegal.[32]

Unlike Silicon Valley, there is a limited safety net for founders at the Frontier. If things don't go well, the company likely won't get absorbed by a larger player; that's because the culture of "acquihires" (acquiring a company only for its team, giving founders a face-saving exit and an attractive stock option package in the new host company) is much less prevalent. Failing often means really failing—firing all the employees, killing the product, and going bankrupt. In many markets, failure can be a lifelong black mark on careers. As the *New York Times* once wrote about Europe's entrepreneurial ecosystem, "Failure is regarded as a personal tragedy."[33] Failure is much more financially and personally painful at the Frontier. Accordingly, it is not flaunted as a battle scar, but hidden as a blemish.

Unsurprisingly, Frontier Innovators have developed an alternative model.

Camels of the Midwest

Mike Evans and Matt Maloney founded Grubhub in Chicago in 2004. Their vision was to enable small restaurants to offer food delivery. Grubhub focused on sustainability from the get-go. It charges restaurants commissions for every sale it makes, and customers pay a delivery fee. Mike and Matt focused on scaling transactions, but doing so while keeping revenues above their costs (particularly payroll, the largest and most fixed cost). As Mike says, "The company focused on revenue and cash flow from day one, prioritizing these over growth-centric vanity metrics like the number of users or employees."[34]

Grubhub raised what Silicon Valley might consider comparatively meager amounts. Its Series A round was $1.1 million, three years after starting (now the average Silicon Valley Series A among top firms exceeds $15 million).[35] This round was followed by a Series B in 2009 of $2 million, and a Series C of $11 million in 2010. In total, the company raised $84 million in venture capital (eclipsed by Silicon Valley competitors like DoorDash, which has raised $1.4 billion).[36]

Despite the relatively small amounts of capital raised, Grubhub was profitable at every fundraise. Grubhub launched with no outside investment and bootstrapped for the first few years, managing to break even through that time. It raised each round for a specific purpose. For example, its $11 million Series C was to expand to three specific cities.[37] But Mike and Matt did this only after they had created a playbook for the team to follow and achieve unit economics.

In 2014, the company went public on the Nasdaq. In 2018, Grubhub made more than $1 billion in revenue from 14.5 million active users and eighty thousand restaurants in seventeen hundred cities in the United States.[38] Its current market capitalization exceeds $6 billion.[39]

The Frontier Ditches of Death

As Mike and Matt can attest, Frontier Innovators don't avoid growth. Of course not. They are trying to scale a business, after all. Many of these innovators enjoy network effects and enviable rates of growth. However, their scaling trajectory may not have the same perfect exponential hockey-stick curve to which Silicon Valley startups aspire.

Instead, Frontier Innovators focus on sustainable growth from day one. The cash curve does not dip as deeply. Figure 3-3 shows the dynamic.

With a balanced growth strategy, Frontier Innovators can grow in controlled spurts, choosing to accelerate and invest in growth (thus accelerating revenue and cash spend) when the opportunity calls for it. Grubhub's revenue curve had multiple waves, each signifying a mini-growth sprint.[40] Figure 3-4 shows the dynamic.

Growth is achieved in manageable increments, and profitability is either reached again in short order or is within reach if necessary. Consequently, instead of facing a single, large, unsurpassable valley of death, many Camels cross something more akin to a few shallow ditches of death. The curves may not necessarily look as rhythmic as in figure 3-3, and the magnitudes of the dips will vary, deepening for example if a

FIGURE 3-3

Frontier valley of death

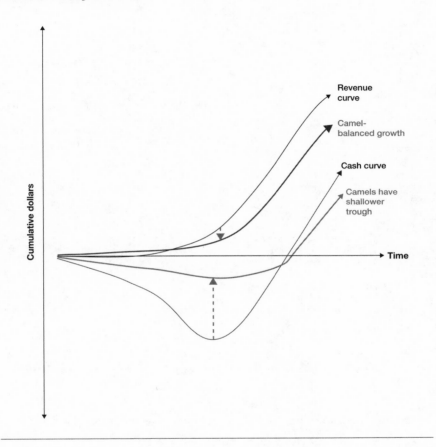

Frontier Innovator raises incremental capital for a particular opportunity. The key distinction here is that Camels preserve the option to modulate growth and head back to a sustainable business if needed.

As Monica Brand Engel, the co-founder of Quona Capital, a leading emerging market investment firm, once quipped to me about this strategy, "breakeven is the new black."[41] This not only is a smart strategy in places with scarce venture capital, but also it can mean the difference be-

FIGURE 3-4

Frontier ditches of death

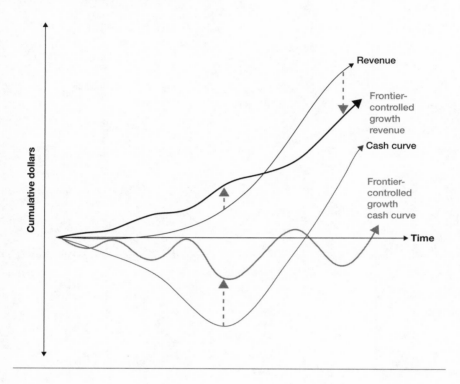

tween survival and failure in the event of a severe shock (such as the effect of Zambia's currency free fall on Zoona's revenues).

Silicon Valley would argue that this approach leads to linear rather than exponential growth, yielding lower returns than an all-out blitzkrieg of growth.

Counterintuitively, however, this is not the case. A study by PitchBook Data demonstrates that venture capital returns in the US Midwest are among the best in the country. Remarkably, among successful exits, nearly half (45 percent) of Chicago investments have provided a multiple on invested capital (MOIC; the capital returned relative to the original investment) of 10x, compared with only 25 percent in the Bay Area. From

2006, the average MOIC was 5.6x for Chicago, outpacing the Bay Area's 4.2x by a significant amount.[42]

In tandem, failure rates at the Frontier tend to be lower. Silicon Valley is quick to say that 90 percent of startups fail.[43] But research from All-World Network, an organization co-founded by Harvard Business School professor Michael Porter, determined that entrepreneurs in emerging markets have an increased survival rate.[44] Troy Henikoff, co-founder of Chicago-based SurePayroll (a leading US internet payroll player) and now a venture capitalist with MATH Venture Partners (which invests in Chicago), says this of his portfolio: "For a portfolio of sixteen companies, you would expect that after three years we'd already have a number of failures. However, we have so far had none. Like many companies in the Midwest, our portfolio has had much stronger survivorship."[45] Anecdotally, the same is true of my own investment portfolio in emerging markets.

These impressive outcomes are the result of a concerted strategy that balances growth with sustainability and resilience. To accomplish this, Frontier Innovators manage costs, charge for the value they create from the get-go, ingest capital on their terms, understand the levers for action, diversify the business plan, and take a long-term outlook.

Manage Costs

Frontier Innovators manage costs through the life cycle of their companies. Like Grubhub, they manage the cost curve to better sync with the growth curve. New hires need to be justified by increases in revenue and operations. Investments in marketing need to be scaled at an appropriate pace. Spending levels are modulated so that the business doesn't go too far down the cost curve hole. As Jason Fried, founder of Basecamp, another successful Chicago-based company, explains, "As a technology startup, there are few excuses to not be profitable as a startup. A big part of this is managing your cost structure. Yet managing costs is not something you hear enough about [in Silicon Valley]. If you are not managing costs [and investing only in growth], you're not building a business. You are building a financial instrument, which is not healthy."[46]

It also helps that Frontier Innovators often enjoy an important cost advantage. For startups, the largest cost is people, particularly in the early days. In San Francisco, the cost of living has been skyrocketing, and so have wages (at least for technology workers). The current cost of hiring a software developer in Silicon Valley is double Toronto's average salary, seven times São Paulo's, and eight times Nairobi's.[47] Of course, it is not only wages, but also rent and other operational costs, that are much cheaper in these latter cities.

The combination of leveraging this cost advantage and managing spending levels means that even when innovators face smaller rounds, the capital can go further. A lower-cost base decreases the depth of the cash curve. This means that for a similar investment, a startup in a lower-cost area has a longer *runway* (time to operate before running out of cash). This gives them more time to grow revenues and build sustainability, and it increases their resilience to shocks.

There Is No Free Lunch

Entrepreneurs working in tougher, less-developed markets don't share Silicon Valley's obsession with offering free or subsidized products in service of growth. They charge their customers for their products.

In Silicon Valley entrepreneurs are willing to subsidize their product. *Vanity Fair* explains it this way:

> Start-ups offer free credit to lure in new users who might not be drawn to the service or even know about it otherwise. They can afford to subsidize these services through the influx of venture-capital funding they've received. And because an increase in users is often proof enough that their concept is working— whether or not new users stick around—these start-ups can go back to investors and raise more money, continuing the cycle

until their funding dries up or they find a way to cut their reliance on subsidizing customer acquisition.[48]

Yet this approach can backfire. For example, on-demand food startups that deliver prepackaged meal ingredients have faced challenges in converting new users they enticed with free products into becoming recurring subscribers.[49] Similarly, in the ride-hailing industry, venture capital funding has been accused of saturating the market, supporting copycat businesses, and leading consumers to default to the cheapest options in a rapidly commoditized market.[50] Many behavioral economists have further documented enduring problems with subsidized or free products: users don't appropriately value the product, and later it is hard to switch them to paying for what they formerly got for free.[51]

At the Frontier, innovators charge for the value they offer from the start. Grubhub's Mike Evans explains the dynamic succinctly: "I am building a business, not a hobby. Businesses make revenues, and hobbies don't."[52]

Frontier Innovators understand that a product's price is not a barrier to adoption but rather one of its features, reflecting its quality and positioning in the market. In emerging markets, incumbent solutions are either nonexistent or so dysfunctional that customers are willing to pay— often even a premium—for reliable, safe, and efficient products. Despite lower incomes, customers are not looking for free products. They are looking for something that responds to their needs, treats them with dignity, and, most of all, that works. Zoona advertises its product as "Easy Quick Safe," and not "Free" or "Cheap."[53] After all, it is running a money transfer business for people who don't have a lot of money. To draw customers, innovators have to offer a solution worth paying for, and they will be rewarded if they do.

Ingest Less Capital, and Control the Timing

A Frontier Innovator's approach to balancing growth with sustainability affords them many options over Silicon Valley–style startups. The depth of the bottom curve—the cash flow hole—is not nearly as deep. Therefore, Frontier Innovators reduce their reliance on venture capital.

Taking less venture capital can be better for every type of entrepreneur. When raising capital, entrepreneurs sell parts of their companies. Hopefully, through growth, the valuation will rise, increasing the total value of the pie. Because Camels sell less of their companies to investors, founders have a larger share of the pie at exit, along with greater control of the business throughout.

Take the case of Qualtrics. The company was founded in 2002 by Ryan Smith, Scott Smith, Jared Smith, and Stuart Orgill in Provo, Utah, as an online research company. Initially, its aim was to help schools and companies gather feedback from their students and customers through effective online surveys. The company was run out of the family's basement for a few years. To fund growth, the founders used the company's profits. While many venture capitalists approached them, they declined investments as the company scaled. They did eventually raise venture capital a decade later in 2012, but they did it on their terms, when they didn't need it. By then, Qualtrics was already a multibillion-dollar company.[54]

Today, Qualtrics has operations in twelve countries and serves more than eleven thousand customers (including 75 percent of *Fortune* 100 companies). In November 2018, Qualtrics was acquired by SAP for $8 billion.[55] The founders still owned the majority of the company at exit.

Building successful startups without venture capital is rare but not unprecedented. Qualtrics is certainly in good company. Companies like Atlassian, Mailchimp, and RXBAR all scaled in a similar way. Interestingly, they were all built outside Silicon Valley—in Australia, Atlanta, and Chicago, respectively.

Some Frontier Innovators manage their capital needs by modulating growth. Basecamp has taken an extreme approach to both. By all standards, the Chicago-based company is a success; it has been growing for twenty years, has millions of software developer users, and earns millions of dollars in revenue. It has done this without raising capital. Part of its approach is to manage growth: if a product requires more than the target maximum employee count of fifty people, the company shutters the product, even if it is successful, to stay small.[56] David Heinemeier Hansson, co-founder of Basecamp and creator of Ruby on Rails, noted, "Why is growth inevitable? It won't guarantee longevity, and it doesn't promise profits. And aren't those the two main, economic concerns of a business? To be ongoing and to make money? When I look at [Basecamp] I can easily satisfy those basic, economic demands: We're still here, and we're still making plenty of money."[57]

Of course, this is not meant to suggest entrepreneurs should avoid venture capital (full disclosure: I am a venture capitalist). Indeed, the vast majority of Camels depend on outside investment. However, Camels are afforded the luxury of *choosing* whether, from whom, and on what terms to raise venture capital (or other types of capital). Like Mailchimp or Basecamp, they can choose not to raise venture capital. Or like Qualtrics or Atlassian, they can choose to raise money for a particular purpose or at a particular point. In chapter 10, you will discover how venture capitalists are also rethinking the model and adapting it to better suit the needs of innovators.

Understand the Levers for Action

At the Frontier, existential threats could come at any time and from anywhere. The Zambian kwacha crash was one such existential threat for Zoona.

Frontier Innovators are intimately aware of these risks, and so they make sure to prepare as much as possible. They understand the necessary levers for action and ways to react in times of crisis. In Zoona's case, Keith Davies had overinvested in a detailed financial model that forecast many economic drivers on the vibrancy of Zoona's booths, as well as the resulting cash needs of the business under multiple scenarios. As Keith explains it, "We were able to understand with confidence and show our investors and partners a range of potential outcomes, and how our business would fare in each."[58]

When the crisis hit, Zoona acted fast. It assessed the impact of the massive devaluation on the business and then called investors and made a plan of action—including rightsizing the company, slowing booth investment, and modulating various cost lines. As a stopgap, the company received a small capital injection and actively tracked the evolving situation.[59]

This approach helped Zoona survive the currency crisis. However, it was by no means the company's last challenge.

Don't Put All of Your Eggs in One Basket

In financial planning, we are taught to not put all our eggs in one basket, but rather to diversify assets and geographies. Yet entrepreneurs are hyper-concentrated, often with their life savings and livelihoods entirely intertwined with their ventures. In Silicon Valley, startups operate like mosquitoes, having a singular focus. Frontier Innovators often take a more financially sane strategy—reflective of the complexities of their ecosystems—by building diversification in to their geography and product mix.

Take the case of Frontier Car Group (FCG), a leading used-car marketplace in emerging markets. As co-founder Sujay Tyle says, "We spread our risk across the world. We narrowed it originally to five markets (Mexico, Nigeria, Turkey, Pakistan, and Indonesia), which will serve as regional hubs. If they work, we will expand. If they don't, we have a portfolio."[60]

Some markets, such as Turkey, struggled. Others, such as Nigeria, faced currency crises. Accordingly, FCG toggled the level of investment by geography. In Nigeria, the company limited exposure until the currency stabilized, and in Turkey it shut the operation down. It also doubled down on what was working. Its strongest geography was Mexico, and from that launching pad, it has now entered four markets in Latin America. As of summer 2018, FCG's transactional platform had sold fifty thousand cars and had expanded to eight markets.[61] So far, FCG has raised nearly $170 million, including a Series C in May 2018 led by Naspers.[62]

Similarly, VisionSpring, a global social enterprise that offers eyeglasses to the poor, built diversity in to its business and market mix. VisionSpring has three business lines: sales to wholesalers, sales through intermediaries, and direct sales (in partnership with local nonprofits for distribution). It is active in six markets. This effectively means that there are eighteen businesses, each at a different level of maturity and scale. The more-mature ones support the others.[63]

These approaches are synergistic with other themes covered in this book. In chapter 2 you learned how Frontier Innovators can operate a horizontal stack, offering multiple, self-reinforcing product lines, and in chapter 5 you will explore how Frontier Innovators operate in multiple markets. As you will see, these strategies are proactive approaches to growth and often necessarily reflect the nascent ecosystems in which Frontier Innovators operate. They are also implicit diversification strategies.

There is evidence that the diversification strategy is effective in building resilience in emerging markets. Research published in *Harvard Business Review* explains that "highly diversified business groups can be particularly well suited to the institutional context in most developing countries. [They] can add value by imitating the functions of several institutions that are present only in advanced economies. Successful groups effectively mediate between their member companies and the rest of the economy."[64] In markets where there is less judicial redress for customers who are wronged, a trusted brand helps. After building a successful reputation on the back of one market segment, multiline businesses leverage this trust elsewhere.

Similarly, in markets with limited capital markets, diversified players cross-fund businesses to support high-potential ventures. In markets with limited training, multiline businesses can keep their best talent and offer them valuable experience across the organization. Relatedly, this strategy also helps innovators mitigate labor market inflexibility (e.g., it's hard to fire people when business needs change) by letting them rebalance human capital across a broader range of activities.[65]

Although the study was particularly concerned with large, diversified groups—such as the chaebols of Korea, grupos of Latin America, or business houses of India—the logic is the same for Frontier Innovators. In especially challenging operating environments, companies having multiple business lines fill institutional voids. As you saw in chapter 2, the approach of building multiple businesses is often not a choice but a necessity given the lack of local infrastructure.

Yet the portfolio approach can go too far. One of the reasons Silicon Valley advises against this strategy for startups is that building fast-growing startups is extremely difficult and requires a massive amount of effort and dedication. It often requires the metaphorical 110 percent focus. As any founder will tell you, building one startup is demanding enough. Being spread too thin across multiple projects is a recipe for mediocrity in each. At its extreme, this dynamic presents itself in certain developing ecosystems as a phenomenon called *portfolio entrepreneurship*, whereby entrepreneurs start a series of unrelated subscale businesses. This practice, often a result of a fear of failure (rather than a clear-eyed resilience strategy), manifests itself when entrepreneurs hedge their bets to save face if any one business fails. Yet it also leads to low likelihood of big success in any one business.[66]

Therefore, the lesson should not be about building diversification for its own sake or in an ad hoc manner. Rather, it is about building a portfolio strategically, and when necessary. A portfolio of activities can be both self-reinforcing and self-balancing. *Self-reinforcing* means that success and learning from one area (say, an emerging best practice for Frontier Car Group to manage fraud) supports the rest of the business. *Self-balancing* allows for managing risk if any of the segments are not working or are facing particular risks, without threatening the whole (in Zoona's case, the currency crisis was particularly challenging because the company had only just begun to scale outside Zambia).

Of course, this strategy is primarily to counter extremely challenging ecosystems. It is often more operationally complex and resource intensive. Therefore, in comparatively stable markets, such as those in the United States, a more concentrated strategy may be advisable.

Take a Long-Term View

Frontier Innovators focus on sustainability over growth-at-all-costs. Consequently, they take a longer view of success.

Analysis of startups in Asia, Africa, and Latin America suggests that the average time to exit is more than thirteen years, and exit times can drag on far beyond that.[67] That's about double the exit times in Silicon Valley, where average time to exit is six to eight years (although unicorns are now tending to stay private longer in Silicon Valley).[68]

Ryan Smith of Qualtrics explains: "This is not a five-year game. It is a twenty-year game. In the early days, we had a good business, but our big breakthrough came in years thirteen through seventeen when we switched to enterprise." For Smith, giving new initiatives time to mature was critical: "Every successful bet we made looked terrible when we started. Everything took longer than we expected. The ability to wait and the flexibility to stick with it was crucial."[69]

This dynamic is particularly true in emerging markets. When advising founders operating in developing markets, I suggest survival as the number 1 strategy. This gives you time to evolve the business model, find a product that resonates with customers, and develop a machine that can deliver at scale. There may be competition. The race is not always about who gets to market first. It is about who survives the longest. Achmad Zaky, co-founder and CEO of Bukalapak, an Indonesian startup valued at $1 billion, boiled this approach down (and added an animal to our menagerie) when he quipped, "We are like cockroaches. They don't shy away from eating anything. They can outlive a nuclear blast. They just survive."[70]

A longer-term outlook decreases the trade-off between growth and risk and allows for resilience. As Mike Evans notes, "It took us ten years to IPO. We could have shrunk that to eight by prioritizing growth over profitability. But we would have increased risk by seven times. We chose sustainability."[71] Grubhub took longer than it otherwise could have to get to an exit but did so with higher resilience; the company was able to absorb risks and challenges along the way.

Supposedly, Albert Einstein once said, "Compound interest is the most powerful force in the universe." A long-term view gives Frontier Innovators the opportunity to grow their ideas to maturity and reap the compound benefits of that growth.

Why It Matters

News headlines lead us to believe that venture capital is plentiful and only looking for a home. Just look at SoftBank's eye-popping $100 billion Vision Fund. It would appear that the unicorn-chasing strategy is unstoppable, at least for now.

But that misses the point.

Compared with Silicon Valley–style startups, Frontier Innovators operate in more challenging ecosystems, with far fewer resources available, much greater risk of experiencing external shocks, and much greater downside in case of failure. Their business models reflect these realities.

Despite Frontier Innovators' best efforts and use of every trick in the book, these challenges remain existential threats for even the best companies. After successfully weathering the Zambian currency crisis, Zoona diversified into new markets and experienced a period of growth. Recently, however, a sudden and seismic shift in the competitive landscape upended its unit economic assumptions, forcing it to adjust its business plan and seek a new round of venture capital from skittish investors wary of the markets in which Zoona operates. As it did in 2015, it is tapping in to its inner Camel and navigating these new challenges—another round in the endless boxing match for survival at the Frontier.

But Zoona's story is not unique to the Frontier. Some areas in Silicon Valley also face an uphill battle raising capital, especially if their business models do not fit the standard mold; for instance, the cleantech industry remains a black sheep.[72] We know, of course, that the good times never last and that the US economy is also susceptible to shocks.

Certain pockets of Silicon Valley are catching on. A movement called Zebras Unite (yes, another alternative animal name for startups that are not unicorns) is focused on raising awareness for the range of startups for which the Silicon Valley unicorn-chasing growth strategy is not appropriate. The movement now has more than forty chapters and fifteen hundred members around the world.[73]

Indeed, it seems that building sustainable and resilient businesses is a good idea for entrepreneurs of all stripes and humps.

4.

Cross-Pollinate

Connect Ideas and Networks from around the World

Silicon Valley thrives on the stereotype of the twenty-two-year-old college dropout building a company in a garage—combining youthful passion and a dose of grit to challenge age-old industries.

The stereotype is the stuff of legend. The storied founders of the world's most successful tech companies support this trend: Apple (Jobs, twenty-one, Wozniak, twenty-six), Microsoft (Gates, twenty-one), and Facebook (Zuckerberg, twenty).[1]

Yet prizing youth comes at a cost. Silicon Valley is known for its "tech bros"—the young, behoodied warriors often accused of building products and services to do tasks Mom doesn't do for them anymore.

This should not come as a surprise. An entrepreneur builds companies based on their life experience. And a twenty-two-year-old's experience is short, local, and often myopic.

At the Frontier, a typical innovator's lived experience is longer and spans geographies, sectors, and industries. This diversity in experience explains the issues they choose to tackle and the unique approaches they employ.

The Road Less Traveled

Idriss Al Rifai is no stranger to challenges. He grew up in Iraq, but when the first Iraq war started, his family fled to Paris. Now he speaks with an unmistakable French accent. When Rifai was eighteen, he played professional basketball, ultimately representing France on its national team, playing alongside Tony Parker. Reflecting on why he left basketball, Idriss quipped, "I wasn't Tony Parker." He later joined the French Special Forces, where he led operations across Chad, the Democratic Republic of Congo, Mali, and Somalia. He was eventually recruited to become an adviser to the defense minister of France.

However, Idriss had always dreamed of returning to the Middle East and starting his own business. To equip himself, he pursued an MBA at the University of Chicago and then joined the Boston Consulting Group's Dubai office.

Settling into his new life in Dubai, Idriss realized that critical business infrastructure he had seen elsewhere was lacking. His new job required him to procure items from all over the world, but often he could not get his packages delivered. The driver didn't show up or would get lost, or the package would get delayed for any number of other reasons. As in Nairobi, there were no street addresses in certain parts of the city.

Dubai's existing delivery infrastructure could not cope with the growth in e-commerce markets. For one thing, the United Arab Emirates faced an acute undersupply of drivers. To complicate things, e-commerce had to rely on customers paying for their items with cash on delivery, because large swaths of the population had no access to financial products (as in many emerging markets).

The system was fragile and unreliable. When customers ordered items online, merchants hoped for three variables to work in their favor: first, that the address existed; second, that customers would accept the delivery (having not yet paid, customers could reject packages if they changed their minds); and third, that customers would have cash to pay for it. If any aspect did not go according to plan, the drivers would be unable to complete the delivery and the merchant would eat the cost of the returns. Unsurprisingly, this was a huge burden to e-commerce players.

To solve this challenge, Idriss founded Fetchr, a last-mile logistics company for the Middle East. Using an app, consumers can better track when packages will be delivered and can be ready to accept them. Drivers can be much more effective through trip planning and route optimization.

Not Your Typical Silicon Valley Entrepreneur

Although Idriss's personal story is exceptional, it illustrates key qualities many Frontier Innovators share.

Like Idriss, Frontier Innovators often have significant lived experience; they rarely start their businesses at age twenty-two. Indeed, the average founding age among leading startups in Latin America, Africa, and Southeast Asia is thirty-one.[2] Idriss was in his mid-thirties when he started Fetchr.[3] Emerging-market entrepreneurs also tend to have more educational and entrepreneurial experience. An analysis of the portfolios of more than forty accelerators around the world revealed that entrepreneurs in emerging markets have 1.65 university degrees on average (compared to 1.45 in developed markets) and worked at an average of 2.8 companies prior to founding their new organizations (often reporting to the CEO or executive director in previous roles).[4]

It is not just age that matters, but what Frontier Innovators do with their additional years. Many of the most successful Frontier Innovators have lived and worked in multiple countries. Of the ten unicorns (a term I'll continue to use herein as a metric of valuation rather than endorsement of the philosophy) built in Southeast Asia over the past ten years, eight had founders that had studied, lived, or worked abroad.[5] Unsurprisingly, a similar overrepresentation exists in Latin America, where well over half of the founders of Latin American unicorns had worked or studied abroad.[6]

Even those who did not have global experiences early in life cultivated them later. Among a sample of founders of leading unicorns across Latin America, India, Southeast Asia, and Sub-Saharan Africa, 23 percent belong to global fellowships or leadership development programs, including Endeavor or World Economic Forum, and 22 percent joined global accelerators.[7]

Frontier Innovators are thus cross-pollinators. They bridge information across geographies, industries, and sectors to create novel business models or solutions. Unsurprisingly, at least for those outside the Valley, being a cross-pollinator drives performance.

Cross-Pollinators Access the Innovation Supply Chain

Innovation is moving in integrated global flows. The *innovation supply chain* describes the phenomenon by which the best ideas traverse continents and improve with successive waves of adaptation.[8] Cross-pollinators leverage the innovation supply chain to find multiple sources of inspiration for their models.

Ride sharing, for instance, started as an innovation pioneered by Uber and Lyft in San Francisco. Startups rapidly exported the model across the globe and adapted it, sometimes significantly, to reflect local needs. Gojek, the ride-sharing app from chapter 2 that is now the dominant local player in Indonesia, did not merely replicate Uber. Rather, Gojek's approach improved upon the ride-sharing model, maximizing driver engagement throughout the day by not only transporting people but also delivering food, packages, and even financial services.

Gojek's strategy incorporates inspiration from China as well. China's technology ecosystem rivals Silicon Valley in many ways. In payments, Ant Financial (Alibaba's $150 billion financial technology affiliate) operates the world's largest mobile payment platform, Alipay. To pay or send money via Alipay, users leverage the social network and unique QR codes (a computer-readable graphic that embeds simple information or an online link). Tencent's WeChat (Alibaba's archrival) has created an entire ecosystem of products and services, spanning payments, ride hailing, shopping, and food delivery on its social network. Both are ubiquitous in major Chinese cities.[9] Replicating WeChat and Ant's functionality, Gojek evolved its model to include a payment platform as part of a broader super-app—one platform to rule them all, with the ambition to offer consumers every possible service in one place.

The multidirectional exchange of ideas continues, and in this case has gone full circle. Some of Uber's recent product launches, such as Uber Eats and its Uber credit card, seem more akin to Southeast Asia's model.[10] Fittingly, Uber recently repackaged these products into its own super-app.[11]

Frontier Innovators tap in to information about which innovations are thriving, along with where and why that's the case. With this data, they are better positioned to conceive of innovative models.

One approach is to focus on "superconductor" locations such as Silicon Valley. In this way, learning from the Valley is still of value. As JF Gauthier, CEO of Startup Genome, told me, "Talk to ten seasoned global venture capitalists in Silicon Valley. They probably have met a meaningful subset of the startups in your space globally. Talk to fifty, and you probably will get to know of a good portion of the ecosystem."[12] That's because many innovators from around the world have also come to Silicon Valley and met the same venture capitalists.

Of course, Silicon Valley is only one of many hubs that matter. China is emerging as a global leader, and certainly some of the pioneering models in e-commerce and fintech outshine what we're seeing in the United States. Kenya remains the place to go for innovation in mobile banking on non-smart phones. Toronto and Montreal are artificial intelligence hubs. Minneapolis is a thriving health care hub. Tel Aviv is a leader in security. London is a leader for fintech. If you are a Frontier Innovator trying to understand leading trends that can catalyze your business, or identify emerging threats to your nascent organization, superconductor locations will help you find answers rapidly.

Cross-pollinators combine their own lived experience with multiple ideas to conceive of their business models. For Idriss Al Rifai, building Fetchr required an understanding of what was possible, both by having firsthand experience of the issues and by bridging insights from multiple industries. Idriss was inspired by efficient last-mile delivery systems pioneered by the largest e-commerce players in the West.

In markets with limited street addresses, Fetchr leveraged advances made by emerging-market ride-sharing players that had perfected GPS-linked addressing and route optimization for their on-demand fleets. The solution also required insights from emerging-market financial services—most crucially, cash-based collection models—to facilitate deliveries for the unbanked. Finally, Idriss faced an acute driver shortage and so had to build an immigration strategy, which he developed in close consultation with experts who supported construction players in the region who similarly faced human capital shortages. Doing all this simultaneously required both the precision of a military operation and the competitiveness of a professional athlete. To devise his solution, Idriss also employed the strategic problem-solving skills he gained in consulting and leveraged his knowledge from working in remote parts of the world as well as his experience with government bureaucracy.

Similarly, Zola's model combines multiple technological and business model innovations. Its home solar systems, targeted at the 800 million Africans living offgrid, are sold on a pay-as-you-go basis rather than purchased outright, making the program more affordable. The financing model required a lender's ability to assess credit. In markets where most consumers don't have credit scores, this was made possible by advances in alternative data credit scoring that were gaining steam in other emerging markets. If customers don't pay, the solar systems can be turned off remotely. Advances in mobile phone technologies and internet of things (IoT) from Silicon Valley and elsewhere allowed Zola to place chips in the devices and remotely control and diagnose them. The units themselves were made affordable largely by economies of scale in solar panel and battery production globally, for the most part from China. Finally, the dominance of small transactions necessitated digital payments, which meant integrating mobile money—an African-born innovation. Devising this complicated model required combining multiple technologies and insights into a coherent whole.

To build successful businesses, Frontier Innovators balance an understanding of these global trends while rooting themselves in the local market and the needs of their customers. You'll explore these joint dynamics in the next two sections.

Cross-Pollinators Tap Scarce Resources

Cross-pollinators' experience can provide them access to a global network that pays meaningful dividends. Nowhere is this more evident than with access to innovation's two most precious resources: capital and talent. As you will see throughout this book, in many markets there is a shortage of one or the other, and often both. The best Frontier Innovators are able to tap their global networks to devise solutions to these challenges.[13]

Idriss leveraged his global network to find capital around the world. So far, Fetchr has raised more than $100 million from leading Silicon Valley venture capital firms, European investors, and local venture capital firms. Similarly, Zola leveraged its founder's global network to attract investment from diverse actors around the world, including impact investors in New Zealand, global development organizations, European corporations, and venture capitalists from Seattle, San Francisco, and London.

A cross-pollinator's network also gives them access to proprietary sources of talent. In the next chapter, you will explore how Frontier Innovators position themselves to be multimarket from the get-go, and in chapter 6, you will learn how this sometimes translates into distributed organizations and teams.

Marrying Cross-Pollination with Local Context

A cross-pollinator's perspective brings unique insights and resources to a problem. Of course, successfully building a business requires marrying this perspective with a deep and nuanced knowledge of the local problem you're solving. Bridging the two makes the magic happen.

My favorite example comes from the world of online matchmaking in India. In 1996, Murugavel Janakiraman, who had been working in Silicon Valley, observed the rise of online news and classifieds. Inspired by these platforms, as a small side project he started a basic news website to offer a forum for the Tamil community in India and around the world.

When Murugavel launched the site, he was dismayed to see low user traffic. However, the matrimonial section, which was added as an afterthought, was surprisingly active.[14] At the same time, he had the good fortune (in retrospect) of being laid off from his Silicon Valley role during the internet crisis of 2000. Murugavel decided to double down. He moved back to India to pursue the traction behind the matrimonial section full-time.

That's when BharatMatrimony (the flagship brand of Matrimony.com) was born.

As younger generations of Indians transitioned from the countryside to cities and overseas, the traditional arranged matchmaking process was breaking down. Living away from parents and extended family, singles needed another solution to find their wives and husbands.

Digital dating services were proliferating around the world. However, what worked elsewhere would need to be adapted to the unique local Indian context. As Murugavel was building Matrimony.com, his peers elsewhere were confused by the features he was implementing, thinking they were either overkill or unhelpful, even at times destructive. For example, families occupy a key role in the Indian marriage world. For the site to offer a credible solution, it not only had to help users find potential matches but also had to allow parents to have an active role in the process.[15] In only 60 percent of cases, adult children are the primary users (often in consultation with their parents). In many cases, parents are the principal users on behalf of their offspring.[16]

Murugavel had to further customize the product for specific requests. Cautious parents wanted more than to read about the suitor's work status, education, and income; they wanted validation of these claims. Therefore, Murugavel created an additional service that validates users' degrees through the platform.[17] Matrimony.com also translated the site into multiple local dialects and created sub-brands for individuals who were looking to focus their search within their community, religion, or linguistic preference. And because Indian families value physical meetings with family present, an online-only experience was insufficient. Matrimony .com created three hundred brick-and-mortar locations to facilitate the process.

Today, Matrimony.com has more than four million users, arranges more than a thousand marriage matches daily, and is public on the National Stock Exchange of India. There are fifteen language-based domains catering to different regions of India, each with its unique language and cultural nuance.[18]

Murugavel is a cross-pollinator who combined best practices from Silicon Valley with his unique knowledge of the local market.

Similarly, as Mudassir Sheikha, co-founder and CEO of the Middle Eastern ride-sharing behemoth Careem (whom you will get to know in chapter 11), explained to me, "When Careem expanded to Iraq, we had to adapt to the fact that the country turns off internet and data during national high school exams so the questions don't get leaked. The local team figured out the hack of allowing riders to make their bookings before this shutdown occurs."[19]

For both Murugavel and Mudassir, adapting to the local context was the only possible path to scale.

Where the Frontier and Silicon Valley Must Do Better

Cross-pollinators' outsized success is built on diversity—diversity in experience, culture, and worldview. But often, attaining a globe-spanning skill set and network is possible only for the most privileged members of society. In this way, diversity remains limited across much of the innovation landscape—both in Silicon Valley and at the Frontier.

In US venture capital, 90 percent of decision makers (partner level, primarily) are male.[20] Fewer than 20 percent of technology startups have even one female founder, and female-led startups received less than 2 percent of the capital available in 2018.[21] This is not just about gender. In the United States, 1 percent of venture-backed founders were black, 2 percent were Latinx, and 3 percent were Middle Eastern (regardless of gender).[22] Similarly, the majority of Frontier Innovators, particularly those who reach scale and gain international attention, are men.

Regretfully, this book is an example of this shortcoming. When looking for interview subjects, I came into contact with far fewer women, perhaps because I was not looking hard enough or not correcting the bias of my trusted sources strenuously enough. In any case, this gender imbalance unfortunately is also documented in this text. My hope is that by the time I write the sequel, the industry will have made meaningful strides in the right direction. To truly unlock the world's entrepreneurial talent, we need an environment that enables all genders and people of all backgrounds to succeed. Nor can we sit passively by and wait for these conditions to develop. For starters, diversity, equity, and inclusion initiatives are growing in both popularity and sophistication in the corporate and nonprofit worlds, and joining and furthering these conversations is a great first step for those in positions of power. Solving this at the most senior levels is critical. Research by Kauffman Fellows indicates that startups with at least one female on the founding teams hire two and a half times more women than their less diverse peers.[23]

There are some interesting bright spots in the gender imbalance of the founder landscape in the Arab world. As *MIT Technology Review* notes, more than 25 percent of Middle Eastern startups are founded or led by women.[24] Hala Fadel, co-founder of Beirut-based Leap Ventures, says it is because the region has no male-dominated legacy in the field. Because so few career paths are open to women and because the unemployment rate is often very high, starting technology startups, often from their own homes, is an attractive opportunity for women.[25]

While Frontier Innovators bring greater ethnic and cultural (and occasionally gender) diversity to the world of tech innovation, dramatic economic inequality in their home countries often enables their success as cross-pollinators. Accessing international education or working in challenging roles at global consulting firms or investment banks is often a re-flection of privilege. Becoming a founder is itself a reflection of a certain level of opportunity and an ability to take financial risk. In many markets, institutional capital is scarce, and early capital is often nonexistent. Startup capital often depends on family and friends. In most emerging markets, with hollowed-out middle classes, raising early capital requires wealthy connections.

The prevalence of startups in Sub-Saharan Africa that are founded by expats from Europe and North America also raises important questions about white privilege. In these markets, white expats often enjoy comparatively greater access to capital and networks, even though locals have a far deeper understanding of their own problems and opportunities. Drawing attention to this imbalance is not meant to undermine or undervalue expat founders' herculean efforts, but rather represents an effort to open space for constructive dialog on changing the status quo.

As American paleontologist Stephen Jay Gould once said, "I am, somehow, less interested in the weight and convolutions of Einstein's brain than in the near certainty that people of equal talent have lived and died in cotton fields and sweatshops."[26] Innovation at the Frontier will benefit immensely from the talent of people from all economic strata and all genders. Empowering those people as contributors and leaders will be transformative everywhere.

Immigrants: The Ultimate Cross-Pollinators

Lin-Manuel Miranda said it best in his musical *Hamilton*: "Immigrants, we get the job done!"[27] Immigrants are the ultimate cross-pollinators, bringing life experience from another country or geography. Like Murugavel and Idriss, and like Xavier Helgesen of Zola, repatriates and immigrants have had disproportionate success in scaling innovations and kick-starting ecosystems.[28]

For definition's sake, *repatriates* are citizens of a country that choose to return after spending meaningful portions of their careers abroad (much more than one school degree or a single international job experience). *Immigrants* are citizens of various countries who settle elsewhere.

At the Frontier, repatriates are often among the early set of entrepreneurial successes. For instance, in India, a large part of Bangalore's leaders of the first wave of startups were "boomerangs"—repatriates who had spent significant time in other geographies, often in Silicon Valley.[29] They brought global learning home with them, enhancing their local ecosystems and enabling subsequent waves of homegrown aspiring entrepreneurs.

In this day and age, immigration has become a hot button issue in the United States and internationally. Yet the data is unequivocal, in the United States just as much as at the Innovation Frontier: immigrants play a central role in technological innovation. Between 1995 and 2005, immigrants co-founded 52 percent of all technology startups in Silicon Valley (and represent 25 percent of all entrepreneurship in the United States writ large).[30] Immigrants' role in the most successful startups is equally notable. According to a recent study by the National Foundation for American Policy, more than 50 percent of US-based unicorns were founded by immigrants. These fifty companies have a collective market capitalization of nearly $250 billion, which, for perspective, exceeds the stock markets of Argentina, Colombia, and Ireland.

Further, more than 80 percent of US unicorn companies have an immigrant in a key executive position.[31] This includes some of the best-known companies in the world, such as Houzz, Instacart, Palantir Technologies, Robinhood, Stripe, Uber, WeWork, and Zoom. This of course also includes Silicon Valley's golden child, Elon Musk, who co-founded four unicorns—Tesla, SolarCity, PayPal, and SpaceX—and recently also launched Neuralink and The Boring Company. Musk was born in South Africa and immigrated first to Canada and ultimately to the United States.

Our learning on cross-pollinators provides yet another counterargument to the troubling anti-immigrant narrative that is permeating politics in the United States and around the world. As Jeremy Johnson, co-founder of Andela and 2U, once told me, "The Statue of Liberty reads, 'Give me your tired, your poor, your huddled masses yearning to breathe free.' This is the most exceptional thing that we do [in the United States]."[32]

Removing the Hood

Stepping into the shoes of Frontier Innovators helps Silicon Valley challenge and reevaluate its own stereotypes.

Silicon Valley's obsession with youth and its outward ageism is misplaced.[33] Yes, Jobs, Gates, and Zuckerberg were young when they started their businesses, but research from the National Bureau of Economic Research suggests they are outliers and not the average. The average technology startup founder at founding is forty-two years old, and among the most successful (the top 0.1 percent), the average age is forty-five.[34] Research indicates that when a startup's founders work at a company for twenty years or more, it is more likely to be a top performer in its local startup ecosystem.[35]

Even among the founders of the most successful companies, performance improves with age. Five-year multiples (the price an investor would pay for a dollar of revenue or earnings) peaked in early middle age for Bill Gates (thirty-nine), Jeff Bezos (forty-five), and Steve Jobs (forty-eight).[36]

More-experienced founders are the ones who typically scale successful businesses. Immigrants occupy a central role. More-diverse gender, economic, and other representation is needed to realize the promise of innovation both in Silicon Valley and at the Frontier. After all, inspiration requires combining a range of ideas to create something new, and increasing the diversity of those ideas is what cross-pollination is all about.

5.

Be Born Global

Target the World from Day One

If you ask around in Silicon Valley, you'll find many people who can give you a step-by-step guide to starting a company. If you're not already located there, the most obvious (and often unspoken) first step is to move to Silicon Valley. It offers access to a unique culture and gives you proximity to talent, customers, and acquirers.

Once you're there, it is disturbingly simple to follow precedent and best practices when making a range of seemingly complex business decisions. Where should the company be based? Silicon Valley. Where and how should it be incorporated? As a Delaware C corporation.

How should the technical team be built? Locally from the ready talent pool. The best computer scientists graduate from Stanford, a forty-minute drive away.

Where should the product be piloted, and where can the first customers be found? If customers are businesses (B2B), then the ready local business market in California should be the first target (including other startups in the Valley). If customers are individuals (B2C), then they can easily be found among local tech-loving residents. The earliest adopters—businesses as well as consumers—are concentrated in the San Francisco Bay Area.

Where should the market scale? The United States is a $21 trillion economy, and the largest technology and software market globally.[1] For most startups looking for a niche to target, the United States is sufficiently large. California alone, the fifth-largest economy in the world, is a large enough starting point.

These decisions may be simple for entrepreneurs in Silicon Valley. But for everyone else, there are no obvious answers to these questions.

Frontier Innovators don't share Silicon Valley's myopic local view. They build their startups in a different way: they are "born global." There are three dimensions to being born global: the founder, the company, and the team. In chapter 4, you explored how Frontier Innovators themselves are born global cross-pollinators. The second dimension, covered in this chapter, is the way Frontier Innovators build companies that can sell in multiple markets and capture global opportunities. The third dimension, covered in chapter 6, is the way they build distributed teams, leveraging talent from wherever it is most available.

Critical to Success at the Frontier

Among the most successful startups at the Frontier (particularly among smaller countries or geographies), expanding to multiple markets is directly linked with success. Among the ten unicorns built in Southeast Asia over the past ten years, seven scaled rapidly internationally. Of the three that stayed local (for now), two were based in Indonesia, Southeast Asia's largest market with over 264 million people.[2] Perhaps symbolically, when Garena, a Southeast Asian technology unicorn, filed for an IPO in 2017 on the Nasdaq, to reflect its pan-regional presence, it changed its official name to Sea (now also its ticker symbol).[3]

Frontier startups expand to other markets early in their life cycles. In the Southeast Asia sample, the average startup entered its second country by year four and its next market within another year or two.[4] In Africa, among a sample of the most valuable technology companies, 64 percent had launched into a second market by year four.[5]

Being born global is increasingly a Frontier imperative, as UiPath's founders know well. Founded by Daniel Dines and Marius Tirca, UiPath is Romania's first-ever unicorn. UiPath offers robotic process automation (RPA), which, through artificial intelligence, allows computers to learn repetitive tasks and, over time, automate them. For example, an insurance company that needs to transcribe physical claims from its clients into its internal evaluation system can use RPA to automate the process and free its staff to work on the higher-value tasks of evaluating claims. Similarly, an accountant who needs to categorize clients' particular expenses in repetitive ways can use RPA to automate the task.

Daniel and Marius opened the original business in 2005, focusing only on the Romanian market. A decade later, UiPath was still subscale and primarily a consulting firm. But in 2015, the founders decided to shift their strategy, offer a technology platform, and focus globally. They partnered with Ernst & Young to distribute UiPath's solution to the Ernst & Young corporate ecosystem.[6] Once UiPath opened the global aperture, it rapidly expanded beyond the embryonic Romanian ecosystem, becoming a global powerhouse.[7] Three years into its platform model, UiPath was operating in eighteen countries. The company now has more than a thousand employees and has raised more than $1 billion in capital from leading venture capital firms such as Accel, Sequoia, and Google's CapitalG.[8]

UiPath is perhaps the fastest-growing enterprise sales company of all time.[9] A key driver, as Daniel explains it, was its ability to master global sales from the moment the founders decided to go global.[10]

What's Old Is New

While the phenomenon of being born global is new in startups, it has been documented as a strategy in more-traditional industries. In 1993, McKinsey & Company published a report documenting the rise of

SMEs—small and midsized enterprises, typically with less than $100 million in revenue—having a global focus.[11] Small exporters in Australia started selling internationally almost from the beginning, often in the first two years.

At that time, the strategy of building a multimarket sales model from the get-go flew in the face of conventional wisdom. Best practice was to internationalize incrementally, starting with a domestic focus and then selling through intermediaries over time.[12] Eventually, seeing enough traction, companies might establish an international subsidiary, but often in places that were culturally most proximate.[13] With enough success, they could then become major foreign sellers.

McKinsey uncovered a generation of SMEs that were born global. As its report and decades of subsequent academic research demonstrated, a different approach to building successful companies existed—and was working.[14]

What's playing out now at the Frontier is a similar rejection of conventional wisdom. Frontier Innovators are selling in multiple markets early in their journeys. Indeed, mastering this strategy is fundamental to their success.

Drivers of the Multimarket Model

For Frontier Innovators, there are a few intertwined reasons that being born global is increasingly a strategic imperative.

The first is a realistic assessment of the addressable market. The size of a company's total addressable market (TAM) is a key metric by which venture capitalists gauge a startup's potential. Unfortunately, in many (though certainly not all) emerging markets, the local TAM is too small for the company to scale to a meaningful size. However, for strategic entrepreneurs, the smaller the local market, the larger the total market. Entrepreneurs in Estonia or Singapore are forced to think globally, whereas startups in India and Brazil often focus locally. As Daniel observes, "Being from this remote part of Europe helped us think big."[15] Having a small local market allows startups not only to sell in multiple markets but also to start from anywhere.

Being born global can also function as a learning strategy. It helps innovators improve the core product, evolve the business model, and benefit from economies of scale. Divyank Turakhia, founder of the Dubai-based global advertising technology company Media.net (which he sold in 2018 for $900 million to a Chinese consortium), explains: "Different markets have different margins and different risk profiles. Some may seem on the surface as less attractive relative to others that may be growing faster and have higher margins. But being present in them now still makes sense as you learn about markets and build relationships."[16] By expanding across markets, the whole organization is forced to improve and build a product offering that is competitive everywhere. Over time, this generates economies of scale. Divyank says, "As you upgrade your technology and product, you will get higher margin in those you're not as competitive in today."[17]

Ultimately, being a multimarket company translates into an offensive advantage. Frontier Innovators who are born global can lay out their stakes first in the most-attractive markets, increasing the cost for second movers. When Zola, which you met in the introduction, expanded from East Africa to West Africa in Ivory Coast and Ghana, it was staking out a claim in the most attractive markets. There are other startups that offer a home solar system solution similar to Zola's. But if competitors were similarly looking to expand, it could make more sense for them to look elsewhere.

Born global startups can often outcompete single-market-only players. They can rely on profits from some markets to concentrate resources to fight in the most-competitive markets. Compounded by cost advantages conferred by global economies of scale and the learning from which they've benefited, born global startups are uniquely positioned to win.[18]

In many ways, staying local is not an option. Other companies from elsewhere will eventually arrive on the scene. Therefore, for Frontier Innovators, being born global is often a requirement to survive.

As they say, the best defense can be a strong offense.

It Doesn't Work for Everything

At this point in the discussion, being born global may seem like a natural strategy. Yet its application is nuanced. Many startups have learned this the hard way.

Uber expanded rapidly around the world. It entered Singapore in 2013, and China in 2014.[19] Seemingly as fast as it expanded, though, it started to retrench to its core geographies. In 2016, after spending more than $2 billion and with no profits in sight, Uber exited China and sold its local operations to the national player, DiDi, for $7 billion.[20] In Southeast Asia, a similar story played out, and Uber sold its operations to Grab (itself backed by DiDi).

Why is it that some models seem destined to be truly global while others are not? Three drivers explain whether certain players come to dominate markets globally while others remain more regional or local.

The Nature of the Network Effects

The first success factor is centered on the nature of network effects. *Network effects* reflect the phenomenon that the value of a service or product increases as more people use it. Some startups have global network effects, while others have more regional or even local network effects.

Google, for instance, has become a global standard in search engines, in part because searching the internet has global network effects. The value of information isn't regional. North American users get greater value from the platform when knowledge from Europe or Asia is cataloged. The value of information is global, and thus winners have tended to enjoy global monopolies. Facebook enjoys a similar dynamic. Relationships aren't only local but also international (particularly among the university students where the company began), and thus the value of the platform increases globally.

In contrast, there are business models that have regional or local network effects. Ride sharing is one. While there are globe-trotters who value having a single app they can use to summon a car in any city, for the vast majority of users the value of the transportation app is local. Of course, there are network effects: the more drivers who are on the app, the more users who will want to join, and vice versa. However, these network effects are localized. That's one of the reasons the ride-sharing industry is unlikely to have a global winner emerge. Local players, be it Gojek in Indonesia, 99 in Latin America, or Careem in the Middle East, are equally placed to create the right network effects to dominate their local or regional markets.

Resource Intensity

The second driver that predicts whether global models succeed relates to resource intensity. Where there is higher resource intensity, global winners are more likely to emerge, whereas models that are more asset light are more likely to be local or regional. Cloud computing is a great example. Amazon Web Services (AWS), as well as Microsoft Azure and Google Cloud, have amassed leading positions, together enjoying approximately 50 percent of the global market.[21] These global players dominate because offering a cloud computing product is extremely resource intensive. Amazon and Google must purchase, maintain, and staff server farms and must build software to manage and secure them. Amazon's capital budget for this has been in the billions of dollars over the years. This leads to classic economies of scale: the high-fixed-cost investment can be spread over a larger client base, at progressively lower prices, in turn cementing the economies of scale. These markets trend toward global monopolies.

The same is true of hardware startups. These often require much larger capital investments upfront so that they can go through safety testing and build the products at scale. Yet once they work, they often enjoy sustainable monopolies. No wonder Elon Musk's SpaceX is only one of a small handful of successful space startups (and now delivering payloads to space for governments and corporations around the world).

A similar dynamic exists in certain markets where access to limited, highly specialized talent is required. For example, in the artificial intelligence market, the most precious resources are data scientists and datasets. There is a shortage of available talent specialized in machine learning and artificial intelligence. The best companies have the most-advanced technology and the largest datasets. This in turn attracts the best players. The best players cement and accelerate the technological advantage. This situation will likely yield some global winners.

As for ride hailing, it's not very resource intensive upfront. Sure, the app manager must pay a lot to recruit drivers and attract riders over time. Yet this is a much smaller comparative investment than the actual technological development that a company like SpaceX would have to undertake for a new rocket. Therefore, it is much easier and cheaper for local competitors to launch and gain share in the ride-hailing business.

Local Complexities

The third predictor of whether startups become truly global relates to local complexities—and in some cases veto-like dynamics that exist in certain markets or industries. For instance, companies like Facebook and Google enjoy leading market positions almost everywhere on the planet. The most glaring exception of course is China. This is driven by a regulatory moat, because the companies' websites have been blocked by Chinese regulations (and the government-controlled Great Firewall). In their place, local alternatives have blossomed. Baidu has become the local search leader, and Tencent has a dominant platform in messaging.

Of course, an outright government ban is an exceptional barrier. Yet much more subtle complexities exist as well. Many industries have specialized local regulations that make it challenging to port models across borders. Financial services is a prime example. Most countries impose strict standards on institutions that want to become custodians of their citizens' savings or provide them with credit or insurance products. That's why historically fintech has been a local game, although this is slowly changing.[22]

Strategies for Frontier Innovators

Every industry is unique. Before going global, Frontier Innovators must evaluate their particular industry dynamics and understand the likelihood that a global, regional, or local model will win the market.

Assuming that resource intensity is high, network effects are global, and there are limited local complexities, then Frontier Innovators should scale as fast as possible to responsibly capture as much global share as possible before someone else does. If the opposite is true—if there are regulatory barriers, low resource intensity, or more regional network effects—then Frontier Innovators should instead focus on their regional or local markets. Figure 5-1 illustrates these principles.

Most markets are somewhere in the middle—for example, markets with high resource intensity but few global network effects, or vice versa.

FIGURE 5-1

Local versus global winners

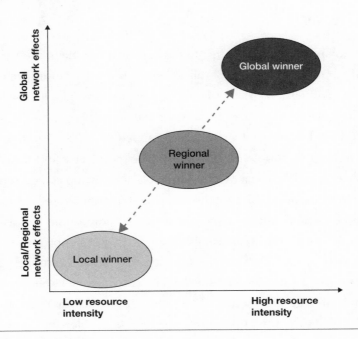

Understanding this dynamic is critical to determining your strategy. Ultimately, any course of action will be an educated bet.

If the decision is to be born global, then a few strategies are essential for success. This includes prioritizing and then staging expansion, developing a product that localizes easily, and building an organization that functions across markets. Let's explore each in turn.

Born Global Market Selection

Being a multimarket company doesn't mean taking a shotgun approach and expanding haphazardly from Mauritius to Mongolia or Botswana to Bali. The first step for an entrepreneur is determining the market selection, prioritization, and staging strategy. Frontier Innovators start thinking about these questions from day one and refine them over time. A key early question is whether some markets are testers and others are must-win.

Tester Markets

Broadway is famous for testing its shows in small markets before committing them to the big stage. Similarly, using market laboratories can be a powerful strategy. SkyAlert, which operates an earthquake early-warning system, took this approach. In most earthquakes, people do not die from the shaking but rather from getting trapped or crushed under collapsing buildings. Technologically, it is possible to perceive and distribute an early warning, because a quake is first felt near the epicenter and travels outward from there. Through its network of distributed sensors, SkyAlert promises its users a head start to evacuate buildings and can work with companies to automate security protocols (e.g., gas shutoff).

SkyAlert began in Mexico City, which Alejandro Cantú, its CEO, describes as his innovation laboratory. The early versions were focused on research and development rather than commercialization. Developing SkyAlert in Mexico City was much more affordable than other major cities for product innovation. Salaries were cheaper. Cost of acquisition was cheaper. Mexico was Cantú's early base of operations and testing ground, but, to scale, he will look elsewhere, starting with the United States.[23]

Must-Win Markets

For some Frontier Innovators, there are certain markets that are must-win, without which they will never reach scale. In Southeast Asia, Indonesia is often a linchpin. In the Middle East, as Fadi Ghandour—co-founder of Aramex and an investor in many local leading startups and whom you will meet in chapter 11—explained to me, "To win in the region you need to win Saudi Arabia. It is the largest market."[24] Ned Tozun, CEO of d.light, explains it similarly for the global solar lantern market: "We absolutely needed to crack India. There are other markets that are less price sensitive. But India is the most price sensitive and one of the largest. We had to win India. Otherwise, we'd lose the world."[25]

The must-win market may not always be a place. In some industries, it could be a particular set of anchor clients (e.g., to win in the sea shipping market requires partnering with one of the few large global shipping conglomerates) or a high-profile subsegment of the market. It is crucial to identify these industry dynamics and target these must-win markets.

Building a plan for future expansion early on is critical. For Zola, its decisions about market expansion were backed by detailed quantitative analysis. Zola executives ranked prospective new markets according to a variety of criteria, which included factors like market size (e.g., total energy spending, population size), level of corruption, macroeconomic risks (e.g., political stability, inflation, the ease of doing business), ability to pay (e.g., GDP per capita and mobile money penetration, which is key to getting repaid digitally), customer demographics (e.g., access to the grid, rural versus urban population density, each of which has unique customer uptake behaviors), consumer behavior (e.g., who would be likely to try new products), logistics (e.g., road penetration, import taxes), ease of doing business (e.g., the time it takes to open a subsidiary, the simplicity of hiring), and culture (e.g., the language spoken and the importance of local connections).

It often makes the most sense to expand from an established anchor market to similar markets in the region. Scaling across countries is much easier if they are proximate, not only physically but also culturally and administratively. Zola considered many options for a second market and ultimately decided on Rwanda, which was physically proximate, was easy to do business in, and had a geography where the team already had operational experience. From there, the company decided it was important to have an outpost in Western Africa, so it headed to Ivory Coast—a small market in and of itself, but a foothold in another region.

Frontier Innovators must make a concerted effort to plan how they will scale their enterprise across markets. Of course, the plan should not be set in stone. Things change. However, it is crucial to understand which markets can serve as testers, whether any markets are must-win, and what an expansion rollout might look like over time. These decisions drive hiring plans, capital raising, and, of course, product development.

Build an Adaptable Product, and Localize

Like successful entrepreneurs around the world, Frontier Innovators think deeply about building great products that customers value. Unlike most of their Silicon Valley counterparts, however, they layer a global mindset into their product development from the get-go. Products are built with an architecture that can be modulated for different price points, adapted to local languages, and tweaked to reflect varying customer needs. If executed well, this inherent flexibility allows startups to scale globally at a rapid pace.

Zola demonstrates this product adaptability. The basic product is a home solar system, which couples a solar panel with a charging box (installed inside the house) and adds a variety of compatible, high-efficiency appliances (e.g., lights, fans, radios). If customers want to increase their system, they can simply plug a new solar panel in to the box and add other, higher-intensity appliances like fans or televisions.

This focus on products and customers was instrumental to Zola's growth. While Rwanda and Tanzania share a border and similar electrification rates and product demand, Ivory Coast and Ghana are wealthier on average and have higher electrification rates.[26] In West Africa, customers sought systems not for baseline lighting but as backups to the grid, or to power a broader range of appliances like televisions. These systems needed to be more powerful. Zola's flexible architecture, which required a considerable upfront investment (far more than if it simply offered a one-size-fits-all system), allowed its model to successfully sell in the Ivory Coast and Ghana markets without a complete reengineering.

Some Frontier Innovators go one step further and decentralize a portion of the product development team, allowing individual markets to customize the core product for local demand and needs. For Frontier Car Group, which you met in chapter 3, technological development is centralized in Europe, but individual countries have flexibility in adapting products to meet local market needs.

Building a flexible product is essential to scale across markets. So is building a flexible team.

Build an Organization That Can Grow across Markets

Launching in different markets is a challenging endeavor that requires an adept leadership team. Companies typically aim to combine an internal global expansion expertise with localized ownership strategies when they develop their teams.

Some Frontier Innovators assemble a specialist team to help build new geographies and carry the culture across borders. Whereas the core team is focused on ensuring that the company's product or service resonates within the current footprint, these specialist teams excel at scaling across borders while preserving the organization's unique advantages.

Matt Flannery is no stranger to creating global operations. In 2004, he co-founded Kiva, a nonprofit that offers microfinance loans to individuals in emerging markets. Now Kiva has more than three million borrowers and nearly two million lenders, operates in more than eighty countries, and has funded more than $1.2 billion in loans (with a remarkably high 97 percent repayment rate).[27]

One of Kiva's early barriers to growth was the limited availability of capital: growth in the number of borrowers required a commensurate growth in lenders. This realization inspired Matt to found Branch, which offers microloans to consumers in emerging markets. Via an app, and leveraging alternative digital data, Branch offers its users, primarily underbanked customers in developing countries, access to credit at lower rates than available in the informal system. Branch was launched in 2015 and already has more than four million customers. It has issued more than fifteen million loans and has distributed more than $500 million.[28]

As it expands to new markets, Branch sends small "swat" teams to get the local business off the ground. Branch entrusts global expansion to these teams. Like the elite police SWAT teams after which they are named, these are teams of high performers, typically young teammates thirsty for a global experience who have already spent meaningful time at home offices understanding the business. Their directives are clear: register the business in the new market, get a local lawyer, secure office space, register the app, get the first few customers, and find local leadership for the new operations.

At Branch, the swat teams' last responsibility is to hire and integrate a local leader. In doing so, the team looks for candidates with a mix of entrepreneurial spirit, leadership skills, and strong cultural alignment with the rest of the organization. The specialist teams are responsible for leaving behind a cohesive and global culture engrained in the new local management team.

Local leaders should ultimately lead the operation. A product should rarely be copied and pasted from one region to the other; it often requires a combination of local adaptation, appropriate positioning, and relationships with ecosystem players. To adapt it to local needs takes local expertise.

Born Global: The Bottom Line

For Frontier Innovators, being born global is often a necessity rather than a choice. Their local market may not be large enough to sustain the company at scale. By taking a multimarket approach, Frontier Innovators piece together a large opportunity from fragmented regional markets.

A born global strategy is not only an offensive move to capture market share but also a defensive one. If you don't go global, your competition will, and it will come to you. As you learned in chapter 3, Frontier Innovators focus on resilience by building a portfolio of activities, and one key way is by serving multiple markets.

As Louis Pasteur said, "Chance favors the prepared mind."[29] In this case, building a born global organization favors the prepared. As you discovered in chapter 4, fostering a global, cross-pollinated mindset and network among the leadership team is key. In chapter 6, you will explore how Frontier Innovators build distributed teams, leveraging the best of multiple ecosystems.

In the coming wave of technological innovation, entrepreneurs won't look to Silicon Valley for best practices on managing dispersed operations from an early stage. They will instead aspire to emulate the entrepreneurs on the Frontier, who have been doing this for years.

6.

Establish a Distributed Team

Tap Talent from across the Globe

Entrepreneurs in emerging ecosystems face a tough decision: Should they go where the customers are but where finding the right staff will be more challenging? Or should they optimize for places where team building is easier but that are farther away from the customer base?

Zola faced this exact conundrum. As founders Xavier Helgesen, Erica Mackey, and Joshua Pierce were considering launching their platform, they realized there was no "natural" place to start the business. On the one hand, it made sense to stay put in London, which has easy connections across Africa. On the other hand, the technology talent pool in London was much smaller in comparison to the wealth of Silicon Valley engineers specializing in batteries and solar panels.

And then there was the option of Tanzania. Erica speaks fluent Swahili and had previously managed a large nonprofit that operates across East Africa. The team knew that in the early days, it would be important to be close to their customers and intimately understand their challenges, as well as build relationships with key local stakeholders. Tanzania, therefore, was a logical first market. The country was ripe for electrification: fewer than 15 percent of Tanzanians had access to the grid in 2010.[1] It also had one of the fastest-growing mobile money ecosystems, which is critical infrastructure for managing payments. Third and most important, Erica knew the country well and had a local network.

But for every advantage, Tanzania had an equal drawback. It is a large country (more than double the size of California) and sparsely populated, with poor infrastructure and roads, a situation that makes for costly distribution. It had a nearly nonexistent startup ecosystem, with a limited number of programmers and little venture capital.

In many ways, Silicon Valley made more sense. Zola's product would require significant technological innovation, and San Francisco had a budding clean-energy technology sector with a large talent base. The team had a strong network there as well. But Silicon Valley is a ten-hour time difference and twenty-four hours of travel away from Tanzania. And the distance is not only physical: startup life in San Francisco is radically different from the Tanzanian reality of blackouts, brownouts, and unpaved roads.

The Zola founders decided to build their operations in a distributed manner. They combined local distribution on the ground in Africa with Asian manufacturing, European logistics, and research and development in Silicon Valley. They started in Tanzania to develop the product in close proximity to users. After they had a basic product, they built an R&D team based in San Francisco to access the best solar energy and battery talent from companies like Tesla.

As Zola built its supply chain, it created close partnerships with firms in Asia to source its solar system hardware. When Zola expanded across Africa, it built an operations team in Amsterdam, which shares a common time zone with and good transportation links to its current and planned future markets. In short, Zola built a distributed organization from the get-go and has doubled down on that approach with every passing year.

Increasingly, Frontier Innovators are not choosing a single location. Instead, they are building the piping of their organizations in a globally distributed manner.

Distributed as a Strategy

Distribution refers to an organizational structure in which the team is dispersed in multiple locations.

This strategy counters Silicon Valley's conventional wisdom, which suggests that the integration of engineering, product development, and strategy is essential to spur creativity. Steve Jobs exemplified this ethos, going so far as to place office bathrooms in a central location to catalyze spontaneous interaction among departments. When Marissa Mayer took over at Yahoo, one of her first directives was to ban remote work. While there are certainly valid reasons to avoid being distributed, however, times are changing.[2]

The Distributed Spectrum

There is no one-size-fits-all model for distributed organizations. In its simplest form, a distributed organization may place the technology development team and sales team in different geographies. At the extreme, an organization may choose to build its teams entirely remotely and may not even have formal or central offices. Figure 6-1 highlights a range of options, which you will explore in turn.[3]

Earth and moon models are perhaps the most centralized among the distributed options. A dominant headquarters (Earth) tends to be the center of the organization. As the organization enters a new phase or market, a moon, or hub, is launched.

Peek Travel is an example of this strategy. The company was launched in San Francisco to offer a marketplace for activities, similar to the way OpenTable allows customers to book restaurant tables directly. Over time, Peek evolved to offer a booking-management solution for merchants. To sell this solution, it built out a dedicated sales team and effort and launched it in Salt Lake City. This became a moon with a specialized function. The company will launch other moons over time for other

FIGURE 6-1

Range of distributed organizations

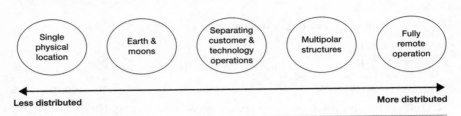

Single physical location · Earth & moons · Separating customer & technology operations · Multipolar structures · Fully remote operation

Less distributed   More distributed

specialized functions. Similarly, Gojek, profiled in chapter 2, has centralized operations in Indonesia but has separate distribution offices across its markets.

A second model of distributed teams involves separating the customer-facing operations from product and technological development. Some refer to this approach as *reverse offshoring*, particularly when customer operations are in developing markets and technological development is elsewhere.[4] Branch, which you met in chapter 5, embodies this approach. It delivers microlending products and services across emerging markets but centralizes product development in San Francisco. Similarly, Frontier Car Group (from chapter 3) has its product and technology development in Germany, with local sales offices in multiple countries.

Some firms go one step further and build a *multipolar* model, in which different regions run different core functions. Zola's model reflects this structure. Fetchr (from chapter 4) built a similar multipolar model. Since technology talent is limited in Dubai, Fetchr formed an eighty-person team across Jordan and China. Its sales and customer service are in Egypt.

Sometimes, multipolar models are self-sufficient hubs, each with its own unique functions. Cimpress and Globant, which you are about to meet, employ this model.[5] Each separate location enjoys relative autonomy and self-sufficiency.

Finally, some companies are fully remote, more akin to a flat network. Basecamp, InVisionApp, and Zapier, all formally based in the United States, have employees all over the world. Although remote companies can have a "head office" (as Basecamp does in Chicago), they are in name only; the team is free to work from anywhere.

When I refer to a distributed team, I mean employee location and regional office specialization. A related but separate topic pertains to decision making; some distributed companies are centralized, with power sitting in a particular location, while others are decentralized, with decision-making authority delegated across the organization.

As a general rule, as companies become increasingly distributed, decision making also becomes decentralized. However, this is highly dependent on the internal dynamics of the company, the type of product it is building, and the markets it is serving. Therefore, recommendations on decentralized decision making are not within the scope of this chapter.

Advantages of Distributed Structures

Frontier Innovators build distributed teams because they confer unique advantages. Through distributed models, Frontier Innovators draw on a diverse pool of human capital, manage costs, often increase team integration, and prepare the foundation for future expansion.

Drawing on a Diverse Talent Pool

One of the central advantages of distributed teams is the flexibility it gives you to tap the best talent regardless of location. Some regions have particular centers of excellence. Building in a distributed manner allows organizations to leverage these best-in-class ecosystems. For instance, while there is a shortage of machine learning programmers in the Bay Area, Toronto and Montreal are becoming hubs. Launching an office in these cities can tap that vein.

Certain regions are also known for behavioral skill sets. Peek built its inside sales division in Salt Lake City before even raising its Series B. Ruzwana Bashir, Peek's CEO, explained: "To find the best talent with the highest return on investment, we picked Salt Lake City. Within a two-hour radius, there are multiple top universities with dedicated sales programs. Their students have worked with many of the great local enterprise technology companies."[6]

In fact, many sales-driven companies scale successfully out of Salt Lake City. Dalton Wright, a partner with Kickstart Seed Fund, says that the city's sales expertise "is partially founded on the resilience, strength, and experience of its residents. Many young Mormons go on two-year missions, and, as any missionary does, they receive rejections all day, every day. They bring an unflappable and relentless mindset back from their missions, and many go on to become leading executives and salespeople in rapidly scaling tech companies."[7] Peek is one of many companies, including Qualtrics, Podium, and MasteryConnect, that rely on Utah's sales expertise.

Building a remote structure is arguably the most extreme way to tap global talent. Zapier, a Missouri-based startup that provides automation for websites, was an early pioneer. Its staff of 250 is fully remote, across twenty states and seventeen countries. Wade Foster, Zapier's co-founder and CEO, explains that the strategy has serious advantages:

> You have access to a worldwide talent pool. If you restrict yourself to thirty miles from your headquarters, you're going to have a hard time hiring. And you see this now in the barrier where Google, Facebook, Apple, they price out any other employer because they can afford to . . . The Bay Area challenge is really, really competitive. But when you open yourself up to remote, you're able to work with folks from all over the world, and so that makes it a lot easier to find great folks.[8]

In the first year since instituting its "delocation" package, Zapier's employment applications have increased 50 percent, and retention is up meaningfully as well.[9]

Building remote teams (and distributed teams more broadly) is associated with increasing diversity. According to research by Remote.co, an industry association, remote companies have a greater percentage of female leaders: some 28 percent of remote companies have female founders, presidents, or CEOs (compared with the 5.2 percent of S&P 500 companies that have female CEOs).[10] The study attributes this to a few factors, including greater work flexibility, the ability to balance multiple responsibilities, and decreasing bias (working remotely obfuscates preconceived notions of what a leader looks like).[11]

Managing Labor Cost

Often, the primary reason for distribution is to access a broader talent pool beyond the home market. Building distributed companies is also a powerful way to manage labor and other costs.

The Bay Area has the highest rents in North America and unsurprisingly also commands some of the highest salaries. In many places in the United States and around the world, tech talent is much more affordable. In Silicon Valley the average engineer costs $124,000, but in Chicago the cost is $90,000, and in Cleveland it is closer to $75,000.[12] The cost advantage only increases in places like Canada that also benefit from a cheaper currency.[13]

Lower labor costs can profoundly impact a startup's viability, as explored in chapter 3. Early-stage venture rounds are geared to helping founders find a fit between product and market. This often involves learning and pivoting. The largest cost for startups at this stage is salaries to support technology development. For a similar round size, lower salaries mean innovators have many more months to experiment, increasing the probability of successfully finding a sustainable business model. This advantage only compounds as the company scales.

Distributed models can help employees be at their best as well. Take the case of InVision, which was founded by Ben Nadel and Clark Valberg in 2011. InVision provides users with tools to research, design, and test products. The company has more than five million users, including 100 percent of the *Fortune* 100—organizations like Airbnb, Amazon, HBO, Netflix, Slack, Starbucks, and Uber.[14]

InVision built a remote organization from the start, in part to better leverage a global workforce. An internal analysis credits the approach with enabling InVision employees to enjoy a better work-life balance. They can avoid long commutes and work from an environment that allows them to avoid distractions or be more present at home.[15] In this way, distributed models generate happier and more productive employees. InVision is now worth nearly $2 billion and has raised more than $350 million.[16]

Being More Integrated, Not Less

The tech sector is challenging the Jobsian notion that in-office connectivity is irreplaceable. Jasper Malcolmson built his company Skylight in a distributed way from the start. Skylight has no official headquarters or offices of any kind. As Jasper sees it, "By being distributed, we're actually even more connected."[17]

In his home, Jasper's desk has two screens, along with a high-resolution microphone and high-fidelity speakers. These come standard for all employees. On his left screen, he sees an array of live feeds of his colleagues at work. Whenever he wants to make a conference call, ask a question, or just say hi, he double-clicks on a colleague's face to open a live microphone link. "Open offices decreased barriers to in-office communication. In many ways, through technology, we've lowered them even further," Jasper reflected.[18]

Being distributed alerts companies rapidly to challenges—like a breakdown in communication or lack of collaboration—and forces them to react and adapt quickly. Kevin Fishner, the chief of staff of HashiCorp, a distributed company that was recently valued at nearly $2 billion, explains:

> There is a popular understanding that a remote company is different than a "regular company" or whatever you want to call it. It's not necessarily different, but it does make your weaknesses more obvious. All companies have communications, collaboration, and alignment challenges. Making these challenges more obvious can be a strength, since it allows you to see them and fix them quicker. Of course, you do have to fix them in order for this to be a strength.[19]

A distributed structure doesn't necessarily mean disavowing in-person connectivity. To the contrary, distributed firms structure in-person interaction. This includes regular retreats, weekly live videoconferences, and an integrated digital communication platform that emphasizes live interactions.

Training to Expand Markets

Being distributed is often a natural consequence of being multimarket. As companies scale across geographies, they naturally build out multiple offices around the world. But things go in the opposite direction as well, since distribution confers a surprising advantage. Building a distributed organization early on forces companies to build and manage communication across geographies, to trust distant colleagues with more autonomy, and to foster a shared culture across the organization. Expanding internationally requires exactly the same skill set. Many entrepreneurs confirmed that building a distributed team prepared them to scale internationally.

Of course, building a successful distributed organization is no easy feat. In the next section, you'll explore several strategies for success.

Effectively Building a Distributed Organization

The best Frontier Innovators implement strategies regarding the kinds of people they hire, the incentives they put in place, the technological tools they employ, and the internal processes and culture of the firm. Let's explore each in turn.

Hire for Distributed Teams

Building in a distributed way theoretically means anyone can be your employee. The reality is that not everyone will be a fit to work remotely or at a satellite office.

Frontier Innovators often select candidates based on demonstrable independence. For example, Zapier focuses on employees who have a "default to action" and are able to drive outcomes independently, according to CEO Wade Foster.[20] Jason Fried, CEO of Basecamp, underscores the importance of employees who are great communicators, particularly via written communication, since that ends up being a key format.[21]

Hiring is further complicated as the global range of an organization expands. Frontier Innovators look to hire candidates who thrive across cultures and geographies. For Matt Flannery, CEO of Branch and founder of Kiva, hiring candidates who value global culture and impact is paramount. This means prioritizing those who have traveled extensively, according to Matt. As he puts it, "I like candidates that have been beyond the typical tourist places. One candidate told me recently she lived and worked in Guatemala. That signals both a sense of adventure, but also a good heart. Someone that was focused on impact. We hired her."[22]

The ability to work in a distributed context can also be tested within the hiring process. Recruiting can be done entirely by videoconference (even if the candidate is local). Many Frontier Innovators ask candidates to complete assignments to test how they collaborate with others at distance. Chapter 7 focuses further on how Frontier Innovators hire by testing for character and behavior. Testing for candidates' performance in a distributed context is an example.

Incentivize Distribution

Frontier Innovators eschew traditional Silicon Valley perks. Instead, they use compensation and incentives to reinforce values like global connectivity. Branch offers its employees the option to work from any of its many global offices and pays for flights between locations. Teammates are thus better integrated across the geographies, know their colleagues across the world, and have some understanding of the different local markets. Matt credits Branch's global culture as a key catalyst for the company to iterate rapidly and adapt to local contexts.

Basecamp offers its employees annual vouchers for vacations so that they have the opportunity to connect with their families and to travel, leaving their remote locations. As Jason explains, "We encourage our employees to travel. This is not work travel but personal travel. This is more genuine."[23] InVision offers its remote employees a preloaded credit card to pay for coffees and lunches to encourage them to get outside during their work day.[24]

Reinvent Processes and Culture

Taking a distributed approach requires building it in to both the strategy and the culture of the firm, as Globant did.

Founded in 2003 in Buenos Aires, Globant is an IT and software provider and a NYSE-traded public company worth more than $3 billion, with more than $400 million in revenues and a sprawling workforce of nearly ten thousand people in forty offices.[25] As Martín Migoya, Globant CEO and co-founder, explains, "We built a distributed organization from the beginning. In our second year, we opened our second office. In our third year, we opened a third location. By year four, we started opening multiple offices a year."[26]

To manage a distributed organization, Martín wanted new tools. "A new kind of company needs a new type of operating system," he says.[27]

Globant reinvented company processes around its organizational structure. To reinforce values, Globant created "Star Me Up." The platform allows anyone at the company or its customers to give employees "stars" for doing anything that aligns with the company values. On the one hand, it serves as a crowdsourcing mechanism for the best employees. On the other, as Martín views it, it is a powerful attrition prediction engine. Those employees who are not active users of the tool are most likely to leave, and thus can be proactively engaged.

Similarly, Martín believed a traditional annual evaluation process would not work in a distributed context. He replaced it with an internal system called "Better Me." Through the platform, employees receive reviews after any interaction, either in person or remote. Globant has also experimented with an internal "Tinder for ideas" to allow employees across the firm's offices to surface new ideas or processes. The most promising suggestions are elevated to senior management.

Other companies have seen value in Globant's tools for distributed organizations. "Star Me Up" and "Better Me" have more than two million users at a range of companies.[28]

Structure Integration

Day-to-day interaction is of paramount importance for successful teams. Therefore, connectivity is structured into the fabric of distributed organizations. At Zola, the time difference between San Francisco and Tanzania is a whopping ten hours. To create as much overlap as possible, the San Francisco teams start very early and the Tanzanian teams work late. To foster a personal connection, calls are videoconferences.

InVision has made this overlap formal. Employees work "core team hours," with at least a four-hour overlap in the 10 a.m. to 6 p.m. EST window. Although employees can be anywhere, they are at least working part of the day at the same hours.[29]

Remote companies also look to re-create informal water cooler interactions digitally. Globant uses an internal Instagram-style photo-sharing platform for staff to share cultural moments across the firm. Zapier created a range of chat-based channels in its internal communication and regularly matches employees with random colleagues around the firm for virtual "coffee dates." HashiCorp instituted a "chat roulette" to spur new relationships inside the company.[30]

Internal communication should be done in a manner that is equally accessible to all. Team announcements can be via videoconference (even if there is a physical meeting room where the announcement is made) and recorded for others to view.

Of course, distribution should not minimize the importance of frequent face time. Mark Frein, the former chief people officer at InVision, has found that "in-person time is important. People get used to the idea of getting on a plane to work on a deal, but most meetings can be done by video. When we do bring people together, we focus on having people getting to know each other and building strong bonds." Successful distributed teams find time for this kind of in-person connectivity. InVision holds one company-wide retreat annually, as well as individual team meetings.[31] For Branch, this means an annual retreat in Africa. Basecamp, which is fully remote, does a twice-yearly retreat.[32]

Invest in Technology

Building a decentralized culture is easier than ever in our high-tech, globalized world. Language barriers are decreasing as more people become multilingual, often including English. Digital translation services have improved significantly and now are often free. Videoconferencing quality has improved so dramatically and the costs have fallen so steeply that some people argue remote conferencing is preferable to meeting in the same physical space.[33]

There are now a range of tools that facilitate remote work, but this requires investing proactively in technology.[34] Skylight's Jasper Malcolmson estimates that each installation for a new employee costs a few thousand dollars. This includes multiple screens, high-bandwidth internet, a camera, a microphone, and other office setups. It also includes a range of subscriptions like Zoom Rooms.

These may seem like large absolute numbers. Yet these costs still pale in comparison to office expenses.

Distributed Models: The Key to Silicon Valley's Future

In 2018 and 2019, Amazon's decision to expand from its single base in Seattle, along with its multistage process to select the new location, dominated technology newsrooms. The first stage of the saga was the call for applications from American cities. More than two hundred applied, eager for the promised fifty thousand new jobs and $5 billion in construction investment.[35] Stonecrest, Georgia, even offered to create an adjacent town called Amazon.

The company decided to split the prize between Long Island City in New York and Crystal City in Virginia—that is, until public backlash forced it to pull out of New York.[36]

The heated drama about Amazon's second headquarters illuminates a broader trend. Rising costs have made Silicon Valley and other major startup ecosystems increasingly expensive. Even well-paid software engineers can't afford studios in San Francisco.[37] Many are leaving: surveys in San Francisco report an astounding 46 percent of residents intend to leave in "the next few years."[38] Yet talent remains the most critical resource for companies. In response, even venerable Silicon Valley institutions are considering deployment of distributed teams in different locations.[39]

US startups like Automattic, Basecamp, GitHub, GitLab, InVision, and Zapier provide successful role models of companies relying on large distributed teams. Buffer's "State of Remote Work Report" highlights a shift in attitudes: today 90 percent of entrepreneurs claim they support remote work.[40] Remote work is on the rise; Mary Meeker's "Internet Trends 2019 Report" shows that 5 percent of the American labor force works remotely (nearly double the 3 percent in 2000), representing more than eight million Americans. Nearly 50 percent of the US workforce has spent at least some time working remotely.[41]

Some venture investors argue that distributed teams may have as big an impact for startups as the cloud once did.[42] Boris Wertz, founding partner of Version One and board partner with Andreessen Horowitz, summarizes this trend: "Among our Silicon Valley-based portfolio companies, not a single company past 'A' does not have a distributed team."[43]

The Triple Threat

Over the past three chapters you have explored three aspects of the born global nature of many Frontier Innovators and their companies: cross-pollination, being multimarket, and building distributed teams. Combining all three of these approaches can lead to a powerful and successful result.

Take Robert Keane. Originally from Buffalo, New York, Robert was a cross-pollinator. After an international career working in multiple countries, in 1994 he started Bonne Impression—a printing business that had a distribution partnership with Microsoft—in the second bedroom of his Paris apartment just after graduating from INSEAD, the international business school. At the time, the cost for small businesses to print marketing materials was astronomical; a typical minimum of five thousand brochures cost $1,000.[44]

But growth stalled after Robert exhausted Microsoft's client roster. He realized scaling the company with its current business model was going to be challenging, if not impossible.

Robert saw another option. He envisioned online in-browser publishing, which would allow small businesses to self-design and order their printing via e-commerce—an offering that was far ahead of its time. In-browser publishing complemented another innovative technology by which algorithms would automatically aggregate many individually small print runs to radically decrease the cost to produce each run. Robert had to decide whether he'd abandon the current direct marketing catalog-based strategy and bet the company on this new internet-based distribution model.

He decided to bet, and the company took off. In 1999, Robert re-branded first to Vistaprint, sold the consultative business in Europe, and moved the company to Boston. "We always were thinking global. In this case, we retrenched to be even more global," he explains.[45]

Robert built a distributed organization and a multimarket sales strategy at the same time. The headquarters and technology development were based in Boston (given the higher concentration of developers), and the customer service team was centered in Jamaica (for English customers) and Tunisia (for speakers of Romance languages). Early logistics development was based in the Netherlands. Canada served as the first core production facility, leveraging its proximity to and connectivity with the United States. The next production facility catered to the growing European business and was located in Germany. This distributed structure was economical, and it allowed Vistaprint—now renamed Cimpress—to tap the best talent from specialized centers and leverage cost differentials across regions.

Cimpress survived the dot-com crash, even as many of its competitors that had raised considerably more money did not. Robert credits his company's survival to "the luck of not having raised enough capital, which forced us to cut back until we were cash-flow positive."[46] The company outlasted its more profligate, better-funded competitors.

Today, Cimpress is operational in more than twenty countries, and more than half of its revenue comes from outside the United States, including Europe, Asia, and Australia.[47] It is a Nasdaq-listed company with a multibillion-dollar valuation and more than twelve thousand employees around the world.[48]

Cimpress took a multimarket sales approach and built itself in a distributed way. Robert credits his success in part to his global experience, and to the multicultural and international culture he built. As he reflects, attitudes have clearly changed. "When we started, building a truly global value chain as a small startup was highly unusual. Today it's more common, even in Silicon Valley."[49]

Like Robert, when Frontier Innovators take the leap of faith to cross-pollinate, be born global, and adopt a distributed structure, it pays off.

Build A-Teams

Don't Hire Just A-Players

In Silicon Valley, a kind of mythology permeates stories about founders.

Jobs and Wozniak's fight against IBM to invent the personal computer has become as much legend as history. Elon Musk's personal crusade to rid the world of fossil fuel dependence through SolarCity and Tesla, populate Mars via SpaceX, and solve metropolitan congestion with Boring approaches the fantastical in scope and vision. The story of Mark Zuckerberg and his friends building Facebook is immortalized in *The Social Network*, a film that grossed over $200 million.[1]

These singular founders are the legends on which Silicon Valley is built.

But in their pioneering efforts, they were never truly alone. Each led a small army. Apple now has eighty thousand employees, Tesla thirty-eight thousand, SpaceX six thousand, and Facebook twenty-five thousand.[2] Talent, perhaps even more than capital, is the critical resource for a startup's success—even the ones associated with legendary founders.

So crucial is this resource that Silicon Valley startups don't have "human resources." Instead, they have "human capital." Leading Silicon

Valley thinkers run the gamut on best-in-class approaches to building and growing teams. Accepted strategies have coalesced into a kind of science, and books, articles, workshops, and class sessions continue to cover the topic ad nauseam.

A central idea is now engrained as dogma: hire only A-players. Every young founder in the Valley knows that hiring the most experienced and most qualified players—those who have already demonstrated excellence in a particular function at a startup in a similar stage of development—increases the odds of success. For example, for any direct-to-consumer retail brand, there are plenty of professionals who have developed an SEO (search engine optimization) strategy, which entails ensuring a particular website has the most favorable ranking on Google and other search engines, or who have figured out optimal marketing spending, through to a successful exit and billions of dollars in sales. According to Silicon Valley best practices, founders must recruit these immensely qualified specialized candidates for their roles and, in so doing, create a culture of performance—ultimately unlocking a self-perpetuating cycle whereby the company will attract more high performers over time.

This idea is predicated on the richness of Silicon Valley's talent pool. Every year, Stanford and Berkeley graduate 1,500 engineering students apiece, and they refill and expand the ranks of the more than 150,000 computer scientists and software developers working in California.[3] Silicon Valley companies also have unparalleled access to graduates having expertise on the business side. Stanford alone has 130 classes on entrepreneurship, many of which focus specifically on tech innovation.[4]

Career paths and roles are well defined at startups: engineering specializations—along with particular job categories spanning project management, product marketing, product design, and business operations—have solidified. Google, Facebook, Twitter, Uber, and Yahoo all have dedicated product manager training and rotational programs.[5] Product managers have their own organization: the Silicon Valley Product Management Association reaches more than five thousand Silicon Valley–based members of the product management community.[6]

But here's the rub: in Silicon Valley, companies and employees see their relationships as short-term affairs. Retention rates are among the lowest in the United States. More than 13 percent of staff turn over every year, and in certain job categories like user design, the rate is well above 20 percent, which translates to short employee tenure.[7] Employees are taught that career development is self-directed. They rotate through a range of companies, seeing best practices and bringing them into their next firms—growing as leaders all the while.

To keep employees engaged, Silicon Valley's primary retention tool is economic: stock options. Through these widely distributed and well-understood instruments, employees can participate in the growth of the company by owning the right to purchase stock at a predetermined price and see it increase in value as the company grows. This perk can create substantial wealth. Famously, Google's part-time masseuse—who was also an early recruit making $450 per week—became a millionaire from her stock options.[8] However, the value of a stock option is predicated on growth. If companies don't grow, they don't have value. Since there are so many job opportunities in the Valley, if a particular company doesn't appear to be a rocket ship, the allure of another great idea will win over a talented player.

Because the candidate pool is plentiful in Silicon Valley, high employee turnover is seen as a nuisance but built in to the business model. In their book *The Alliance*, Reid Hoffman, Ben Casnocha, and Chris Yeh suggest that Silicon Valley startups should think of employees as being on "tours of duty." Employees and startups are in a temporary "alliance." The company aligns its needs with employees' current career motivations. In the authors' conception, only a few tours are "foundational"; longer-term roles that provide continuity are reserved mostly for senior employees.[9]

This situation creates a model of human capital focused on constantly replenishing the ranks of an elite mercenary team.

At the Frontier, however, hiring Silicon Valley's version of A-players—those "been there, done that" candidates—is not a realistic goal. There just aren't enough of them. Therefore, Frontier Innovators adopt unique

strategies to build A-teams in emerging ecosystems and offer their recruits compelling, longer-term careers.

The A-Team of One Great City

A band of my youth, the Weakerthans, once wrote a tongue-in-cheek song
about our shared hometown, called "One Great City." Its refrain? "I hate
Winnipeg."

That's where we are headed.

Joshua Simair is CEO of SkipTheDishes, a Winnipeg-based startup
in the food delivery space. Joshua grew up in Prince Albert, a working-
class city of thirty-five thousand in northern Saskatchewan, the Canadian province adjacent to Manitoba. Joshua attended the University of
Saskatchewan in the "big city" of Saskatoon (population: three hundred
thousand), where he graduated at the top of his class.

In a weirdly small world, Joshua, like me, left his Canadian prairie
alma mater to pursue an undergraduate exchange program in Rouen,
France. Subsequently, we both moved to actual big cities to work in investment banking at the Royal Bank of Canada (he to London, and I to
Toronto). Joshua recalls feeling out of place for most of his career: "When
I was an investment banker, I was struck by how polished, how smart, and
how confident my peers were. They were such high performers, and I was
intimidated. In my high school, if you didn't do drugs you were the good
kid. When I moved to London, I sold my car to buy my suit."[10]

In 2011, Joshua decided to apply his learning from metropolitan innovation to create a meaningful business for the Canadian prairies. "Working in the big cities like London and Toronto, I saw people who saved
time everywhere," he said. "In dense city environments, they ordered
food, picked it up, or had it delivered, and went home to spend more time
with their families or work on their businesses. The same options were
not available in small Canadian cities."[11] Joshua decided to build out those
options. With his brother and a few other co-founders, he launched Skip-
TheDishes and headquartered it in Winnipeg, Manitoba. SkipTheDishes'

mission was to partner with restaurants to offer home delivery in smaller cities in the United States and Canada.

From the outset, Joshua knew that finding human capital would be one of his biggest challenges.

On the one hand, although there is abundant talent in Winnipeg, there have been few scaled startups in the city. Thus, there is a limited trove of experienced professionals who have already scaled startups like SkipTheDishes. New hires would all need to be trained. The talent limitations are compounded by the constant risk of brain drain to the larger economic centers.

The Frontier Talent Challenge

Winnipeg is like many parts of the Frontier: the prospect of hiring only Silicon Valley–style, experienced technologists is a distant dream.

This dearth of expertise does not reflect a lack of inherent ability, intelligence, or drive on the part of people at the Frontier. Indeed, some of the most talented individuals I know are from my hometown. Capacity and merit are evenly distributed across the world. Unfortunately, opportunity is not.

Availability of trained and experienced talent is a near-universal pain point for Frontier Innovators. In a survey, more than half of Frontier Innovators reported that recruiting and retaining talent represent their most acute challenges—twice as many as those who selected availability of capital.[12] In a similar study of more than six hundred entrepreneurs in emerging ecosystems, more than 60 percent responded that their inability to access the right level of talent would critically impact their businesses. Significantly, 75 percent of those with rapidly scaling startups (which need new talent at a faster pace) categorized lack of available talent as the single most important barrier to their businesses. The research indicates that this is the only challenge that becomes more acute over time as team size grows.[13]

Startups live and die by the quality of their talent. In many markets there is a massive undersupply. Consider computer engineers: currently, the University of Manitoba in Winnipeg has a total of two hundred under-graduate students in computer engineering, far fewer than what Joshua estimates is required for the ecosystem.[14] In developing markets, the need can be more dire.

Finding engineering talent is not the only human capital challenge that Frontier Innovators face. Shortages across key operational roles—like finance and sales—often result in companywide unmet needs.[15] This is compounded by the fact that without a culture of startups, the best candidates look to work at more-stable employers (that also pay more).

In emerging markets, it can also be a reflection of a limited job-training ecosystem. In Kenya, while universities pump out an enviable 800,000 graduates each year, only about 70,000 readily find jobs in the formal economy; opportunities to receive the kind of on-the-job training and apprenticeship available in more-developed markets are slim.[16] The remaining 730,000 often take years to find jobs, working in the infor-mal economy in the meantime. The same dynamic applies in emerging innovation ecosystems around the world: there are simply far fewer ex-perienced product managers, marketing executives, or supply chain or operations analysts.

One solution is having candidates relocate from somewhere else. This can also be a challenge. As Amanda Lannert, CEO of Chicago-based Jelly-vision, reflects, "Candidates that consider moving for startup roles look around at the ecosystem. If there are few local alternatives if things don't work out, that increases the candidate's perception of risk."[17] Of course, Winnipeg-based startups, like those in Chicago, have an additional bar-rier in recruiting outsiders: winter. It is frequently colder in Winnipeg than at the North Pole or even on the surface of Mars.[18]

No wonder Joshua considers Winnipeg "one of the hardest places to recruit from and to recruit to."[19] Yet he overcame these challenges and occasionally turned them into advantages. SkipTheDishes now has food orders exceeding $1 billion per year and has become one of the largest employers in Winnipeg, with three thousand employees in five offices in the city (and this excludes the much larger delivery force). The majority of Joshua's original employees grew alongside the company and stayed through to the company's exit, a remarkable feat for startups. The company was recently purchased for $200 million by Just Eat.[20]

Strategies to Build and Scale Top Teams

Frontier Innovators like Joshua use five key strategies to build and scale top teams. They test candidates for behavior and capabilities, develop a proprietary talent pipeline, leverage global distributed options, take a growth mindset to retention and training, and think critically about compensation and perks.

Moneyball: Testing Candidates at the Frontier

The 2002 Oakland Athletics (A's) professional baseball team is famous for its innovative player sourcing strategy. With a limited salary budget of only $44 million (about 40 percent of the budget of the New York Yankees), the California club was at a considerable recruiting disadvantage. However, instead of relying on a network of scouts, as was customary at the time, the A's relied on impartial statistics. On-base percentage and slugging percentage (a weighted batting average) were the metrics most correlated with players scoring runs. The A's rooted their decision criteria in these two metrics, thereby discovering undervalued and occasionally ignored talent. Ultimately, the team made it to the playoffs in 2002 and 2003 and inspired an entirely new method of player recruitment which has become an industry standard.[21]

Philosophically, Frontier Innovators take a similar approach. They look beyond traditional recruiting and assessment approaches to find diamonds in the rough.

This is in part a reflection of practical reality. At the Frontier, traditional résumé filtering and interview-based recruiting techniques can be exercises in frustration and futility. Where startup ecosystems are nascent and there are fewer trained candidates, hiring someone with the perfect résumé is simply not a practical goal. In developing markets with high unemployment, job postings are overwhelmed with applications. In Tanzania, for instance, Zola's job postings consistently receive hundreds, if not thousands, of applications, although few candidates have directly applicable experience. Where large informal markets exist, résumés are typically laden with professional experience that is difficult to compare or calibrate.

At the Frontier, innovators focus on character, behavior, and demonstrated skills rather than the perfect résumé. Joshua explains, "We focused on high-performance people, people that won competitions in athletics, maths, public speaking, chess, or things like that. We tried to uncover the hidden gems."[22]

At the extreme, some Frontier Innovators institutionalize large-scale, automated recruiting strategies based on demonstrated capabilities and skills.

Meet Mark Essien, founder of Hotels.ng, a prominent Nigerian startup that offers the country's leading online booking platform. Mark's biggest barrier was not sourcing hotels for the platform but finding teammates. Historically, Mark's human capital team had the impossible task of sifting through unending piles of résumés. Candidates without shiny résumés never had a chance to prove their worth. Many of the best candidates in Lagos, Nigeria's capital, had already been discovered and were working with leading startups or large companies. At the same time, the best candidates in the smaller towns around Nigeria did not have the right networks, connections, or pedigrees to be discovered.

So Mark launched the HNG Internship, an online internship that serves as a digital filtering mechanism that can reach far beyond Nigeria's capital. The company screens candidates without meeting them, through a multiple-round, task-based, impartial recruiting process.

The process starts when Hotels.ng posts a job in the internship task manager. The recruiter assigns prospective recruits a series of computer science problems via Slack (a digital chat program). Candidates who pass one round of testing go on to the next phase. Those who fail are eliminated. Over time the problems get more difficult, and thus the list is winnowed. When 95 percent of candidates have been eliminated, the final few are interviewed and a subset are hired.

The program is evenings only and not meant to be all consuming for candidates, who likely have other full-time responsibilities to manage. Hotels.ng also wants to make sure no one drops out for financial reasons. They pay everyone in the pool a stipend as they progress.

Mark has forged partnerships to fund his program at greater scale, including with state governments in Nigeria as well as various corporations. He thinks that, over time, this structured candidate-testing platform could become an industry standard. The first internship class had seven hundred applicants. The last batch increased nearly sixfold, to four thousand. Hotels.ng hired the best twenty-five, predominantly from outside Lagos. Given the demand for workers at Hotels.ng, these numbers will likely only continue to increase.

For technical roles, like computer scientists or accountants, a skills-based testing approach like this one works well. However, assessing potential job performance is more challenging and nuanced for team-based roles that involve creativity, relationships, and strategy.

Here again Frontier Innovators have a solution. They are pioneering the implementation of behavior-based models to understand a candidate's character, aptitude, competence, and projected performance.

Paul Breloff and Simon Desjardins, both formerly investors in Frontier enterprises, observed that, universally, hiring represented the most important bottleneck across their portfolio.

They founded Shortlist to solve this challenge. Shortlist is a recruiting platform focused on competency-based hiring. The company has created more than a thousand digital modules to evaluate how candidates perform in simulated real-life work environments. When a candidate applies for a job, they encounter a customized scenario based on the company, industry, and role they are applying for, and they perform tasks that shed light on their capabilities and motivation levels.

Shortlist is in high demand among startups at the Frontier. It now has more than six hundred clients in Africa and India. And that's after a mere $3 million in funding.[23]

Building the Candidate Pipeline

Hiring based on capabilities and behavior assumes local talent is readily available. Sometimes, either because they operate in nascent ecosystems or have already exhausted available sources of talent, Frontier Innovators go one step further and actively build and train their pipeline.

Executives at Shopify, a Canadian e-commerce enabler based in Ottawa, realized the company had maxed out its traditional recruiting channels. CTO Jean-Michel Lemieux wanted to increase the pipeline of candidates, so in 2016, Shopify launched the Dev Degree. In partnership with Carleton University in Ottawa, the company created a de novo work-integrated academic degree. Reflecting Benjamin Franklin's words, "Tell me and I forget, teach me and I may remember, involve me and I learn," the Dev Degree marries traditional education with on-the-job practical experience.[24] Over four years, students complete an honors degree in computer science and gain more than forty-five hundred hours in practical work experience—double a typical co-op or internship-based program—at one of Canada's most successful technology companies. Each semester, students take three classes and work directly at Shopify for twenty-five hours a week. Students receive academic credit for the work experience, as long as they complete a practicum report reflecting on what they learned after every term. What's more, Shopify covers the four-year tuition cost and pays the students a salary for the time they work.[25]

Shopify's new program serves a dual purpose. On the one hand, Shopify is able to create a proprietary talent pool pipeline—finding, testing, and attracting the best of the class organically. On the other, this program benefits all participating students and the startup ecosystem more broadly by offering accessible and affordable practical lessons on the front lines of a world-class technology company.

Although still in its infancy, the program seems to be working. The first cohort of the program (itself a small pilot of eight students) will graduate in 2020 (subsequent cohorts are twenty-five each and will soon be much larger). All graduating students receive an offer to work at Shopify full-time. Impressively, gender diversity in the program is much more balanced than in traditional engineering programs. In recent cohorts, 50 percent of candidates are women, compared with fewer than 20 percent in computer science degrees on average.[26]

Shopify predicts that among candidates it recruits from the program, onboarding will be more rapid, since the students already know the role and the company.[27] As Jean-Michel explains it, "The technology industry is upending other industries, yet university programs have remained virtually unchanged. When we hire computer engineers, who have spent four years learning in school, we have to invest another full year training them to real-world applications. In this program, students have already been working in lockstep with us, and will hit the ground running."[28]

Other universities are already looking to implement similar programs. In late 2018, Shopify expanded the program to a second university: the Lassonde School of Engineering at York University.[29]

For Shopify in Ottawa, the major talent bottleneck was a lack of programmers. Elsewhere, the bottleneck may be different, but a similar pipeline creation approach is possible.

For Bridge International Academies, a startup that operates a network of more than five hundred ultra-low-cost private schools in multiple emerging markets, serving more than one hundred thousand pupils, its bottleneck was a shortage of teachers. Its unique "school in a box" model offers centralized lessons, technologically enabled school operations, and back-office support. To increase its teacher pipeline, it created a teacher's academy, the Bridge International Training Institute. The eight-week curriculum trains recruits on a combination of theoretical aspects of teaching, hands-on experience in classrooms, and instruction on how to work within the Bridge model. Bridge also implemented a similar model for other roles in the organization such as recruiting managers.[30]

Similarly, for Zola, the availability of trained sales and service people in rural Africa served as an early human capital bottleneck for its rapidly growing operation. Zola created a similar academy, offering a boot camp in business, sales, and service best practices in Tanzania, where the company recruited the best graduates.

Building the pipeline is often yet another manifestation of having to build the full stack, as you explored in chapter 2.

Looking to the World for Talent

Frontier Innovators must leverage the best talent from wherever it arises. This often means looking beyond the current location for talent.

Immigration (both in-country and international) is a powerful tool. For SkipTheDishes' Joshua Simair, sudden shifts in the political landscape transformed Winnipeg into a strategic recruitment location. After the US Trump administration nixed the Obama-era entrepreneur visa program (and adopted an aggressively anti-immigrant foreign policy), many countries around the world created new accelerated visa programs, sensing an opportunity to recruit talent that might otherwise have landed in the States. SkipTheDishes was able to leverage a Canadian immigration program designed to attract immigrants to smaller provinces: quotas are allocated by province, and Manitoba had many available slots. Joshua aggressively recruited prospective immigrants and brought them to Manitoba through this program.

SkipTheDishes' approach is certainly not unique. Shopify sourced top engineering talent it discovered in competitions around the world. Idriss Al Rifai from Fetchr built an entire immigration team to increase the size of its pipeline for drivers, recruiting drivers from Pakistan, India, the Philippines, and Nepal and bringing them to Dubai and Saudi Arabia.

In parallel, and as discussed in chapter 6, Frontier Innovators can leverage a distributed strategy to build teams in multiple geographies. Companies like Basecamp, InVision, and Zapier have gone to the extreme and become fully remote.

Taking a global lens to talent, whether one relocates candidates or builds a distributed model, is an effective way to increase the available talent pool.

Don't Churn and Burn: Retain and Grow

Silicon Valley accepts high employee turnover as a necessary by-product of its strategy of hiring only A-players. Perhaps because Frontier Innovators invest so much more in finding and training candidates, they take a longer-term view of the relationship. Brittany Forsyth, Shopify's senior vice president of human resources, explains: "Unlike companies in San Francisco, where there is a plentiful supply of talent, and as a result people move around from company to company, for us, our strategy is to work with employees over the long term. We want them to know that they can do their life's work here. We want them to know: if you invest in us, we can invest in you."[31]

In many Frontier ecosystems, employees are more loyal than those in the Valley. Chris Gladwin is founder of Cleversafe, which was sold to IBM in 2015 for $1.3 billion.[32] Chris reflected on the Chicago ecosystem, saying, "One of our key advantages was much higher employee retention. It is certainly different than in the Bay Area. We've experienced median retention of ten years."[33]

Some of this retention is structural. Because Frontier Innovators operate in nascent ecosystems, employees (like innovators themselves) have fewer options, so mutual dependence and mutual alignment for a long-term relationship is more likely.

Creators and the Multi-Mission Athletes you will meet in chapter 8 can harness their powerful visions to find and hire mission-aligned employees. These employees stay 50 percent longer than at other companies and are more likely to become high performers.[34] In interviews with leaders of hundreds of startups, the one unanimous sentiment was the importance of passion. Giving employees an opportunity to channel their passion drives retention. This trend will become increasingly important as millennials come to represent a larger part of the workforce. A recent study of three thousand professionals in the United States discovered that more than 85 percent of millennials would take a pay cut to work for a mission-aligned company (versus only 7 percent among baby boomers).[35]

Frontier Innovators also take a proactive approach to retaining and promoting employees over the long term. David Levine is CEO of Mr Beams, a Cleveland, Ohio–based startup that was acquired by Ring, which later was sold to Amazon for $1 billion. David incorporated candidates' personal development in the recruiting process for key hires.[36] He recalls that for an early product leader hire, Ryan Hruska, he developed a PowerPoint presentation, explaining the vision of the company, changes it would make over time, and ways his role would evolve. The pitch had Ryan start as a product engineer. Over time, he would lead and launch a few products and evolve into a director-level product manager. As David explains it, "Ryan achieved everything in that PowerPoint presentation, and much more. We mapped it out early."[37] Ryan has been with the company (now Ring) for nearly five years and now is director of product. David sees him as one of the company's future leaders.

To help their employees grow, Frontier Innovators look to institutionalize training grounds and connect their employees with mentors. Adalberto Flores, CEO of Kueski, a leading financial inclusion lender in Mexico, travels to San Francisco to meet investors and other companies on a regular basis. On every visit, he invites his high performers to join him. Through his network, Adalberto helps them meet peers at Silicon Valley startups.

Brittany Forsyth herself is a characteristic example. When she joined Shopify in 2010, she was the twenty-first employee; at the time the company was an early-stage startup in Ottawa that had yet to raise a Series A. She was hired as the office manager. She had a background in human capital, so she started helping out on the side. As soon as the company raised its Series A and started hiring fast, Brittany's role shifted to human capital. To help Brittany grow, Shopify encouraged her to take courses, seek mentors, and travel to other ecosystems. Now, as the SVP of human capital, Brittany is responsible for Shopify's entire four-thousand-person workforce. Shopify is now a $30 billion company that is traded on the Nasdaq.

Reward Employees with What Matters

To attract candidates, it can be tempting to look at Silicon Valley and try to replicate the superficial perks of its startup culture—free lunches, afternoon yoga classes, unlimited vacation policies—or its stock options' potential financial incentives. But these often miss the point.

The best Frontier Innovators look to offer perks and financial compensation that reflect their unique strategy, organization, and location. As you saw in chapter 6, Branch supports interoffice mobility, sponsoring travel for its employees to work from any of its many global offices. The travel perks support a global culture. Employees self-select to work at companies with these kinds of benefits.

At the Frontier, it can be challenging to replicate stock options, Silicon Valley's de facto financial retention tool. Employees are less likely to understand them or seek them out. Joshua witnessed this firsthand. He wanted to give SkipTheDishes equity to a number of his employees before the acquisition so that they could benefit from the windfall. He offered it to more than seventy of his ninety-three employees, many of whom had no equity before the deal. "It was rushed when we were giving it out," he said. "Many of our employees were scared they were getting screwed. They had seen *The Social Network* and saw how Zuckerberg had treated his co-founder. So many people turned [the stock options] down. They didn't understand the model."[38] To complicate things, in certain countries stock options aren't legally allowed, either for tax reasons or structurally.

A preference for cash over stock options is perhaps not an irrational position for employees at the Frontier; after all, exits are less proven and take longer. For the moment, stock option usage is low in Frontier ecosystems. This dynamic manifests itself even in more-developed European ecosystems. A study that surveyed more than seventy companies across European startup ecosystems and analyzed more than four thousand option grants determined that expectations for stock options were much lower across Europe than in the United States, with tremendous variety by country. On average, European employees owned half the options of their Silicon Valley counterparts.[39] The statistics are even more striking in emerging ecosystems.

Of course, offering fewer stock options does not obviate the need and desire of Frontier Innovators to offer their employees a stake in the business (or of their employees to have such a stake). In interviews, innovators consistently profess a desire to offer ownership—often universally—to their employees.

To do so, many Frontier Innovators are experimenting with new models of employee ownership that are better aligned with their growth profile. Lyndsay Handler, CEO of Fenix International, an energy startup based in Uganda, built phantom shares (code-named "Fenix Flames"). Part of her motivation was channeling the level of commitment and dedication many of her employees were demonstrating. As she explains it, "Many of our staff in Africa were not rich by any standards, yet were asking to invest their savings into the company."[40] Fenix Flames resemble direct stock ownership more than options, which means they are easier to understand and, importantly, benefit employees even if the company doesn't have exponential growth. Lyndsay granted Fenix Flames to every employee, all the way to the installers in remote Ugandan villages. This was a transformative financial investment for many of her staff during the company's subsequent sale to ENGIE, the French energy giant.[41]

It is far too early to tell what emerging best practices of employee ownership will ultimately look like, and various models are bound to continue evolving. Frontier Innovators continue to experiment with perks and compensation that align with their startup's strategy and look to retain employees over the longer term.

A-Teams, Not Just A-Players

For growing startups, strong teams are both their most important asset and their biggest challenge. Silicon Valley has created a rich science of recruiting and retaining top players. It focuses on identifying and recruiting top talent (A-players) and replacing them as they churn rapidly. But few human capital markets have either Silicon Valley's breadth of talent or depth in any field.

What works there rarely translates elsewhere. Places like Singapore or Toronto have the strength of Silicon Valley's talent but, given their countries' smaller sizes, lack its depth. Emerging ecosystems in Latin America or Africa have a more restricted pool of experienced talent.

It is hard to overstate how much of a barrier finding, training, growing, and retaining top talent at scale can be for startups anywhere, but particularly at the Frontier.

Slowly, though, progress is being made.

What leading Frontier Innovators have in common is a philosophically distinct approach to managing their human capital. Frontier Innovators look to build A-teams, recruiting based on capabilities and behavior rather than résumé experiences. These entrepreneurs actively build out a talent pipeline when one does not exist. They look to the world for resources, through either promoting immigration or building distributed models. And, of course, they look to retain and grow their teams over the long term, providing them with a set of aligned incentives and compensation.

In Silicon Valley, there is increased talk about expanding to more-affordable places, increasing diversity by looking beyond traditional sourcing methods, managing decentralized teams across geographies, and increasing retention over a longer term.

The newest and best approaches in this field will not be invented in Silicon Valley. They are already under way at the Frontier.

8.

Train to Be a Multi-Mission Athlete

Combine Impact and Profit-Based Goals

The rise of mixed martial arts (the combination of multiple fighting techniques like karate, boxing, jiu jitsu, and judo) represents a turning point in the history of hand-to-hand combat. Historically, the best fighters in any one discipline would face off against their counterparts in the same discipline, but this changed in the 1990s, when competitors using mixed martial arts techniques began to win the Ultimate Fighting Championship (UFC). A mixed approach is now standard. The best fighters are not experts in any one technique but in many fighting styles.[1] In addition to being one of the fastest-growing sports, mixed martial arts has become a standard training practice in elite military units around the world.[2]

A similar evolution is happening in the mindsets of Frontier Innovators.

The most successful Frontier Innovators are not solely focused on growth and financial returns; they consider social impact a central goal from the start, a stance that is reflected in the problems they're tackling as well as the customers they serve. Like UFC champions, many if not most Frontier Innovators are "Multi-Mission Athletes" who use a range of techniques to hit multiple targets. More often than not, their financial and social returns are inextricably connected.

Ali Parsa, founder of Babylon Health, exemplifies this mindset. Ali grew up in Iran. After the revolution of 1979, he fled his hometown of Rascht due to his political views. He left alone, without his parents. In a grueling overland journey, he traveled to Pakistan and eventually made it to Europe and settled in London.[3]

His early days in London were not always welcoming. Undeterred, he excelled in school and eventually earned a PhD from University College London. Ali could have become an academic but chose to be an entrepreneur, building multiple successful ventures over the years.

In 2004, Ali underwent knee surgery. He was dismayed by the experience and felt inspired to deliver better health care and health outcomes. By all accounts, his first venture, Circle Health, was a financial success. A private health care provider, Circle Health had a vision of reinventing the clinical experience; the hospitals were designed by architects, the rooms run by hoteliers, and the menus designed and cooked by chefs.[4] The company went public in 2011 on the AIM (a submarket of the London Stock Exchange) for more than $100 million.[5]

Yet Ali was unsatisfied with the results. The problem? Circle Health was not broadly accessible given the price point, nor was it solving the major pain point in health care: primary care. Ali sees primary care— what happens outside the hospital—as the linchpin of high-quality, accessible health care. In the United Kingdom, as in many places, the health care system is overloaded, and people turn to emergency room visits for their health needs.[6] Emergency rooms thus face long waits due to lack of beds and staff. Ali mused, "What if we could do for health care access what Google did for information?"

That's how Babylon was born. Through its text chat service Ask Babylon, the system can automatically perform routine diagnostic care by combining artificial intelligence and live clinicians. Babylon also offers a more-involved Talk to a Doctor service, which allows patients to speak with relevant clinicians in a live video chat and receive diagnoses and prescriptions from the comfort of their own homes.[7] Babylon recently released Healthcheck, which helps patients to monitor their health.

Babylon Health saw early success through a partnership with the National Health Service in the United Kingdom. However, Ali knew that Babylon would have greater impact in markets with more-limited national health care systems. He next partnered with the ministries of health in Rwanda and Saudi Arabia to offer Babylon as a national service. Ali also teamed up with Tencent to make Babylon available via WeChat.[8] Now Babylon has more than fifteen hundred doctors, engineers, and other staff on the team (and hundreds of part-time doctors) and nearly five million registered users.[9] Babylon recently raised more than $500 million at more than a $2 billion valuation, the largest digital health fundraise in Europe.[10]

For Ali, the social impact of the program is key; it is its raison d'être, explaining both why he started the company and why it is so successful. The majority of Frontier Innovators resemble Ali in this way: they are deeply focused both on building commercially successful, scaled businesses, and on having a positive social impact. This plays out in the products they offer and the customers they target, their interactions across the value chain, and their role in shaping the ecosystem.

Products and Customers

As you saw in chapter 1, Frontier Innovators are Creators who build new industries. Most often, they also create and build in underdeveloped industries where their innovations have a profound impact on community-wide quality of life.

In "A Theory of Human Motivation," Abraham Maslow proposed a so-called hierarchy of needs, arguing that humans focus on achieving needs in a certain order of importance.[11] At the lowest layer of the pyramid are the basic needs we prioritize, which include physiological needs (food, water, sleep, shelter, and sex) and safety needs (personal security, emotional security, financial security, health, and well-being) that underlie the achievement of all other needs, which include social belonging (friendship, intimacy, family), and finally, esteem and self-actualization.[12]

Compared with their Silicon Valley counterparts, Frontier Innovators tend to target human needs that are lower on Maslow's hierarchy. An analysis by the Global Accelerator Learning Initiative (GALI), which shares best practices and learning among innovation accelerators around the world, confirms this trend. By analyzing the portfolios of forty-three accelerators around the world, GALI determined that entrepreneurs in emerging markets are more likely to operate in sectors that include agriculture, energy, education, and financial services.[13]

The same is true among scaled companies. A study by Village Capital determined that of the nearly three hundred unicorns in the United States, only 18 percent are focused on industries that include health, food, education, energy, financial services, or housing.[14] In contrast, an analysis of leading startups in Latin America, Sub-Saharan Africa, and Southeast Asia reveals that a far greater share (as many as 60 percent of our sample in Sub-Saharan Africa) target these basic human needs.[15] The sheer number of revolutionary Frontier companies focused on the lower end of the hierarchy of needs becomes increasingly apparent throughout this book.

At the Frontier, startups tend to focus on the mass market from day one. While they naturally choose particular subsegments to target first, they rarely select the elite. More often than not, this mass market strategy responds to practical reality. Unlike in many developed countries, where there is a bell-shaped normal income distribution that bulges around an affluent middle class, in many Frontier markets the income distribution is heavily weighted toward the middle and bottom of the pyramid (see figure 8-1).

FIGURE 8-1

Frontier market income distribution

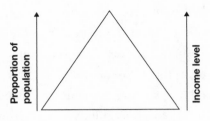

Thus, the only viable customer market at the Frontier is often the mass market.

River on the Go

In 2013, Deepak Garg and Gazal Kalra were thinking about how to help transform the Indian economy.[16] In their work at McKinsey & Company, they were struck by the comparative inefficiency of the Indian logistics system. Road, rail, and coastal shipping are 30 percent to 70 percent more expensive in India than the United States. This inefficient logistics network costs India's economy a staggering $45 billion each year, accounting for 14 percent of India's GDP.[17] Yet the country has an acute shortage of drivers, needing almost double the available supply.

The shortage is a reflection of interrelated challenges. The first is drivers' working conditions. They face unsafe roads, corruption, long hours, and days away from home.[18] Because of the fragmented industry, drivers travel to the delivery location—sometimes over several days—and upon arrival find that there may or may not be a return shipment available. Either they wait for a new load, or they return home with an empty load and are compensated only for one direction. Truck driver wages are low and often volatile, in part due to this dynamic.

To disrupt this vicious cycle, Deepak and Gazal launched Rivigo, based on a logistics model that is centered on drivers (referred to as "pilots") and improves their experience on the road and at home. Rivigo's motto is "Making Logistics Human." Rather than have pilots drive the entire length of a trip, they drive for five or six hours to a relay point. Another pilot takes that load and keeps going to the next relay point, and onward to the final destination. The original pilot swaps their load with another and drives it back to their original relay point, where again it is transferred to another driver. Rivigo's endlessly complex daisy chain allows pilots to return home each day and earn more, because trucks are driven at higher capacity thanks to the company's investment in technology to automate shipment coordination and demand planning.

Rivigo and other Multi-Mission Athletes aren't merely creating jobs; they're increasing the quality of employment throughout their value chains. Job creation on its own is a key aspect of entrepreneurial social impact: Endeavor estimates that fast-growing entrepreneurs, while representing less than 4 percent of the market, create disproportionately 40 percent more of the jobs in the field.[19] Indeed, new firms less than one year old are responsible for more than 1.5 million jobs every year for the past thirty years in the United States.[20]

But as we know, not all jobs are created alike. Multi-Mission Athletes like Rivigo can set themselves apart by building their business models around the needs and expectations of some of their most key constituents—their employees. Rivigo's strategy is working. By the fall of 2018, Rivigo had more than ten thousand trucks in its network, along with team members in five hundred micromarkets to work with suppliers.[21] Rivigo has expanded its logistics services to include cold freight storage, express brokerage, and a freight marketplace.[22] Rivigo completed a $50 million Series D round valued at more than $1 billion, for a total of $170 million in debt and equity raised since its launch only four years ago.[23]

The Rise of the Social Enterprise

For many people, the MMA mindset may sound similar to *social entrepreneurship*—an emergent field that, depending on the definition, spans companies with market capitalizations in the billions as well as small nonprofits. Over the past decade, the field of social entrepreneurship has gained increasing recognition from private funders, public officials, and university professors worldwide. Social enterprise initiatives, courses, conferences, and clubs have become ubiquitous on top university campuses, as young people aim to found organizations that integrate impact and profit. Prominent foundations have developed impact strategies that focus entirely on supporting and scaling social enterprises. Between 2003 and 2018, social enterprises received approximately $1.6 billion in foundation grants globally.[24] In short, social entrepreneurship has become an industry, and a hot one at that.

Perhaps because this important movement has grown so big, it continues to escape a singular definition. The central element of a social enterprise is the use of business-minded approaches to solve social problems. But social enterprises might be nonprofit or for-profit, or they might use a hybrid model; approaches vary widely. Some social enterprises consider scalable or profitable businesses a secondary objective to their desired social impact, while others see profit generation and scale as the engines that drive impact. Each company or nonprofit balances the needs of investors and shareholders with the desire to have a positive impact on customers, the environment, employees, and so on, in its own way.

For the purposes of this book, it is reasonable to say that while few social enterprises are leading technology-based startups, many leading Frontier startups share characteristics of social enterprises. Multi-Mission Athletes are deeply focused both on building commercially successful, scaled businesses, and on having positive social impact at the same time. They are not trading off profit versus impact. They are inherently doing both due to their business models.

This approach represents a departure from Silicon Valley norms, in which most entrepreneurs perceive startups and social enterprises as distant cousins, even though nearly all Silicon Valley founders are convinced of, or give lip service to, their "change the world" ambitions.

To build their balanced businesses, Multi-Mission Athletes focus less on the purity of the intention and more on the construction of the business model.

Impact Tied to the Business Model

What sets Multi-Mission Athletes like Babylon Health and Rivigo apart is the way they build impact in to the business model. Babylon Health's economic and social impact interests are fully aligned: to scale, Babylon will need to convince the NHS and other ministries of health that Babylon demonstrates better clinical outcomes and is more affordable than alternative options. The company also receives immediate feedback from users, who will adopt the platform only if quality of care is high and the experience is convenient.

For its part, Rivigo is able to attract more drivers to the platform when it increases the percentage chance that drivers will return home within twenty-four hours, with a full load in both directions. This outcome in turn increases Rivigo's ability to scale its logistics platform and serve customers effectively across the country.

Creating a business model that aligns social impact and economic best interest is no easy feat. It is so difficult that leading Silicon Valley companies have only managed to implement "do no harm" policies, back-end giving programs, and lackluster corporate social responsibility policies. Take, for instance, Google's promise, "Don't be evil."[25] It commits to treating its customers ethically, even though it is in its (short-term) economic interest, and its shareholders' interests, to maximize profit; this could mean, for example, using customer data in more personally invasive or nefarious ways to sell more ads. When social impact (or avoiding negative impact) runs counter to business interests, instituting an "avoid evil" policy is equal parts reassuring and alarming.

Many companies have good intentions and implement generous programs to give back. The Pledge 1% organization encourages firms to offer 1 percent of any or all of the company's stock, employee time, products, and profits to causes that matter.[26] Some Silicon Valley corporations have created parallel structures that include a charitable foundation arm. Others leverage buy-one, give-one (BOGO) models; for every good purchased, another is donated or sponsored. These models have their heart in the right place, but some of them yield mixed results. The BOGO model in particular has been criticized for its negative externalities. Toms Shoes didn't consider the repercussions of its initial BOGO model for local shoemakers and ended up distorting shoemaking markets across Africa and putting people out of work.[27]

For each of these companies, from Google to Toms, back-end impact is not a foundational part of the business model. If the business does not perform well, it is easy to cut back-end giving. This is not meant to diminish these programs. They are commendable. But a crucial difference remains: each of these approaches gives money *after* the company has made its profits. Impact is not rooted in their business models in any substantive way. As Ross Baird, founder of Village Capital, would say, this is "two-pocket" thinking: one pocket makes money, and the other gives it away.[28]

Multi-Mission Athletes are doing everything in the same pocket.

You Are What You Measure

For Multi-Mission Athletes, impact is directly correlated with business success. But this does not mean they track revenue and assume that impact has correspondingly occurred. After all, as they say, "You are what you measure."

The best Multi-Mission Athletes carefully reflect on their desired impact and decide how to assess success. They then assiduously track, report, and disseminate information about progress toward this goal across the organization. In many cases, the chosen impact metrics align with or are complementary to the company's financial metrics, because impact is part and parcel of the business model. Still, it is a challenging feat, in part because there is no universal, easily quantifiable impact measurement system. Just like Darwin's finches, which varied by island in the Galapagos, a Multi-Mission Athlete's chosen impact metrics are necessarily unique to its industry, context, and business model.

As Deepak Garg explains, "It's the principle of karma. We are focused on giving back and solving the problem. This is our language and our company's shared beliefs. Pilot metrics are leading indicators of our ongoing success."[29] While Rivigo naturally tracks financial metrics like cash flow and revenue, it gives equal weight to its own measures of success in solving the challenge of quality of life for drivers and efficiency in the logistics system. Rivigo therefore measures the percentage of pilots returning home within twenty-four hours and the number of loads filled in both directions.

For consumer-facing companies like Branch, M-PESA, M-KOPA, OkHi, and Zola, where impact is linked to product adoption, key metrics are tied to the number of customers and the level of usage.

For Gojek, impact is about entrenchment in society and the economy. CEO Nadiem Makarim is focused on growing market size (his target is to double or triple the size of any market Gojek enters). Nadiem tracks the incremental earnings of drivers and service providers and the employment opportunities he creates. In Indonesia, Gojek has become the largest income source in the country, with more than one million people earning income through the platform.[30]

Ultimately, metrics are tied to the objectives of the business and the mission. Deepak likens his approach to the banyan tree, which can live for hundreds of years and grow to staggering widths of more than six hundred feet.[31] As Garg explains it, "The banyan tree is the world's longest-living tree. The reason is because of its entirety: its roots give back to nature. Its impact is in and out. That leads to its growth and survival."[32] Multi-Mission Athletes see giving back to employees, customers, investors, and the ecosystem as fundamental to their companies' long-term growth.

Sector-Level Impact

A Multi-Mission Athlete's impact is not restricted to building successful, scalable, *and* socially impactful businesses. Multi-Mission Athletes often take on even broader, sector-shaping roles.

Chapter 1 discusses the mobile banking pioneer M-PESA, which not only has a direct impact on its customers but also has created an entire revolutionary sector. Because of M-PESA, customers can now access a range of formerly nonexistent services. M-KOPA, which offers rent-to-own solar home systems that replace unsafe kerosene lights, would have been impossible without M-PESA because of the prohibitive cost of collecting hundreds of thousands of small payments. A range of other services use M-PESA as well, from new private schools like Bridge International Academies to public sanitation projects.

This ecosystem is a direct enabler of the original business. When applications are built on top of M-PESA, they not only result in more transactions on the system but also reinforce the habit-forming nature of mobile money and, ultimately, the competitive moat it enables. Multi-Mission Athletes are accomplishing similar sector-building feats in education, health care, financial services, and more. As Babylon Health scales, Ali Parsa will enable a range of service providers—like pharmacies, hospitals and other health care providers—to plug in to the system.

Successful Multi-Mission Athletes spur ecosystems in other ways as well. M-PESA demonstrated the potential to develop and scale a mobile money platform, and an entire industry exploded on the back of this innovation. Now there are more than 250 replica mobile money deployments that serve more than six hundred million people worldwide.[33] Demonstrating the success of the model may also inspire a range of replicators in other markets. Similarly, as Rivigo scales, it will enable a range of other platforms to thrive, leveraging cheaper and more-efficient logistics, all while changing the lives of drivers and their families.

Frontier Innovators' impact can further extend to the entrepreneurial ecosystems in which they work, as you saw with Hotels.ng and Shopify's efforts in building the local human capital pipeline. Chapter 11 plunges into the myriad ways Frontier Innovators actively build their ecosystems.

The Multi-Mission Athlete Role Model

The lessons Multi-Mission Athletes offer us are particularly germane today. While Silicon Valley continues its steadfast march toward providing us with the best photo-sharing apps, the Frontier presents a powerfully different perspective and model. This alternative conception is crucial for the United States and other highly developed countries as we increasingly look to business, and particularly innovators, for solutions to society's challenges. And US society is not short of challenges. In the United States, sixty million people are financially underbanked (including 53 percent of African American households, and 46 percent of Hispanic households).[34] More than five hundred thousand people in the United States are experiencing homelessness.[35] Student loan debt has soared to forty-four million borrowers, owing in aggregate $1.5 *trillion*.[36]

The public, the government, and regulators are holding companies to a higher standard than they did even ten years ago. Witness what Larry Fink—CEO of BlackRock, the world's largest capital provider—stated in an open letter to the CEOs of public companies: "Companies must benefit all of their stakeholders, including shareholders, employees, customers, and the communities in which they operate. Without a sense of purpose, no company, either public or private, can achieve its full potential."[37] More recently, the Business Roundtable, an association of CEOs of the largest companies in the United States, redefined the purpose of a corporation, explaining that beyond the maximization of profits, corporations have a role in supporting many external stakeholders including employees, suppliers, the community, and the environment.[38] Whether business leaders will deliver on their rhetoric remains to be seen, but this cultural shift suggests that we have moved beyond generic "do no harm" mission statements and should now expect much more from our companies.

Innovators win when their customers and their supply chains win. Building a Multi-Mission business model, where impact is aligned with profitability, is not easy, but if the model works, it can be a recipe for success and change. CircleUp, a lender for startups, examined the relative performance of traditional companies versus mission-aligned benefit corporations, or B Corps. Among consumer companies, the average consumer brand ranking on their platforms was 5 out of 10, while 75 percent of B Corps had brand rankings of 9 or 10. This translated directly into sales performance as well, with B Corps seeing sales growth rates three times as high as the average consumer company.[39] Researchers at Harvard Business School, Northwestern University, and Causeway Capital determined that firms with good ratings on sustainability issues that directly related to their business models outperformed those with lower ratings and traded at a premium to their peers.[40] It is still early days, but others have documented the power of mission on governance and on the quality of asset management practices at a company.[41]

Being a Multi-Mission Athlete can be a key enabler of many of the strategies outlined in this book. When building A-teams, Multi-Mission Athletes can more easily attract mission-aligned candidates and compete with other firms. When raising capital, they can access a wider and more diverse set of pools, including government and donor capital—although they may struggle to attract those venture capital firms that still erroneously equate impact with lack of returns. When working with the ecosystem, they are more likely to find supporters and sponsors that buy in to the mission and look to support the organization.

Some people argue that balancing multiple missions of scalable businesses and social impact requires trade-offs. For Multi-Mission Athletes, however, there is rarely such a dichotomy.

Many developed ecosystems, including Silicon Valley, are rife with intractable social issues, including homelessness, unaffordable health care, poor public education, and much more. Learning from and adopting the practices of Frontier Innovators not only will help us solve these pressing challenges but also will empower the next generation of Silicon Valley innovators to tackle problems beyond the photo-sharing app. Much as I love my photo-sharing apps.

9.

Manage Risk

Foster Trust: Don't Just "Move Fast and Break Things"

An acceptance of failure and an audacious approach to rapid product and company development represent a cornerstone of Silicon Valley's risk-taking culture. Coined by Mark Zuckerberg, "Move fast and break things" was Facebook's mantra. He notoriously once said, "The idea is that if you never break anything, you're probably not moving fast enough . . . At the end of the day, the goal of building something is to build something, not to not make mistakes."[1]

Therefore, it is just fine if Silicon Valley's products are imperfect. The important thing is getting versions out to customers for testing and then receiving feedback on the idea. Over time, the product will naturally improve as the kinks get worked out.

This culture of acceptance of failure extends beyond the way products and companies are built. It drives Silicon Valley's relationship with society and laws: the attitude to move fast and break things is not exactly conducive to legal adherence. Many role models for young startups realized their success by starting in legal gray areas and operating under the radar as small companies. They look to change the laws as they scale. This was Uber's playbook: enter a city, rapidly scale, and then rely on customer support to have the local laws changed.[2]

But in most emerging ecosystems, Silicon Valley's blasé approach to product risk and company development, or its relationship with the law, does not work. Frontier Innovators view risk—particularly certain risks—as an externality that should be avoided or at least mitigated. This philosophy doesn't mean that you don't take risks. Managing risk is about determining upfront which risks are acceptable and which are nonnegotiable. It involves building a culture of risk management, thinking critically about the potential negative externalities of products, and engaging proactively with the ecosystem.

Life or Death

I once asked David Rosenberg, CEO of AeroFarms, what kept him up at night. Without blinking, he immediately answered, "Rule number one in farming is don't kill your customer." In short, food safety is David's paramount concern.

AeroFarms is a Newark, New Jersey–based startup that is at the forefront of the vertical farming movement. *Vertical farming* is the growing of fruits and vegetables, often in constrained spaces in urban environments, by stacking the plants on top of each other (rather than horizontally, or side-by-side, as is typical on land).

While AeroFarms itself is relatively new (founded in 2004), its approach has been decades of research in the making. One of its co-founders, Ed Harwood of Cornell University, is known for his development of an aeroponics approach to vertical farming. Unlike hydroponics farms, where plants are grown in water, *aeroponics* involves growing plants in the air and feeding them with misted water. Ed accomplished important cost savings and efficiency gains by designing a patented cloth growth media.

Like a well-strung hammock, the cloth holds plants upright. The plant's roots perforate the cloth and grow into the air below, dangling like a marionette's legs. They are misted with water at just the right time and in the right quantity to grow optimally.

Ed's aeroponic insight transformed the traditional vertical farming business model in two essential ways. First, the inputs are lower. Using a mist on the exposed roots is more than 50 percent more efficient than hydroponics (which itself is 70 percent more efficient than growing plants in soil). Second, because there are no water basins, the crops are lighter and therefore stackable. By stacking up to twelve levels of plants to heights as great as forty feet, AeroFarms dramatically improves farm space utilization.[3] The combination of higher stacking and fewer inputs allows for the construction of productive farms in urban environments where real estate is expensive.

AeroFarms expanded in 2011 when David, along with Marc Oshima—who had been working on a vertical farming initiative—approached Ed about merging their respective businesses. Together, the three men combined aeroponics with data analysis and process-driven innovation. By tracking inputs minute by minute (e.g., air composition, temperature, nutrient solution, and water pH) and observing the plant's resulting growth and shape, they continuously improved the method over time.[4]

In addition to AeroFarms' flagship farm in Newark, the company has now built eight farms, has more than 150 employees, and has raised about $200 million.[5]

The foundation of AeroFarms' farming system is food safety. It is a baseline goal for everyone in the company. At AeroFarms, scaling starts with a deep understanding of the potential risk factors and an institutionalized structure and culture of risk mitigation.

This approach is a necessary consequence of the product. For David, a bacterial outbreak in his farms could literally kill his customers. An obsessive concern over food safety is warranted, because his company is reinventing the way food is produced and distributed.

Providing a safe product is table stakes; if AeroFarms fails on food safety, it will fail on everything. It is this understanding of and attitude toward risk that differentiates Frontier Innovators.

Different Products for Different Customers

Food safety may seem like an extreme example. Yet it is not an isolated one. As you have seen throughout this book, Frontier Innovators are offering different types of products to a different customer base.

In Silicon Valley, most startups solve customer pain points that aren't a matter of life or death. Therefore, the consequences of failure typically are not catastrophic. These companies tackle problems higher on Maslow's hierarchy of needs. If their Uber app stopped working, the average millennial would take a taxi (if these still exist in a few years), and if Venmo failed, they could get cash at the ATM (if these still exist in a few years). Some firms target the top of Maslow's pyramid, self-actualization, including using and refining talents (e.g., MasterClass) and even transcendence (e.g., Calm or Headspace for meditation). These companies offer valuable services to their users. But they do not have life-or-death consequences to the customer if things go awry.

In this context, it is fine, most of the time, to move fast and break things. It is also much easier to build trust with users if the worst-case scenario is not that bad.

It's different at the Frontier, as you have seen: more startups are solving critical needs or providing missing infrastructure. This includes physiological needs like food (e.g., AeroFarms), light (e.g., Zola), and health and education (e.g., Babylon Health and African Leadership University, which you will meet in chapter 11). Frontier Innovators are also offering products and services to a customer base that has more to lose. These customers are looking for trustworthy products, and it often takes a lot of effort to build their trust.

Frontier Innovators need to communicate their focus on risk management in order to build trust with their customers. In the early days of M-PESA and Zoona, as both were offering a product geared to the underbanked, the companies struggled to convince their users to adopt their systems. A customer's perception of trustworthiness and safety was critical to product adoption, so much so that Zoona built it into its tag line: "Easy, Quick, Safe." Product safety was built in to the product experience, specifically on cash-outs. The ability for customers to withdraw cash from the network of agents was viewed as a prerequisite to convincing them to put it into the system in the first place (many customers' first transactions were small, just to test this ability with different agents). If agents always had cash for customers to pull out of the system, customers would trust the technology and would be more willing to put cash into the system.

Sometimes, building trust may require physical manifestation. Chris Folayan, founder of Mall for Africa, one of the leading e-commerce platforms on the continent, remembers early customers who doubted the online platform would make good on its promises of delivering goods ordered online. Chris had to build a "physical trust network." As he explains it, "People are used to going to the market and meeting their suppliers face to face. In a digital world, this is not possible."[6]

To solve this, Mall for Africa created physical pick-up locations. In the United States, Amazon's edge is its convenience for home delivery. Yet, for Mall for Africa, success came by allowing customers to pick up from the company and see it was a real company. Chris doubled down on building trust with customers by partnering with well-known brands. The combination of being associated with trustworthy brands and demonstrating a physical presence helped drive customer adoption and has made Mall for Africa one of the largest players in the continent.

Frontier Innovators build reliable products that are worthy of trust, and they foster relationships with their customers to build that trust.

Choosing Acceptable Risks

Innovation is an art and not a science. It is often said that entrepreneurs "build the plane as they fly it." There will invariably be high risk in building a startup, whether it is in Silicon Valley, at the Frontier, or elsewhere.

Frontier Innovators start by determining which types of risk are acceptable and which are not—none more so than Dr. Consulta. Founded by Thomaz Srougi in 2011, Dr. Consulta is an ambitious startup that operates a leading chain of medical clinics in Brazil.

Free health care is enshrined in the Brazilian constitution. It covers everything from primary care to long-term hospital visits. Unfortunately, the public health care system is underfunded and has long wait times. As a consequence, more than a quarter of Brazilians have private health insurance, which allows them to access a faster, parallel system. The other three-quarters do not. Dr. Consulta's vision is to offer an affordable primary care alternative to the remaining three-quarters of Brazilians who cannot afford higher-end options. It leverages technology to dramatically simplify many back-end processes and innovate on the medical clinic model to enable doctors to offer efficient, excellent care.

Like many Frontier Innovators offering critical products or services, Thomaz's understanding of risk had serious implications for the way he built his business and scaled its operations. As Thomaz puts it, "On patient safety we have zero tolerance for risk. On everything else, we take highly calculated ones."[7] To deliver medical advice in its clinics, Dr. Consulta hired the best doctors it could find, refusing to compromise on the patient experience. But on everything else, the company looked to experiment and innovate. For example, its pricing, unlike most health care systems around the world, is highly transparent. In a recent *Business Insider* article, this model was likened more to a fast food restaurant than a medical clinic: it "doesn't take insurance and lists its prices like a McDonald's menu . . . At each doctor's office, prices for procedures are listed out. For example, a general practitioner visit costs roughly $30 (110 Brazilian reals)."[8]

When the company creates a new product line, such as the recent installation of MRI machines (a first for clinics in Brazil), it didn't experiment with the machine process, but only with clinic footprint and utilization. Dr. Consulta recently built an analytics platform that reviews patient trends to predict treatment results and improve care (as well as help researchers find better treatments or investigate new therapeutics).[9]

Dr. Consulta built risk management in to its product development as well. It chose to start in the hardest market: a favela in São Paulo. If the model worked safely there, the company knew it would work anywhere, as long as the product was valuable and resonated with customers. Once clinicians mastered it there, the model had sufficient slack to function everywhere else.

Dr. Consulta now has more than fifty clinics, employs more than two thousand doctors, and has served more than one million customers. It has garnered more than $100 million in venture capital funding from investors around the world to scale the model across Brazil.[10] Each of its innovations continues to be done in a siloed and incremental way, keeping patient care as the primary and nonnegotiable objective.

VisionSpring, which looks to offer low-price eyeglasses in emerging markets, built risk management into its planned product evolution. VisionSpring wanted to offer glasses to children, but these required the most operational excellence and manufacturing intricacy. Therefore, the company staged product development to build its capabilities over time and manage the risk of offering a substandard product. It started with reading glasses, followed by prescription glasses for working-age adults. Only after mastering these steps did the company attempt glasses for children.[11]

For Frontier Innovators, high-quality products and services are a direct result of a considered approach to risk: deciding where it is not appropriate to take risks, as with food quality or patient care, while experimenting elsewhere.

A Culture of Risk Management

To cement this focus on quality products and trust, Frontier Innovators often create an organizational culture that manages risks and empowers their employees to act when they see something.

David Rosenberg from AeroFarms built his organization and his team around risk management. To run his business, David reports to his board on seven operational key performance indicators (KPIs): (1) people safety, (2) quality and food safety, (3) yield, (4) operational efficiency, (5) inputs (e.g., nutrients, seed, energy), (6) price, and (7) labor. It is striking that his first two KPIs have to do with safety. After all, and as discussed in chapter 8, you are what you measure. As David says, "If we cannot deliver on people safety and quality, then nothing else matters."[12]

Food safety runs through the reporting structure and is built in to the culture and fabric of the organization. Tim Bender is the head of engineering and reports directly to Roger Post, AeroFarms' COO. Before working with AeroFarms, Tim spent fifteen years in senior leadership positions at ConAgra and ARYZTA, both industry leaders. One of his roles at AeroFarms is to constantly consider safety questions: Where might bacteria grow? What could hamper food safety? What processes need to be put in place to ensure quality?

Each farm has a head of food safety. Checks and balances are integrated into the reporting structure; safety managers report to quality assurance, who reports to the COO and not to the head of a farm. David knew that "there may be trade-offs between food safety and efficiency . . . [so] we put in place an organizational structure that allows for independent reporting, to make sure decisions are long-term focused for the good of all stakeholders."[13]

AeroFarms was conscious it was creating a new food production process and there were no existing food safety industry standards. The best way to decrease risk was regular cleaning. Yet one of AeroFarms' biggest cost drivers is labor associated with cleaning. How much cleaning is enough? David explains:

> When I asked leaders in the greenhouse space, particularly in
> Europe, when they last cleaned their facilities, their answers
> were invariably centered around a particular [negative] event,
> and cleaning as a result of that "event." For us, we decided to
> clean our facilities twenty-five times a year. We don't know if
> that's the right answer, and we're pretty sure we're overdoing it.[14]

AeroFarms' cleaning figure of twenty-five times a year was not determined by policy nor by the head of engineering. It came from the bottom
up; the staff on the safety team suggested cleaning be tied to another step
in their process: harvest times. AeroFarms grows in fourteen-day cycles,
resulting in twenty-five harvests per year. David says, "We are starting
with a realistic and very conservative high bar. We will go from there as
we figure out the right level."[15]

While AeroFarms is on track for sales and plant openings, its commitment to cleaning has left it behind on its labor cost estimates because it
has added the extra cleaning step. For David, it is worth it. The process
may be overkill for now but needs to scale to many types of products.
With food, you can't learn by experimenting with a product that hits the
market.

Building a comprehensive reporting structure for something like food
safety fosters team alignment, creates momentum, and builds habit. As
Charles Duhigg explained in his book *The Power of Habit*, these design
choices go a long way in creating repeatable patterns of behavior. Ultimately, this creates a virtuous cycle that supports not only the evaluation
and mitigation of risks but also organizational health overall.[16]

Considering Negative Externalities

Some people argue that startups must take a further step and proactively
evaluate the potential negative consequences of a technology product at
its inception. The Institute for the Future, in partnership with the Technology and Society Solutions Lab, recently published a guidebook that

describes approaches to planning for and avoiding the potential negative uses of new products. They cover eight principal risk vectors, including truth, disinformation, and propaganda along with risk of addiction to products. They write as follows:

> As technologists, it's only natural that we spend most of our time focusing on how our tech will change the world for the better . . . But perhaps it's more useful, in some ways, to consider the glass half empty. What if, in addition to fantasizing about how our tech will save the world, we spent some time dreading all the ways it might, possibly, perhaps, just maybe, screw everything up?[17]

The manual goes on to offer tactical approaches to building ethical action in to startup product development from the get-go.

Consider what this approach might have looked like at Facebook. Had Facebook's board required a report of the volume of fake news going viral on the platform, the number of fake accounts created, or the siloing of echo chamber discussions on the platform, the company might have avoided some of its unintended, though highly foreseeable, externalities.

A more thoughtful approach to risk also translates to Frontier Innovators' relationship with the law.

Break the Law or Make the Law

One of the most intriguing aspects of Frontier Innovation is the unique way innovators relate with the law in the ecosystems in which they operate. Achmad Zaky, co-founder and CEO of Bukalapak, the Indonesian e-commerce startup you met previously, sums it up well: "In many emerging markets [with high degree of economic informality] there are no rules. Therefore, we are not breaking them. More often than not, we are having open dialog with the government to make them."[18]

Take the case of Uber in the United States versus analogous ride-sharing startups at the Frontier. In developed markets, Uber avoided laws about pickup points and driver background checks; subsequently it saw investigations on its impact, and it lost licenses.[19] It was an unregulated, disruptive force in a regulated, even unionized, industry.

In contrast, in many emerging markets regulated taxi industries don't exist. Instead, some markets have hordes of unregulated, unlicensed, uninsured, untracked, and unidentified taxis. Car-sharing startups like Grab or Gojek in Southeast Asia or 99 in Latin America (and Uber in many of these markets as well) changed that. Drivers must present a photo ID to register and must have insurance to join these platforms. If something goes wrong, not to worry: every ride is tracked. This is by no means a foolproof system. For instance, there have been several reported cases of abductions of female riders in India by Uber drivers.[20] Yet overall, many observers argue it's safer than the informal, untracked alternative.

The same thing applies for a range of businesses. Square, one of the most prominent fintech success stories, created a revolutionary product that allows small merchants to accept credit cards. By providing them with an attachment that connects with their phones, Square frees merchants from the need to purchase expensive sales terminals like those in stores in shopping malls. Instead, Square merchants can use their cell phones and create receipts by email. In the United States, most of the merchants who adopted Square's technology were already formal businesses that filed taxes and were regulated; they just happened to not accept credit cards.[21]

Square replicas have popped up worldwide—such as Clip in Mexico, Yoco in South Africa, and Ezetap in India. For many of the merchants they serve, accepting debit and credit cards represents their first transaction within the formal financial system. These are the shoe vendors at the street markets, the cell phone reseller on the busy street, or the neighborhood corner store in Mexico City, Johannesburg, or Delhi. In effect, they are becoming formal businesses for the first time.

In some exceptional cases, Frontier Innovators have to work closely with governments. As Yousef Hammad from BECO Capital, a leading Middle East venture capital fund, shared, "Governments are heavily involved. Without their buy-in, the private sector would not survive. You would effectively be starting to compete with the government."[22] Yousef was talking about the Dubai taxi industry, which is heavily linked with the government—meaning that Uber or Careem weren't merely displacing a formal or informal industry, but a government-backed one. Working within the established system was therefore not a choice but a prerequisite.

Frontier Innovators aren't simply bringing greater transparency into the industries within which they operate. They often are looking to create the regulatory infrastructure for their nascent industries. AeroFarms' David Rosenberg understands he's pioneering not only a business model but also an entirely new urban farming industry. Therefore, for him, his industry's food must be as good as or better than existing alternatives. As the adage goes, "No one ever gets fired for hiring IBM." In other words, any missteps by AeroFarms, or by any of its smaller competitors, risks alienating early customers and throwing the vertical farming industry back a decade.

Thus health and safety standards are crucial, not only for not killing the customers but also for the company and the sector's ongoing growth. David explains: "If you calculate the press on vertical farming, Aero-Farms, one of the earliest and the current market leader, gets about fifty percent of it. People see us as a thought leader. But press also invites a lot of competition, which we're increasingly seeing. The problem is that many up-and-comers are not even asking risk questions that we've already solved [e.g., how often to clean the plant]. I decided it was part of my duty to organize our peer group."[23] Consequently, AeroFarms co-launched the Food Safety and Urban Agriculture Coalition, which brings together leading vertical farming innovators, sets best practice standards, and lobbies the government for appropriate regulation (and in this case, more-stringent regulation).

Similarly, Zola was involved in the early development of the Global Off-Grid Lighting Association (GOGLA). M-PESA engaged with regulators before even thinking of offering mobile money accounts.[24] Clip, the Mexican payment company, is deeply involved with its regulator, including advising on the recently adopted Mexican Fintech Act (a law that defines how and where innovators can offer financial products and services, within a prudential consumer context).[25] Whether from necessity or smart business practice, Frontier Innovators often create regulation and formalize industries, decreasing risk to customers as well as themselves.

Why It's Important

A seismic shift is under way. Consumers no longer tolerate Silicon Valley's cavalier approach to risk. They are demanding a more responsible approach. Look no further than the recent backlash against Facebook and Twitter for enabling Russia's 2016 US election interference and for the companies' nontransparent use of customer data. Big technology companies are increasingly being called upon to mitigate the negative consequences of their products and to become better corporate citizens. It may be no coincidence that Facebook recently changed its motto to "Move Fast with Stable Infra[structure]."[26] Mark Zuckerberg explained the rationale: "What we realized over time is that it wasn't helping us to move faster because we had to slow down to fix these bugs and it wasn't improving our speed."[27]

The arrogance of Silicon Valley has no place at the Frontier—nor, increasingly, in Silicon Valley itself.

Frontier Innovators do not have the luxury to ignore product or business risk. They are offering fundamentally needed products and services, often to vulnerable populations. Therefore, they carefully evaluate the types of risk they're comfortable taking, build in a margin of safety, consider the negative externalities of their products, and build a culture that supports these aforementioned approaches. Often, since they are creating industries, they look to formalize industries, create appropriate regulation, and engage with the ecosystem to strengthen best practices.

In the last six months of 2018, Facebook's market capitalization tumbled from a high of $630 billion to $380 billion—a nearly $250 billion loss—in large part attributed to its users' and society's decreased confidence in the platform and its attitude toward product risk, in the wake of the Cambridge Analytica and other scandals.[28] Frontier Innovators' more measured approach to risk provides not only a valuable counterpoint to Silicon Valley's brazenness but also an example (and a highly profitable strategy) toward which we should all aspire.

10.

Reinvent Finance

Develop New Venture Models for Tougher Ecosystems

In innovation, perhaps the strongest symbiotic relationship is between entrepreneurs and venture capitalists. Without venture capital, entrepreneurs might have an idea, but no way to get it off the ground. They are willing to sell a portion of their company in return for capital and advice to accelerate it. And, of course, without entrepreneurs, venture capitalists would have no one to do the hard work of building a company.[1] Yet this mutually dependent relationship can fall out of balance.

Carlos Antequera is a former entrepreneur turned venture capitalist. He is intimately aware of the idiosyncrasies of the industry and determined to chart a different path. Originally from Bolivia, Carlos studied computer science and mathematics in Kansas and later worked as a software engineer. After completing his MBA, he founded Netchemia in Kansas, originally as an internet consulting firm to help bring Latin American businesses online and digitize their processes.

Then an acquaintance asked for his help in automating special education for the local Topeka, Kansas, school district. Soon other school districts heard about the product and requested his help. Netchemia found its niche building a talent management platform for school districts to recruit, develop, and train their teachers and administrators. Netchemia then scaled to become a dominant national player in the United States and to serve more than thirty-five hundred school districts, over time helping them with a range of products spanning job boards, applicant tracking, employee records, and performance management.

Carlos built his company without traditional venture capital. He bootstrapped Netchemia for four years until he raised a seed round of $850,000 from angel investors. Many years later in his journey, to support some investments in the business he received a $6.5 million private equity investment, essentially skipping the venture capital stage.[2]

Reflecting on his experience, Carlos concluded that classic venture capital wouldn't have worked for his business. Netchemia had a strong business model, good growth, and highly predictable revenue, but it had neither the potential nor the ambition to scale a hundredfold. As a growing technology business with limited collateral, the company also wasn't a great fit for bank loans.

The venture model did not work for Netchemia, nor does it work for many companies like it. As Carlos explains, "If I had wanted Netchemia to be a fit for a venture capitalist, I would have had to break what I already had. Venture capitalists need bigger markets to invest in. I would have had to move away from a niche market and swing for the fences on a larger idea. But by going to a larger market with no expertise, I would likely lose everything I had so painstakingly built."[3]

In 2016, fifteen years after starting it, Carlos sold Netchemia to a private equity firm. As his next step, he wanted to find a way to financially support more entrepreneurs like him who were building companies like Netchemia that were incompatible with traditional Silicon Valley–style venture capital.

What was it about the venture capital model that was so incompatible with Carlos's desired investments? To understand that, let's first explore the basic principles of classic venture capital typically associated with Silicon Valley.

A Tale of the High Seas

Venture capitalists are specialized investors in startups. They raise funds—pools of capital—which they invest over three to four years; then they help their investments mature and ultimately exit. An average fund has a life-span of ten years. To continue investing, the venture capital firm raises a new fund every time it has finished investing the first one. The general partners (the venture capitalists) invest the capital of limited partners (family offices, pension funds, university endowments, foundations, and corporations) who entrust their capital with the fund. Venture capitalists have a nearly universal business model, which is composed of a fee and profit-sharing system (often referred to as "2 & 20," the typical fee structure for venture capital funds, consisting of a management fee and "carry," explained shortly).[4]

When I ask my students where they think the classic model originated, they often bet on the earliest days of Silicon Valley. But its roots are much older and have nothing to do with tech. In fact, the now-standard profit-sharing structure was pioneered in the 1800s in New Bedford, Massachusetts, for a completely different industry: whaling. While New Bedford was only one of many ports that supported the whaling industry, it dominated the trade on a global scale. As the *Economist* observes, the whalers in New Bedford "did not invent a new type of ship, or a new means of tracking whales; instead, they developed a new business model that was extremely effective at marshaling capital and skilled workers despite the immense risks involved for both."[5] Of the nine hundred whaling ships worldwide in 1859, seven hundred were American, 70 percent of which hailed from New Bedford.[6]

The New Bedford whaling model worked in a strikingly similar way to the modern venture capital system. Whaling agents (the equivalent of modern-day venture capital firms) recruited investors and put up capital to buy and equip the boats. For this, they would receive a share of the profits (a portion of what one could "carry" off the boat). The captains (our modern-day entrepreneurs) often also invested their own capital in the voyage and received a meaningful share of the proceeds. The crew was paid entirely from the proceeds of the voyage, much as modern-day stock options reward startup employees. The timelines were long: boats would return only when the ship was full, something that could often take years, and a meaningful percentage of boats were lost at sea.[7]

Like mid-nineteenth-century whaling, venture capital is a risky investment strategy. Each unique investment in a startup has a high risk of failure; a reputable San Francisco research firm recently predicted that there is a less than 1 percent chance of a Silicon Valley startup becoming a unicorn. Some 70 percent of startups fail.[8]

The risk inherent in the venture capital model is offset by its potential rewards. Successful investments in startups don't increase by 10 percent to 20 percent, as the stock market might, but by 100 or 200 percent, and sometimes much more. Through their funds, venture capitalists make multiple bets and hope that the returns from a small number of winners will more than pay for the losses accrued along the way.

These investments can be highly profitable; to take an extreme example, the Silicon Valley venture firm Accel returned a rumored $9 billion on its original $12 million investment in Facebook.[9] Similarly, when Sequoia invested in WhatsApp, its stake was rumored to be worth as much as $3 billion at exit, more than fifty times the original investment.[10] Although both of these transactions are outliers, they illustrate the economics at work. A few highly positive financial outcomes tend to dominate a venture capital fund's returns and cover the losses from the rest of the portfolio. Overall, venture returns are attractive, averaging 9.6 percent annually over the last ten years, and nearly 20 percent over the last thirty years.[11]

The venture capital structure, however, also comes with its own incentives and particularities, which in turn influence how the innovation industry behaves. Funds have ten years to invest and return capital, a practice that sets the finish line when an investor is looking to exit. Funds are structured with 20 percent carried interest (funds receive 20 percent of the returns they generate for their investors), and so they search for startups that can garner sufficiently large profits that maximize capital gains in the desired timeframe. The 2 percent management fee pays for the operation of the fund.

Unsurprisingly, this model doesn't work everywhere.

The Reality of Venture at the Frontier

Despite its global dominance, the traditional venture capital model does not perfectly translate to the world outside Silicon Valley. Like the Frontier Innovators they serve, venture capitalists in emerging ecosystems face unique challenges.

Of course, a dearth of capital is a key challenge. Whereas Silicon Valley has nearly a thousand venture capital funds, Africa's fifty-four countries together account for fewer than ninety firms (fewer than two per country).[12] Latin America has fewer than 150 firms across the entire region.[13] This disparity also extends to the United States, where the entire Midwest accounted for a mere 0.7 percent of national venture capital investment (versus 40 percent on the West Coast).[14]

Compounding this, macroeconomic conditions, such as those explored in chapter 3, create more uncertainty for Frontier investors and challenge returns. A 30 percent drop in one country's currency would cause a meaningful hit on an investor's return.

Timelines to exit are also longer. Whereas in Silicon Valley, a venture investor can count on a ready corporate acquisition ecosystem and stable IPO markets, in an emerging ecosystem neither is a given.[15] On the surface, the combination of limited capital, dependence on other investors, singularly challenging exits, and macroeconomic risks paints a dismal picture.

Despite these manifold challenges, Frontier venture capital funds are demonstrating viability, and often they are uniquely attractive business models. Cambridge Associates, an investment consulting company, estimates that the average return for emerging-market venture capital and private equity over the past fifteen years is more than 10 percent.[16] Other, specialized indexes suggest that emerging market returns exceed US performance across multiple vintages.[17]

Some of the strategies used by leading Frontier investors to accomplish this feat include constructing a resilient portfolio, becoming born global themselves, and taking a long-term outlook.

Portfolio Resilience

The venture capital portfolio at the Frontier has a distinct risk and return outlook than in Silicon Valley.

Venture capital firms rely on a few investments to carry the entire fund, because for every business idea there will always be multiple companies trying to build it, and only one will end up dominating the market and making money for the venture capital firm. For every Facebook, there was a Myspace. When a business succeeds, startups raise a large sum of capital to capture market share rapidly before anyone else does. The power law, as noted in figure 10-1, describes this paradigm. Unlike normal distributions, in a *power law* the top couple of companies see outsized success, and the remainder see mild to no returns.

The power law translates to venture capital as well. Estimates suggest that after fees, half of all venture capital firms don't return their capital (a zero or negative rate of return), and only 5 percent return more than three times the capital (the equivalent of 12 percent annualized return over ten years). This means that after ten years, half of venture capital firms provide worse returns than comparatively investing in low-interest checking accounts (at a much higher level of risk).[18]

Even when half of firms perform poorly, however, the average industry return remains quite attractive. That's because returns are highly concentrated among a few firms and, within them, in a few deals that generate most of the returns.

At the Frontier, these dynamics are more nuanced and less extreme.

FIGURE 10-1

Normal versus power law distribution

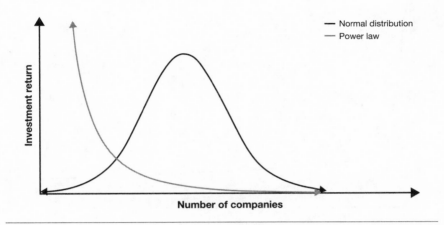

As you have seen, Frontier Innovators are building their companies differently from their Silicon Valley counterparts. While still growing, given that typically there aren't five competitors vying for the number one spot, Frontier Innovators are more concerned with having strong business models and enjoying repeatable growth than with making an all-out land grab. Being a Camel may lower the speed at which outsized success is reached, but it decreases the likelihood of a total bust. Indeed, research suggests Frontier startups have higher survival rates than those in Silicon Valley.[19] This means venture capitalists at the Frontier invest in startups with a lower failure rate.

The downside to lower failure rates is that, so far, stratospheric success is rarer. With the exception of China, no other region has been able to consistently generate as many unicorns, or unicorns as large, as Silicon Valley in the past decade. Globally, the United States has more than half the unicorns, and China accounts for another quarter. Except for Germany, India, the Netherlands, Russia, the UAE, and the United Kingdom, no other country has yet seen two or more unicorn exits. The entire continent of Africa recently saw its first startup IPO: Jumia. Even in the

FIGURE 10-2

Power law at the Frontier versus Silicon Valley

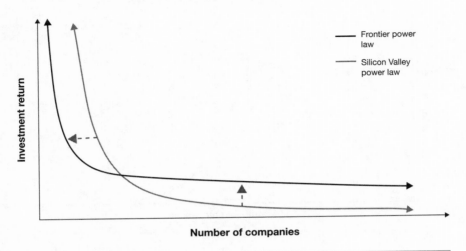

United States, outside California and New York the vast majority of states cannot lay claim to a single unicorn.[20]

While academic research on the topic is still emerging, early data suggests that Frontier venture capitalists have a lower likelihood of *outsized* unicorn-level success, but also a lower likelihood of failure, since they are building profitable and sustainable businesses. This does not mean venture capital at the Frontier does not depend on outsized winners; it does. However, the portfolio mix is different. Figure 10-2 explains this dynamic.

The Southeast Asia venture capital firm Asia Partners studied the Sharpe ratio (the amount of return for a given amount of risk) of venture capital in Southeast Asia relative to other asset classes. Venture capital was among the most attractive across any category and, remarkably, offering the same level of risk-adjusted return as real estate.[21]

To enhance resilience in their portfolios, Frontier venture capitalists also collaborate with other investors. This *syndication* reduces risks in investments in two ways. First, each fund doesn't need to allocate quite as much to a single deal. This allows smaller funds to diversify their portfolios. Second, syndication ensures there are more players around to help fund companies when they raise subsequent rounds.[22] Syndication is also correlated with higher likelihood of exits at higher valuations.[23]

In Silicon Valley, syndication is increasingly uncommon (except at the earliest stages). The size of venture capital funds has continued its inevitable march upward, with many leading investors consistently raising more than $1 billion.[24] As a result, Silicon Valley investors often look to write larger checks (smaller ones would be immaterial to a billion-dollar fund) and acquire meaningful ownership (so that in the event the company is a success, the investor reaps a larger share of the rewards). These dynamics in turn make it harder to syndicate deals or allow other funds to participate.

Frontier investment dynamics such as syndication may signify a "what's old is new" moment for those who have studied the history of Silicon Valley. In the original days of Silicon Valley, most funds also collaborated.[25]

Born Global Diversification

Historically, venture capital was a local game. For good reason: to successfully support entrepreneurs requires deep knowledge of industry pain points, the political and regulatory landscape, and economic dynamics. It's also because Silicon Valley investors prefer to invest closer to home. An analysis of venture capital funds found that nearly two-thirds of a typical Bay Area–based investor's portfolio was in the Bay Area, and 80 percent in the West Coast.[26]

For many Frontier venture capitalists, multiregionalism is intentionally woven into the fabric of the firm. Just like the born global startups you met in chapter 5, many venture firms adopt a multimarket approach from the get-go—out of necessity. Creating a single-market venture capital firm is challenging. Frontier businesses by their nature scale across multiple markets, and thus the winner in any country might be local or originate somewhere else.

Moreover, innovation trends are no longer unidirectional from Silicon Valley and now follow a global supply chain. Compounding this, in more-developing ecosystems (particularly for deals beyond Series A and B, outside the largest emerging markets like Brazil, China, and India), there is rarely enough deal flow to support a single fund. Consequently, firms expand across geographies to find a sufficient flow of deals. Born global startups face competition from everywhere. Accordingly, their investors often organize themselves to invest across borders, spotting trends in other geographies early and helping scale their portfolio companies into global (or at least regional) category leaders.

Cathay Innovation, for example, is a firm that is international by design, with a global footprint and offices across Asia, Africa, Europe, and North America. Its vision is to create a global platform that shares lessons on trends in innovation, includes international corporations to support entrepreneurs, and assists portfolio companies in expanding across markets.

Long-Term Outlook

Time-based constraints (typically in Silicon Valley venture capital) force investors to think within a certain timeline, thereby restricting a startup's growth trajectory and the entrepreneur's needs. This practice runs counter to limited partners' interests, who are focused on long-term maximization of capital.

These time constraints are a major challenge for venture capitalists at the Frontier, where, as you have seen, timelines to exit are longer. To tackle this challenge, the approach I find most compelling is an evergreen fund.

Investors using *evergreen* structures have no fixed timeline to return capital to limited partners and continue to reinvest as profits come back. Naspers, a South Africa-based conglomerate and a leading global Frontier investor, effectively has an evergreen investment structure.

Naspers' first venture investment was in Tencent. Naspers' CEO was looking to acquire a Chinese media company. In 2001, the team stumbled upon WeChat, a communications app that many entrepreneurs were using to communicate. What began as a takeover discussion morphed into an agreement to purchase nearly half of Tencent for $32 million. Nearly two decades later, Tencent's market capitalization is more than $500 billion, and Naspers' stake is worth more than $100 billion (over the past ten years, Naspers' own market valuation skyrocketed from $1 billion to more than $100 billion, largely on the back of this single deal).[27] This investment is arguably the most successful venture capital deal of all time.[28]

Since then, Naspers has invested around the world and has grown its footprint to include offices in Brazil, Hong Kong, India, Israel, the Netherlands, Singapore, and South Africa.[29] Freed from returning capital to investors within a time-bound fund, as a publicly traded company Naspers can take long-term bets, such as Tencent, and hold them to fruition.

Similarly, Vostok Emerging Finance (VEF) was founded in 2015 to invest in financial services startups across the world. VEF is publicly listed on the Stockholm exchange, which allows it to hold positions as long as it needs.[30] As an evergreen fund, VEF can be flexible on stage, investment size, and deal structure. VEF has already invested in a range of early- and late-stage companies across the world.[31]

While Naspers and VEF are publicly traded companies, evergreen funds can be private structures as well. For the moment, neither private nor publicly traded evergreen structures are common. Since the structure is not mainstream, many limited partners are not yet comfortable investing in evergreen funds.[32] Another solution investors are experimenting with is long-dated funds (i.e., longer than ten-year funds).[33]

Although still outside the mainstream, these fund structures signal an important trend within Frontier finance: investors have recognized the need to take a longer-term outlook.

Just as investment tools, portfolio construction, and fund design are changing, so too are the players. New players include corporate and impact investors.

Corporate Investors

Corporate investors are a major driving force behind Frontier ecosystem development. By contrast, in Silicon Valley, large corporate investors take a bifurcated approach. For many, their primary concern is acquiring companies. They watch startups mature and then purchase the ones they deem most synergistic with their operations, or most threatening to their long-term vitality. Facebook's purchase of WhatsApp and Instagram—two rapidly up-and-coming social networks it couldn't replicate nor allow to succeed—illustrates the latter scenario. Some corporate investors go one step further and invest through dedicated vehicles, largely corporate venture capital funds (CVCs). Although CVCs are on the rise in Silicon Valley, traditional investors dwarf them in scale.

This dynamic is reversed in many parts of the Frontier, including in China. In China, powerhouse technology players like Baidu, Alibaba, and Tencent (often referred to by the acronym BAT) are dominant investors and partners of startups. Unlike their Silicon Valley peers, they don't merely invest capital or seek to acquire companies. Leveraging their platforms (such as Tencent's WeChat or Alibaba's Ant Financial, its payment affiliate), they can offer powerful distribution and support through their ecosystems. The BAT investors have backed and partnered with more than a quarter of China's unicorns.[34]

Chinese corporate investors are affecting other ecosystems as well. Ant Financial, itself a rapidly growing startup (at the time of writing, it is set to go public at more than a $100 billion valuation, eclipsing Silicon Valley's largest startup by a wide margin), raised nearly $3 billion specifically to fund emerging-market financial services companies.[35] Tencent reportedly invested $30 billion in companies between 2015 and 2017, including companies like Snapchat, Spotify, Tesla, and Uber.[36]

In Southeast Asia, corporate investors have become important growth-stage investors. They are currently funding the ongoing ride-sharing battle between Grab, a Singapore-based startup that has raised billions and is backed by Alibaba and Softbank, and Gojek, Indonesia's key player, backed by Tencent and JD.com (one of the biggest technology e-commerce companies in China).[37]

Of course, the rise of corporate investment is not only a Chinese phenomenon. Naspers, perhaps one of the largest Frontier investors, is a corporate investor. In fact, the largest venture capital fund in the world is run by a corporate investor. In 2016, Japan-based SoftBank launched the Vision Fund and raised nearly $100 billion to invest in startups around the world. SoftBank recently raised a separate $5 billion dedicated fund for Latin America.[38]

Between 2013 and 2018, CVC investment grew fivefold—from $10 billion to more than $50 billion—and now CVCs participate in nearly a quarter of all deals (versus 16 percent in 2013).[39] There are more than a thousand major corporations with CVCs, including seventy-five of the *Fortune* 100.[40] This number includes everyone from Salesforce.com to Sesame Street. CVCs are increasingly international: 60 percent come from outside North America.[41] If the Frontier is any indication, global CVCs may look less like those in Silicon Valley that invest or acquire, and may instead follow the nurture-and-partner model espoused in China and elsewhere.

The Rise of Impact Investing

Chapter 8 highlights the balancing act Frontier Innovators maintain as they work to prioritize both social impact and business success. Similarly, a cadre of investment firms are increasingly pioneering and scaling impact investment. Indeed, impact investments are a driving force at the Frontier.

Omidyar Network, my previous firm, was one of the first impact investing funds. Omidyar Network has a unique structure, marrying a nonprofit with a traditional LLC venture capital model. This arrangement allows its investment teams to exercise great flexibility in making both grants to and investments in entrepreneurs around the world.

When it started, Omidyar was one of a few funds in a burgeoning sector. Now impact investing is an increasingly crowded field. Many foundations and nonprofits have gravitated to the model, because capital can be returned and reinvested and can support a wide range of institutions. At the other end of the spectrum, much larger, traditional financial institutions are also taking up the mantle. In 2017, the Texas Pacific Group (TPG Capital), one of the leading mainstream private equity groups in the world, closed a $2 billion impact investment fund.[42] The Ford Foundation recently announced that it had earmarked $1 billion from its endowment for mission-related investments. Since the term *impact investing* was coined at a Rockefeller conference in 2007, more than $220 billion in assets has been committed to the impact sector.[43]

Like Multi-Mission Athletes, in emerging ecosystems Frontier venture capitalists increasingly support organizations whose impact is intrinsic to the business model. All investors have an important role to play in supporting Frontier Innovators—and all entrepreneurs—in their quest to create businesses that matter and have transformative impact.

Challenging the Typical Investment Structure

Many of the leading Frontier Innovators profiled in this book, such as Gojek, Grubhub, and Guiabolso, were funded through traditional venture capital structures as well as corporate and impact investors. That's normal. This model is still by far the dominant option.

But many investors at the Frontier are beginning to experiment with new models, including creating new investment structures, leveraging artificial intelligence to source and make decisions, and allowing users to invest.

In 2016, Keith Harrington, a venture capitalist in the US Midwest, was experiencing ever-mounting frustration with the traditional venture capital model. Few companies he was encountering were venture backable. "They were great businesses," Harrington explained, "but they weren't a fit for the traditional venture capital models. By all accounts, they were growing impressively, often over twenty percent a year. This of course is slow for a startup . . . [They] were bootstrapped [having never raised venture capital] and closely watching cash and managing profitability."[44]

Because venture capital found its inspiration in one specific resource industry—whaling—Keith Harrington was exploring other industries for ideas. He struck gold in mining, which relies on a royalty system. Prospectors pay their investors a certain percentage off the top over time. Investors therefore share in the upsides and downsides of the business; they get paid only if the prospectors are successful, and, if things don't go well, there are fewer payments.

Keith joined forces with Carlos Antequera of Netchemia, and Novel Growth Partners was born. The two men proposed an alternative mining-inspired solution to fund startups: a revenue share. Instead of buying equity in the business, they would purchase a portion of a company's revenue for a certain amount of time.

The revenue share structure addresses two challenges simultaneously: lengthy investment duration and the risk of not finding an exit. Unlike the traditional model, revenue shares offer ensured liquidity. To get their capital back, Silicon Valley venture capitalists need to wait for somebody else to purchase their equity, an eventuality that requires the company to be acquired or to go public—outcomes that are far from certain. A revenue share, however, is based on current revenues. For many companies, future revenues in the next two to three years are relatively predictable. Investors get an ensured exit and payouts on set schedules. Entrepreneurs benefit from the control that revenue shares afford them, since investors don't own any stock in the company.

One of Novel's first investments was in MyMajors. Although it was started in 1964, it had recently developed an algorithm to help match college students to academic majors. The software fills a crucial and yet often overlooked niche. As Keith notes, "Most colleges are graduating students in six years or more. The reason is that students flip majors. It's a problem for everyone. Colleges are trying to figure out how to increase retention rates and graduation rates. Students are looking to reap maximum value from their education."[45] MyMajors helps students focus early on promising areas of study.

These types of "novel" revenue share structures are still very early, but they are gaining traction in the venture capital industry and will continue to proliferate. Already, there are at least eight revenue-based funds in the United States. Unsurprisingly, they sprang up predominantly outside Silicon Valley, including in Dallas, Park City, Toronto, and Seattle.[46]

Computerized Decision Making

Artificial intelligence is becoming an increasingly important tool for venture capital sourcing and decision making in both Silicon Valley and the Frontier. More than eighty venture capital firms globally have publicly disclosed their artificial intelligence models. Many others are likely doing this privately.[47]

Because there is less capital available at the Frontier, the distance to travel is longer, and the cost of assessing investment opportunities in different countries is higher, data-driven techniques are valuable tools for investing in Frontier Innovators.

For example, Clearbanc, a Toronto-based startup that offers startups revenue shares, has pioneered an automated process. Startups connect their bank and social accounts, along with detailed transaction logs. The speed and impartiality of Clearbanc's model is particularly striking: startups can receive a revenue-share term sheet in twenty minutes.[48] Similarly, Social Capital (which is no longer raising outside capital) pioneered a model called *capital as a service*, or CaaS, which created algorithms to benchmark and predict companies' performance objectively. If Social Capital's algorithm liked what it saw, the company would write a check for as much as $250,000.[49]

Historically, venture capital decisions reflected an art of analysis and were based on consultation with the fund's partners. Clearbanc and Social Capital's CaaS is algorithmic. It verifies data, makes decisions about funding, and offers advice.[50] By focusing only on impartial metrics, these companies invest in founders who might otherwise be overlooked. Among Social Capital's more than seventy-five CaaS investments, 80 percent of founders were nonwhite and 30 percent were women, spread across twenty countries—statistics far above traditional industry numbers.[51]

It is unlikely that computerization will completely replace the human venture capitalist; nor should it. After all, in startup investments, qualitative factors like deal structure and team dynamics are critical. On Wall Street, hedge funds have perfected the use of artificial intelligence–driven trade decisions to get microsecond edges on the market, but in venture capital, timing is less urgent, and thus there is time for human review. What's more, the human factor between investors and entrepreneurs matters a lot (I remind my students that the average venture capital relationship is longer than the average American marriage).[52] At the Frontier, although artificial intelligence is poised to be an insightful tool, it likely won't be replacing investors any time soon.

The Most Nascent of All: Customers

Arguably, the newest investor at the Frontier may be customers themselves. Historically, in traditional venture capital, investors in startups were disconnected from the user base (e.g., rarely do Uber riders own stock in Uber). In the majority of markets, an investor needs to be accredited (in the United States, a would-be investor must make more than $200,000 in salary or have more than $1 million in liquid net worth) to legally make investments directly in startups.[53] Rarely can employees or users of startups purchase stock (except for stock options). Many founders seek a better way; they want their communities of users to also participate in the benefits that their usage generates.

Innovations in the cryptocurrency space may turn this paradigm on its head. Initial coin offerings (ICOs) are a form of crowdfunding. Unlike an IPO, in an ICO investors do not receive shares in the business, and, unlike traditional crowdfunding campaigns, investors are not promised a particular product or experience. Instead, ICOs represent the sale of a token that grants access to the ecosystem or network that the entrepreneurs are building.[54] The number of available tokens is generally finite, and so as the network becomes more popular, the demand and thus the value of the token rises.

Many have heralded the rise of ICOs as a game-changer for the venture capital ecosystem. In 2017, entrepreneurs raised a staggering $6 billion in ICOs.[55] But if this seems too good to be true, you might be on to something. The legality of ICOs in many parts of the world is still in question. Many ICOs lose money. Shockingly, some estimates suggest that as many as 80 percent of the first wave of ICOs were fraudulent.[56] Of the honest projects, they were often very early stage projects that amassed gargantuan sums of capital with a very limited business plan.[57] Many of these projects will naturally fail. Over the past year, the ICO industry has slowed considerably and regulators have started cracking down on the model.[58] A reckoning in the early ICOs is likely.

ICOs are a very specific part of a much broader trend: the rise of crowdfunding. Platforms like Kickstarter and GoFundMe have provided options for entrepreneurs everywhere to access nondilutive capital and prove demand for their products. In the United States alone, crowdfunding has raised more than $17 billion in 375 separate platforms.[59] By mid-2019, crowdfunding in China had raised eight times the US amount.[60] Recent regulation, including the JOBS Act in the United States, will make it easier for individuals to invest in startups. These models allow entrepreneurs from anywhere to access capital.

Much like the rise of impact investors and corporates, individual investments in startups is certainly a trend to watch and may help bridge a lack of capital over time.

Lessons from Early Advances in Venture Capital

It is still early days for venture capital at the Frontier. The majority of innovators profiled in this book depended on traditional venture capital funding, in part because that was what was available.

Building solutions that work for local ecosystems is paramount. In chapter 11 you will meet Erik Hersman, the founder of BRCK and Ushahidi, two high-profile startups in Kenya. As Erik explained, "You've got to make sure the tail doesn't wag the dog. Today, many startups depend on Silicon Valley for funding, so they tell their story to match the practical reality [of raising capital from existing investors]."[61]

Startup strategy should not be dictated by the subjective constraints of a geographically specific venture capital system that itself is derived from a long-forgotten industry. Silicon Valley has adopted an "if it ain't broke, don't fix it" attitude toward the current venture capital model. But, increasingly, it is where things are broken that we are seeing true innovation. Venture capitalists at the Frontier—entrepreneurs and innovators in their own right—are reinventing the model according to the needs of their investees.

One thing is certain: the next industry standard will not derive from whaling ships on the high seas. Rather, it will emerge on the shores of Frontier ecosystems.

11.

Lay the Foundation
Support the Next Generation of Entrepreneurs

The greatest challenge in building a Frontier startup is operating at the Frontier, especially when you are the first to arrive. As you have seen, Frontier Innovators are tackling tougher problems than their Silicon Valley counterparts are, and they are tackling them in more-difficult ecosystems.

The best Frontier Innovators lead heroic acts of terraforming: laying the building blocks for a future innovation ecosystem and kick-starting ecosystem development. A small minority of these entrepreneurs—those who reach scale and exit early in the life span of their ecosystem—have an outsized impact on these systems, clearing the path for future generations of entrepreneurs and lending them a helping hand. Let's call them the older siblings of their ecosystems.

Older Siblings of Latin America

Hernan Kazah is a quintessential older sibling. He grew up in Buenos Aires and managed brands for Procter & Gamble in his first job out of college. In 1997, Hernan was admitted to the Stanford Graduate School of Business. He quickly fell in love with the technology world and the opportunity to shape a nascent global ecosystem. Instead of staying in Silicon Valley, he partnered with his business school classmate Marcos Galperin, who had the idea of setting up an e-commerce platform for Latin America. It was a bold idea when internet adoption in the region was at a meager 3 percent and there wasn't a single venture capital firm on the continent.[1]

They launched the MercadoLibre platform in 1999. It was not a smooth ride; the company operated in a challenging and hostile ecosystem. Once, fearing both the potential encroachment of US players like eBay and a number of well-funded local competitors, a few of the investors lost confidence entirely. They asked Hernan and Marcos to shut the company down and return to them what little capital was left. The two men had to fight for the life of their company and convince investors of their strategy.

Ultimately, they proved the naysayers wrong. Now MercadoLibre is the largest e-commerce company in Latin America and among the top ten in the world, boasting nearly twenty-eight million customers, more than nine million vendors (several tens of thousands of which rely on the platform as their primary source of income), and more than 181 million products traded.[2] The company went public in 2007 on the Nasdaq, the first Latin American company to do so, and now is worth more than $29 billion.[3]

After the IPO, Hernan transitioned management responsibilities to the up-and-coming leaders at the company. Instead of retiring, he chose to give back to the next generation of entrepreneurs and solve some of the problems he had faced. He partnered with MercadoLibre's former CFO, Nicolas Szekasy, to found Kaszek Ventures. Hernan wanted to provide these entrepreneurs with the mentorship, network, support, encouragement, and, of course, capital that he had struggled to access when he first began. Kaszek Ventures started out investing only its own personal capital but subsequently accepted outside capital. Its most recent fund, its fourth, was more than $600 million.[4] The portfolio includes the companies of leading Frontier Innovators profiled in this book, such as Nubank, Guiabolso, and Dr. Consulta.[5] Many of these companies have a social lens, and they focus in part on giving back to the community as a whole.

In addition to his work at Kaszek, Hernan Kazah served on the board of LAVCA (Latin American Private Equity and Venture Capital Association) and co-founded ARCAP (an Argentinean association for private investing). His profound impact on the ecosystem extends beyond his involvement with ecosystem-building organizations. He and Marcos have mentored dozens of entrepreneurs. The Globant founders, for instance, credit the two men with motivating them to pay it forward again in the next generation.[6]

Just as elder siblings often face unrelenting parental resistance, first generations of entrepreneurs in nascent ecosystems often find it challenging to succeed. As they forge ahead, they create the ecosystem and environment they need if they are to realize success, and, by breaking down barriers, they benefit their younger siblings. Older siblings also look behind and actively help their younger siblings along, just as Hernan has done in Latin America. A few trailblazing older siblings can make all the difference. In Latin America, older siblings from three companies, including Hernan and Marcos, are linked to 80 percent of startups in the region.[7]

Laying the Foundation, One Brick at a Time

Of course, ecosystem building doesn't fall only on the shoulders of those entrepreneurs who "make it," nor does it depend on an older sibling to act as a catalyst. All Frontier Innovators are the architects of their ecosystems, and they are using every tool available to build something that lasts.

Some of the tools they use include promoting startup culture and its acceptance of failure, teaching entrepreneurship and related skills, creating collaborative physical spaces, providing mentorship and financial support in parallel to scaling their businesses, building industry organizations, getting involved in local regulations—and, of course, building highly successful businesses. Let's explore each in turn, beginning with one of entrepreneurial culture's defining characteristics.

Mescal and Failure

Our story starts (as all stories should) with six friends having a conversation over a bottle of mescal. When the topic turned to Mexican startup culture's aversion to failure, the entire group agreed that it was hampering the country's budding entrepreneurial scene. No one talked about the nearly universal experience of *fracaso*—failure. While would-be entrepreneurs dreamed of success, many never started because they had no idea how to succeed and were intimidated by the likelihood of failure. Every person at the table had experienced these emotions. Nor were they alone. As you have learned, failure is not often tolerated at the Frontier.

The group was not new to the Mexican startup scene. Pepe Villatoro, for example, was born and raised in Chiapas, Mexico, one of the poorest parts of the country, but he went on to found a range of startups, including a magazine and a coworking space. He was recruited to launch WeWork in Mexico, which would become one of its fastest-growing markets. In each of these experiences, he endured many failures.

Back at the bar in Mexico City, Pepe and his friends decided to tell all. Perhaps it was the mescal or the cathartic effect of discussing failure out in the open, but each of them left the conversation feeling more comfortable with entrepreneurial risks. Each realized that the outcome of the failures they shared was not that bad. Here they were, years later, succeeding in other endeavors. They left, energized to imagine their next companies, and the group began to meet monthly for honest discussions about risk and failure.

The idea went viral, and so "Fuckup Nights" (FUN) was born. Pepe and his friends created a platform for others to replicate similar events in their own startup communities. The objective was for participants to share stories of their professional or personal failures, all while creating a culture that accepts risk taking and the failure that may ensue. Over the next few years, FUN organically and unpredictably turned into a global platform for entrepreneurs to share their stories of defeat and reflect on what they had learned, thereby helping others learn and avoid the same mistakes. FUN redeemed failed projects and startups by putting their stories to use.

Pepe became CEO of the organization and set out to institutionalize it. He formed a consultancy to work with the network and wrote a manifesto. Later, FUN launched the Failure Institute, which collects and analyzes data on entrepreneurial failures in cities, tracking rates of failure by location, industry, and startup type and calculating trends in the development of resilience in entrepreneurial communities.[8] FUN recently launched academic chapters to destigmatize failure in the education system and is working with more than two hundred corporate partners to help change their cultures and mindsets.[9]

Already, FUN events have been hosted in more than 330 cities in ninety countries. More than ten thousand people have told their stories to more than a million people.[10] It has become a leading distributed entrepreneurial social movement.

Like Pepe and his friends, Frontier Innovators shape cultural perceptions of risk. They may also impact regulations (e.g., punitive bankruptcy laws), decreasing the real costs of failure. Over time, Frontier Innovators can foster a culture that accepts entrepreneurship as a viable profession, supports entrepreneurs in taking risks as they scale their businesses, and enables them to commit fully to one venture.

Of course, acceptance—and celebration—of failure is also a time-honored Silicon Valley tradition, but it is only one part of building an entrepreneurial culture.

Teaching Entrepreneurship

In many Frontier markets, building an entrepreneurial culture involves educating people about how and why entrepreneurship is a viable career path. In extreme cases, it involves introducing the very concept of entrepreneurship.

Geoffrey See, an innovator, entrepreneur, and venture capitalist, founded the Choson Exchange to promote entrepreneurship in North Korea. For the past nine years, Geoffrey has offered targeted workshops to teach business, economic policy, and law. Of course, given the political situation in North Korea, Choson operates in narrow segments. It provides critical training for a burgeoning market-oriented system in which households engage in trade activities and small business. Another option for aspiring entrepreneurs is to open businesses in partnership with a state-owned enterprise. These ventures are "state-owned with a private investor." Typically, the entrepreneur has operating autonomy and shares 30 percent to 70 percent of their revenue with the affiliated state-owned enterprise, depending on what the enterprise contributes to the business.[11]

Choson Exchange focuses on training young entrepreneurs and has already trained hundreds of men and women. Geoffrey also contributed to the establishment of the country's first startup incubator. He partnered with North Korea's State Academy of Sciences (SAS) and attracted more than twenty thousand researchers who are interested in commercializing their ideas. Geoffrey's endeavors include a valuable cultural exchange element: the workshops are staffed by volunteer teachers from all over the world.[12]

For Geoffrey, the entrepreneurial culture needs in North Korea are completely different from those anywhere else on earth. As he explained, "In many markets, the risks to starting a business overwhelm the dream of the potential of the business. In North Korea, paradoxically, success can also be a big risk. Entrepreneurs are worried that the business will get confiscated. Therefore, in the past, they were motivated to take cash out of it and not reinvest in growth."[13] As a result, a meaningful portion of Choson Exchange's work is to valiantly attempt to shape policy and legislation to enable a more stable business environment and better protection of property rights. Through his courses and student exchanges, he is slowly helping build an entrepreneurial community in North Korea.

For the rest of the world, there are organizations like Startup Weekend (now a part of Techstars, an accelerator focused on emerging ecosystems), which aims to create entrepreneurial culture in nascent ecosystems, from Bolivia to Madagascar to Mongolia to Tunisia. Startup Weekend organizes weekend events to demystify the entrepreneurial journey. Over fifty-four hours, the program immerses would-be innovators who are considering starting a new venture into the world of entrepreneurship. The events promise to give participants the opportunity to "experience the highs, lows, fun, and pressure that make up life at a startup," bringing together a unique set of mentors, advisers, and ecosystem participants as part of the setting.[14] So far, Startup Weekend has organized nearly three thousand events for more than two hundred thousand prospective entrepreneurs in 150 countries.

Some Frontier Innovators want to offer both a launching pad and a safety net for potential founders. Yasser Bashir, founder of Arbisoft, a successful technology company in Pakistan, incubates his employees' startups internally. Yasser allows potential entrepreneurs, often his own employees, to become "entrepreneurs-in-residence" while still receiving a salary. If it works, the new idea is spun out into its own entity, and Arbisoft receives equity. If not, the would-be founder can get another job within the company. Yasser has incubated five successful companies.[15] Savaree, a ride-hailing startup for the local ecosystem, was incubated within Arbisoft for eighteen months. It was spun out and ultimately was acquired by Dubai-based ride-hailing platform Careem.[16]

Demystifying, teaching, and incubating entrepreneurship all help entrepreneurial culture grow and thrive. But many regions struggle with a lack of critical educational infrastructure.

Teaching the Skills, Finding the Training

As you have seen in previous chapters, one of the largest resource gaps at the Frontier is the shortage of trained, experienced talent. Both prospective entrepreneurs and their future employees suffer from a lack of opportunities locally to learn necessary skills and gain experience.

Enter Fred Swaniker and his company, African Leadership Group. Fred is fostering the next generation of entrepreneurial leaders for Africa.

Fred once described the arc of modern African political leadership to me this way: "The first wave were those leaders that bravely led Africa out of colonialism in the 1950s and 1960s. The second were the dictators that arose out of warfare, corruption, and lack of governance. Many countries have witnessed the emergence of a third generation of more democratically accountable leadership that has stabilized governments region-wide." Fred says that Africa is now approaching a fourth wave of leadership—one in which the next generation of young Africans tackles complex economic, social, and governance challenges through entrepreneurial solutions.[17] This generation will also build crucial institutions to drive social and economic inclusion and prosperity.[18]

A key challenge stands in the way of this vision: the limited opportunities for the fourth wave of leaders to learn and get trained. More than 120 million Africans will seek to enter the continent's workforce in the next decade, and they are sure to be looking for meaningful and competitive opportunities.[19]

One major bottleneck is university capacity. To train this generation of emerging young leaders, Fred launched the African Leadership University (ALU).

Fred is not new to the education and leadership development space. Born in Ghana, at a young age he fled with his family during a time of political turmoil, first to the Gambia and then to Botswana. His mother, herself an entrepreneur, built a grade school there. By the age of eighteen, Fred was serving as headmaster of the school, having just completed high school himself.[20]

Nearly fifteen years ago, after completing his MBA at Stanford in 2004, Fred launched the African Leadership Academy (ALA) with the hope of creating the premier high school on the continent. The competitive two-year program is open to only 250 students per year. Roughly 85 percent of the students attend virtually for free, the tuition funded through donor-backed forgivable loans. The loan agreement stipulates that the student must return to Africa to work for at least ten years after completing university; otherwise, they must fully repay the approximately

$60,000 in total tuition.[21] So far, ALA has graduated 983 students from forty-six African countries.[22] They have gone on to attend some of the best universities in the world, and many are already back in Africa tackling challenges in refugee camps, entrepreneurial finance, and primary school education.[23] In addition, Fred launched the African Leadership Network to connect influential leaders from across the continent.[24]

ALU is his boldest venture yet. It is not a traditional university. For one thing, the curriculum was built to cultivate specific "twenty-first century skills" (skills like leadership, entrepreneurial thinking, quantitative reasoning, critical thinking, and communication) required in the market. The learning model is project based and student driven. Rather than choose majors, students at ALU choose a mission from a set of fourteen "grand challenges and opportunities" facing Africa and the world, which range from governance and health care to urbanization and wildlife conservation.

Fred also worked with leading corporations to develop customized curricula and guarantee employability of ALU graduates.[25] For example, there is the ALU School of Insurance, which prepares students for careers at partners like Swiss Reinsurance, Africa Reinsurance, Allianz SE, and Liberty Mutual.[26] Similarly, ALU's computer science program integrates technical skills with leadership so that students practice not only coding but also the entrepreneurial thinking required to develop and scale new products.[27]

So far, ALU has raised $80 million and has campuses in Mauritius and Rwanda.[28] Fred sees opportunities for South-South knowledge exchange and hopes to expand in India and Brazil. If he succeeds, he will have made an important dent in creating the fourth generation of leaders in Africa and beyond.

After fledgling entrepreneurs take advantage of all these opportunities and get started, the next ecosystem challenge is to help them find one another.

Creating a Physical Space for Culture and Partnership

In 2010, Erik Hersman, one of the early pioneers of the Kenyan technology ecosystem, turned his attention to the problem that Kenya's community of entrepreneurs, technologists, and investors was disjointed. Erik's belief that proximity breeds strength, improves communication, and creates community motivated him to found iHub in 2010.

A coworking space in the middle of Nairobi, iHub is open to entrepreneurs, programmers, investors, and anyone else interested in the technology community. Since its inception, more than 170 companies have grown and connected in the space, which now boasts sixteen thousand members. iHub also offers a range of services to its members—including innovation consulting services as well as a testing lab (so that entrepreneurs can test their apps on various types of phones)—and hosts a research center and a number of corporate partners looking to connect with the ecosystem.[29] Additionally, iHub runs more than twenty events per month that cater to individuals at all stages of the startup and tech community.[30]

iHub helped catalyze the Kenyan ecosystem by giving people in the burgeoning entrepreneurial movement a location to come together in community. It has since inspired others to replicate its success in other geographies.[31] Erik has gone on to lead other initiatives, including founding BRCK, a startup whose ambition is to increase internet access in Africa.

Tighter-knit entrepreneurial communities can assist with another key challenge: finding a co-founder. Entrepreneur First (EF) is an innovative startup launcher and talent investor focused on solving this problem. CEO Matt Clifford explained its rationale: "In Silicon Valley, conventional wisdom is that you can't start a startup with a stranger. In many ecosystems, network density is weak, making it hard for talented people to find the right co-founder for them in their network. We wanted to shift this dynamic. We lower the bar to starting with a stranger, but also lower the bar to get out."[32] EF is focused on the Frontier, with locations in Bangalore, Berlin, Hong Kong, London, Paris, and Singapore.

In the early phases of the program, entrepreneurs are encouraged to work with many people and identify compatible working styles quickly, in a process much akin to speed dating. If things don't work out, no problem, and on to the next idea. The data suggests EF is on to something. In its eight years of existence, it has launched more than two hundred companies, collectively worth more than $1.5 billion.[33]

The opportunity to bounce ideas off of others who are going through similar challenges is a critical advantage of proximity. It can also enable another key element of fostering entrepreneurial culture: mentorship.

Mentorship in Parallel

They say it takes a village to raise a child. The same is often true of startups: a strong mentorship community directly impacts success. An analysis of the Bangalore startup ecosystem found that mentorship from leading innovators doubled the odds that a startup would succeed.[34] In Argentina, a similar analysis of mentored entrepreneurs determined that they grew revenue and jobs nearly three times as fast and sixteen times as fast, respectively, as their peers. Mentorship also feeds on itself: entrepreneurs who receive mentorship are eight times as likely to mentor others.[35]

In Silicon Valley, mentorship follows the ladder of success: founders receive mentorship from those further up the ladder and, if they become successful, mentor the next generation located a few rungs down. In many emerging ecosystems, however, the ladder is not yet crowded enough. The existing cohort of successful founders is far less robust, and in some cases nonexistent.

Frontier Innovators therefore often build their own companies and generously support others *in parallel*, becoming angel investors and advisers to up-and-coming startups while still scaling their own. Take Ben Gleason, whom you met in chapter 2. Almost as soon as he started

Guiabolso, he started investing in other entrepreneurs and giving them advice. Similarly, Erik Hersman is an active investor in the East Africa ecosystem at the same time he is running his own startup BRCK.

A study that sought to explain the take-off of the New York tech ecosystem uncovered a similar phenomenon. More than a quarter of co-founders of startups in New York were also angel investors in other companies. Entrepreneurs represented nearly half of the total angel investments in the ecosystem—an impressive number, given that most entrepreneurs are investing everything they have into their own businesses and taking serious pay cuts.[36]

Some Frontier Innovators have made it their singular mission to fulfill the mentorship need for entrepreneurs. Endeavor is one of most successful organizations tackling this challenge. Founded by Linda Rottenberg and Peter Kellner, Endeavor identifies leading entrepreneurs (typically at companies that are at the beginning of scaling), matches them with some of the best mentors in business in their local market, and supports them through their scaling phase of development. The organization creates local chapters that raise money primarily from the local business community. The centralized office manages information sharing, specializes in particular industries, and helps select entrepreneurs through its global selection process. Endeavor's model hopes to create a virtuous cycle: success stories inspire new entrepreneurs to join its ranks and attract capital, thereby feeding the next generation of entrepreneurs and mentors, promoting entrepreneurship at the ecosystem level.

Endeavor is twenty-two years old and has supported nineteen hundred entrepreneurs (of sixty-five thousand applicants). Its track record is enviable; Endeavor companies generate more than $20 billion in annual revenues and have created more than 3 million jobs.[37] While Endeavor's roots are decidedly in emerging markets, having started in Latin America and expanded across Africa, Asia, and the Middle East, Endeavor is now bringing its model to developed markets as well, including in early startup ecosystems in Europe and the United States.

Setting Standards, Creating Regulation

Frontier Innovators often need to build collaborative structures to give themselves, and their nascent competitors, a voice at the table and in the industry at large. In some places, this looks like an industry association, such as the Food Safety and Urban Agriculture Coalition (FSUAC), co-launched by AeroFarms. Another such organization is GOGLA, whose members include Zola, Fenix, d.light, and M-KOPA; its mission in the offgrid energy space is to "build sustainable markets, delivering quality, affordable products and services to as many households, businesses and communities as possible across the developing world."[38]

Collaboration can also take the form of a standard-setting body, a lobbying organization, and other forms of direct engagement with policy makers to advise them on how to regulate their industries. Adolfo Babatz, CEO and co-founder of Clip, worked with the Mexican government on the country's new financial technology law. Similarly, Tayo Oviosu, founder and CEO of Paga, the leading mobile payments company in Nigeria, actively engages Nigeria's central bank on mobile banking and financial inclusion regulation. These varied permutations play a critical role when the ecosystem is not used to working with startups or, worse yet, is hostile toward them.

Clearly, Frontier Innovators are engaging proactively with the question of how to build their ecosystems and approaching the issue from many different angles. Every contribution is a necessary part of the whole. That said, building a highly successful company can be one of the most exponentially powerful things an entrepreneur can do for a local ecosystem.

Older Siblings of the Middle East

Back in the 1980s, Fadi Ghandour's goal was to build the FedEx of the Middle East. He co-founded Aramex, and by the 1990s, it was a one-stop shop for its customers as well as the best provider of domestic, express, and freight services in the region. In 1997, Aramex was the first Middle Eastern company (outside Israel) to hold an IPO on the Nasdaq. Now Aramex employs more than fifteen thousand people in more than six hundred offices and sixty-five countries. The company is a leader in comprehensive logistics and transportation solutions worldwide.[39]

But Aramex is only the preface to the tale of Fadi's contribution to his regional ecosystem.

Maktoob, the Middle East's first technology startup success—and Fadi's most celebrated investment—started as a wrinkle in Aramex's first IPO. When the company went public in 1997, bankers identified a small investment in a loss-making entity that seemingly had nothing to do with the core business of the company. The bankers suggested selling it before the IPO, and Fadi decided to purchase the stake himself.[40]

The subsidiary was, of course, Maktoob, an early webmail service (think Hotmail) that was unique in offering support in Arabic. Maktoob was founded by Samih Toukan and Hussam Khoury alongside Aramex as a website development company and grew rapidly under Fadi's mentorship. In 2009, the company was acquired by Yahoo for $164 million, at the time the largest acquisition in the region.[41]

Amazingly, this story repeats itself one more time. One of Maktoob's small internal projects was a marketplace called Souq, an online auction website hoping to become the Amazon of the region.[42] The project became a company, and it tailored its model to the region, developing alternative payment methods, in-house logistics, and multimarket operations. In 2017 it was sold to Amazon for $580 million and now operates in seven countries, serving more than 135 million customers.[43]

Fadi, Samih, and Hussam each used his outsized early success to support his ecosystem in a unique way. Fadi has become an investor and mentor to the next generation of startups, launching Wamda Capital to work with entrepreneurs. Samih is a founding investor in Oasis500 (the largest incubator in Jordan) and, with Hussam, a regional investor through Jabbar. Endeavor studied Maktoob's direct impact and found more than twenty companies that have received mentorship from its founders, gained direct investment, or were founded by former employees. Its indirect impact has been even wider. And Maktoob was only the beginning.

One of Fadi's other investments was Careem, the local ride-sharing leader. It was purchased in 2019 by Uber for $3 billion, the most successful startup exit ever in the Middle East (excluding Israel).[44] This sale represents a watershed moment for the region. As Chris Rogers, an investor with Lumia Capital and co-founder of Nextel Communications, explains, "As the region's first unicorn and now its first multi-billion-dollar exit and largest acquisition by over a factor of five . . . Careem's exit is sure to motivate top talent in the region to more aggressively pursue entrepreneurial endeavors. Already we see Careem alumni building the next generation of exciting regional startups."[45] The direct and indirect effects of this unprecedented exit are predicted to have a far-reaching impact in the region.[46]

Success Enables Exponential Success

Older siblings like Fadi and Hernan equip the next generation of innovators with the skills, networks, credibility, and capital to launch their own ventures. These older siblings accomplish this just by bringing their scaled companies to an exit, even before they engage in the proactive ecosystem-building initiatives explored earlier in this chapter.

Their successful companies, like Maktoob, MercadoLibre, and Careem, act as informal schools of entrepreneurship. Endeavor studied job creation in startups and determined that a small percentage of companies drive most of the employment growth in any given region. In Nairobi, for instance, eight companies—fewer than 1 percent of the more than 650 local technology companies—scaled to more than one hundred employees between 2008 and 2018.[47] These eight companies represent more than 40 percent of the startup job creation and more than two-thirds of total venture capital raised in the country. Similarly, in Bangalore, alumni from

Infosys have founded and scaled more than two hundred companies.[48] Older siblings scale their companies, and these companies become entrepreneurial schools (and badges of credibility) for a new generation.

In addition, employees of scaled companies often receive an infusion of capital at the time of exit because of the sale of their stock options. This capital enables them to start or invest in the next generation of startups. When Flipkart was purchased by Walmart, more than one hundred of its employees became millionaires. Many of them will join the next generation of angel investors.[49]

Often, older siblings themselves become part of the next generation of entrepreneurs. Research from AllWorld Network suggests entrepreneurs in emerging markets start 25 percent more companies than their West Coast counterparts.[50] More than 80 percent of the emerging-market founders in its study had an intention to start another business in the next two years.[51] For example, after starting his first business before he was eighteen, Divyank Turakhia, the Indian and Emirati entrepreneur you met in chapter 5, went on to found three others, selling them for between $200 million and $1 billion apiece.[52] André Street founded his first company at the age of fourteen, going on to start and sell five others before his most recent success, Stone Pagamentos, a Brazilian payment processor that recently was listed on the Nasdaq and has a market capitalization of more than $8 billion—all before the age of thirty-five.[53]

Unsurprisingly, older siblings were critically important in the rise of Silicon Valley as well: more than two thousand companies—including Instagram, Palantir, WhatsApp, and YouTube—can be linked to eight individuals who co-founded Fairchild Semiconductor back in 1957.[54] A staggering 70 percent of public Bay Area technology companies have some link to Silicon Valley's metaphorical patient zero, Fairchild.[55]

More recently, a group of thirteen former PayPal employees and co-founders has become a driving force in Silicon Valley. The so-called PayPal mafia includes Elon Musk (founder of SpaceX, Tesla, SolarCity, and The Boring Company, among others), Peter Thiel (co-founder of PayPal, later Palantir), Jeremy Stoppelman (co-founder of Yelp), Reid Hoffman (PayPal's COO, later founder of LinkedIn), Russel Simmons (PayPal's software architect, later co-founder of Yelp) and many, many more.[56] The PayPal mafia has so far been linked to more than $30 billion in businesses.[57]

These days, Silicon Valley enjoys a self-perpetuating machine. However, at the Frontier, each new older sibling plays a catalytic role in accelerating their Frontier ecosystem's momentum.

The Multiplier Effect

Of course, Fadi, Hernan, and other older siblings didn't just build successful companies and then retire. As you have seen, they are taking leadership positions in their growing ecosystems, as culture carriers, capital providers, mentors, advisers, and advocates.

Older siblings' efforts are often compounding, having a disproportionate impact on their ecosystems. Endeavor refers to this phenomenon as the "multiplier effect."[58] As successful older siblings scale, they support many leaders of the next generation, who then go on to do the same. Each generation builds on itself.

Hitting the Inflection Point

It is hard to predict which companies will scale. As Hernan once told me, nine of ten times in building MercadoLibre, the company would have been unsuccessful. Yet a certain number of innovators will succeed, and they will go on to inspire and enable the next generation, which smooths the path for the next generation, and so on, often exponentially.

Looking at China, after its first unicorn scaled in 2010 it took five years to reach its fifth, and the very next year the count skyrocketed to twenty-one. As shown in figure 11-1, a similar dynamic is happening after a similar number of unicorns were created in India, the United Kingdom, and Latin America.[59]

Looking at startup ecosystems around the world, there seems to be an inflection point after a critical mass of three to five older siblings bring

FIGURE 11-1

Cumulative number of startups valued over $1 billion by geography

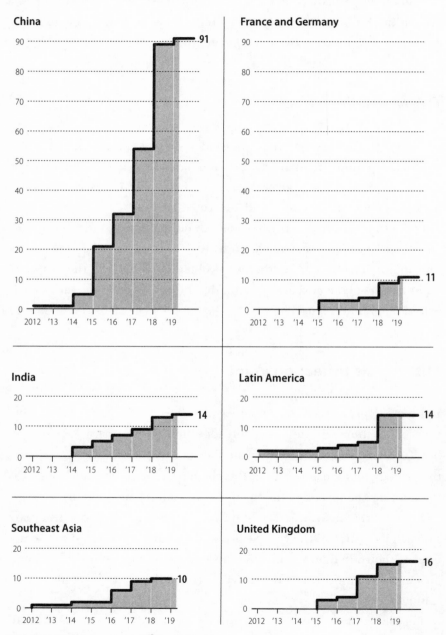

Note: As of Q1 2019, based on publicly available data.

FIGURE 11-2

Unicorns accelerate post inflection point

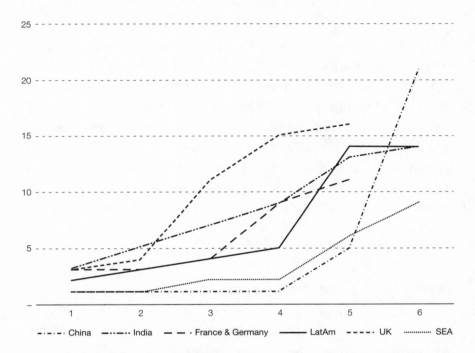

Note: China total cutoff, today over 100. LatAm start time started later given longtime historical successes.

their companies to exit, depending on the size of the market (larger markets seem to have a slightly later inflection point). Because most available data focuses only on companies valued at more than $1 billion, figure 11-2 maps the unicorn count from the year the first unicorn appeared in each geography.[60]

We are starting to see a similar inflection point being reached in a few emerging ecosystems.

While I can't pinpoint an exact reason this phenomenon manifests itself, I have three hypotheses. First, when there is one critical success, it can easily be explained away as an exception. As Daniel Dines mentioned, UiPath was occasionally dismissed as an aberration of the Romanian ecosystem. Having a few successes from a particular ecosystem demonstrates repeatability and thus increases the relevance and power of the role models.

Second, as you will explore in chapter 12, the power of capital and people lies in networks. Increasing the effect of older siblings is not linear but exponential: once there is a critical mass, there are many more network connections to be made.

The third hypothesis concerns human capital. As Amanda Lannert, CEO of JellyVision, explained, "The Chicago ecosystem is rapidly changing, because we've had many recent success stories. Potential recruits considering moving to Chicago have to make the calculus about what happens if things don't work out. If there are many successful technology companies, the risk is lower. And so, a rising tide rises all boats."[61] As more innovators successfully scale, their impact across the industry is compounded.

Laying the Foundation, Together

Frontier Innovators play a direct and active role in creating the building blocks of an ecosystem. This includes laying the foundations of an entrepreneurial culture through initiatives like FUN and iHub and educating prospective entrepreneurs with programs like Choson and Startup Weekend. It also means providing skill training through programs as does ALU, mentoring and supporting the next generation as do Hernan and Endeavor, and creating ecosystem infrastructure through industry organizations like GOGLA and FSUAC. Frontier Innovators also bring up the next generation of entrepreneurs through informal schools of entrepreneurship like MercadoLibre, Maktoob, and Careem—often in parallel with developing their own ventures.

As you have seen, a select few Frontier Innovators play the disproportionately powerful role of older siblings. These entrepreneurs become role models for the next generation, and their scaled businesses train new generations of leaders. These older siblings often take an active role in giving back, as investors, mentors, and supporters.

But no older sibling (metaphorical or otherwise) succeeds without a wider group of supporters: family, friends, teachers, and good Samaritans. Similarly, ecosystem participants have a much wider role to play in helping entrepreneurs, and, by extension, their ecosystems, succeed. Chapter 12 offers concrete recommendations for all ecosystem players, including employees, corporations, philanthropies, government actors, and beyond.

12.

It Takes a Village

How the Rest of Us Can Help

Developing entrepreneurial ecosystems is a top priority for nations worldwide. Policy makers are looking to spur local innovation and support job creation. Corporations are looking to revitalize age-old processes and infuse them with technology, all while giving back to their local ecosystems. The social and philanthropic sectors hope to leverage innovative solutions to address seemingly intractable problems.

As you learned in chapter 11, Frontier Innovators are at the forefront of building their ecosystems—but they can't do it alone. Everyone has a role to play, including the government, local corporate leaders, investors, the social sector, and other ecosystem participants.

This chapter details strategies for anyone looking to support Frontier Innovators. Before we start, it is helpful to review the current best thinking on innovation ecosystem development.

Theories of Ecosystem Development

Traditional theories of entrepreneurial ecosystem development fall into three broad subsets: input-driven models, network-driven models, and entrepreneur-driven models. Let's look at each in turn.

Input-Driven Theories

Input models focus on the conditions under which entrepreneurial ecosystems succeed. For example, the World Bank ease of doing business rankings focus on the policy environment and its influence on the simplicity and ease of starting businesses. Others measure a more comprehensive set of markers. For instance, the OECD Entrepreneurial Ecosystem Diagnostic Toolkit's rubric measures fifty-seven separate metrics, including access to debt capital, tax incentives, local graduation rates, and access to telecom and infrastructure.[1]

Similarly, the agglomeration of demand model considers the economies of scale in acquiring specialized resources as a sector grows. This theory suggests that resources like entrepreneurship-focused lawyers, venture capitalists, and specialized tax accountants who understand stock options are more likely to exist in sectors that scale: the ecosystem can support the fixed shared cost of increasingly specialized resources, labor, infrastructure, and knowledge.[2]

While input models catalog the magnitude of specific conditions and measure the vibrancy of a system already in motion, they typically fail to explain the magic that catalyzes exponential ecosystem growth. As Chris Heivly, co-founder of MapQuest and a global ecosystem builder with Techstars, once told me, "If building an ecosystem was as easy as finding the right ingredients, wouldn't everyone have done it already? Silver bullet solutions unfortunately don't work."[3] Thus, input-focused theories fall short of explaining why some ecosystems enjoy virtuous cycles and others do not.[4]

Network-Centric Theories

To explain virtuous cycles, a second school of thought explores the role of *networks*. Network economics are well understood among technology entrepreneurs. A network's value increases as more people use it; Facebook is not valuable if there is only one person on it. Harvard Business School professor Michael Porter developed a theory on network-driven regional innovation advantages. He suggests that innovation sectors thrive when there is an intersection of multiple players, including suppliers, governments, and competing companies that help create clusters of advantage and, over time, innovation ecosystems.[5]

For others, the value of networks lies in the ability of an ecosystem to share ideas, best practices, and strategies horizontally. In her book *Regional Advantage: Culture and Competition in Silicon Valley and Route 128*, AnnaLee Saxenian provides an explanation for Silicon Valley's rise. Thirty years ago, it was unclear whether Silicon Valley or Boston's Route 128 would become the dominant US innovation ecosystem. At the time, both ecosystems were similar in size, were proximate to top universities, and had abundant access to talent. Saxenian argues that the key determinant of Silicon Valley's success was the combination of horizontal network effects and a culture of transparency.

Silicon Valley's culture (unlike Boston's) promoted information sharing at every level of organizations and among organizations. Therefore, close horizontal social networks defined by wide information sharing took shape. San Francisco's advantage was compounded by relatively lax employment practices (e.g., noncompete clauses in employment contracts are not enforceable), making it much easier for employees to move between companies and for best practices to propagate across the ecosystem. The result: much more porous functional barriers between firms in Silicon Valley (versus Boston, where information was shared top down) and thus much stronger network effects. Therefore, the value for someone to plug in to the Silicon Valley network was higher and thus the ecosystem won out.[6]

Others have focused on networks that form due to geographic and cultural concentration. In his book *The Creative Class*, Richard Florida argues that innovation stems from intellectual creativity, which is largely driven by engineers, academics, and artists. Innovators want to live among people who are tolerant of new ideas and open to pushing creative and artistic boundaries. They also want to live around each other. Therefore, the value of a local network increases as more people contribute their skills and values, in this case of tolerance and openness. Once a region reaches a critical mass, it earns a long-term competitive advantage.[7]

Network-driven approaches successfully explain what makes a startup ecosystem endure and how a region cements its advantage over time. However, as with input-driven models, creating the individual nodes or the foundation of a network doesn't explain how it takes hold, or why. The magic is in kick-starting the network—the activation of the connective tissue between people and firms.

Entrepreneur-Centric Models

A third set of theories explores this magic kick-starting effect. In their book *The Rainforest*, Victor Hwang and Greg Horowitt describe entrepreneurial ecosystems as the product of complex organisms. Whereas traditional policy makers focus on ecosystem development in the way a postindustrial manager would build a factory, Hwang and Horowitt argue instead that startup ecosystems are developed organically. They cannot be planned.[8] The key input for these ecosystems is to foster the right culture and enable entrepreneurs to grow and shape their ecosystem.

More recently, in his book *Startup Communities*, venture capitalist Brad Feld proposed the Boulder thesis. Feld's fundamental principle is that entrepreneurs must lead the startup community. Government, academics, corporations, investors, or other outside actors cannot kick-start an entrepreneurial ecosystem alone. Feld argues that the entrepreneurial leaders of a startup community must have a long-term commitment to the geographic region itself. At the same time, the community must be inclusive and welcoming. The boundaries of the ecosystem should be porous, allowing companies and individuals to flow in and out. Experimentation should be encouraged; the best ideas are supported, and failures are shuttered quickly. Finally, Feld writes that the startup community must have continual activities to engage the community.[9] Chapter 11 in this book explores this topic in detail, showcasing the many ways entrepreneurs, and in particular older siblings, build and kick-start the ecosystems in which they work.

But entrepreneurs do not build ecosystems alone in a vacuum. Others play critical roles, from ensuring basic table stakes—a nod to the necessary input and network preconditions that most ease the burden for entrepreneurs—to taking more-tactical approaches to supporting entrepreneurs in emerging ecosystems, including fostering opportunities for cross-pollination, facilitating access to both financial capital and human capital, and investing in entrepreneur-friendly infrastructure and regulation.

Rooted in the lessons of innovation at the Frontier covered so far, the suggestions in this chapter build on existing ecosystem development theories to suggest strategies for all ecosystem builders at the Frontier.

Table Stakes

The input-focused theories are correct in that certain ingredients are necessary for an ecosystem to take hold. Throughout this book, you have explored many of the disparate macroeconomic, currency, or political challenges many Frontier Innovators face.

While economic advice is beyond the scope of this book, macroeconomic uncertainty (e.g., inflation, economic growth, etc.) unquestionably decreases an entrepreneur's interest in and ability to take risks. Currency depreciation makes raising capital all the more challenging. Political volatility complicates strategies such as being born global. The business climate is important, too, as exemplified by the World Bank's ease of doing business rankings. If an environment is rife with corruption or unfair competition through monopolies, it effectively functions as a tax on innovation.[10]

Legal systems can be an important innovation catalyst. If bankruptcy laws are hostile to entrepreneurship (e.g., if debt follows founders past startup failure), entrepreneurs won't even want to start. Similarly, flexible employment laws motivate entrepreneurs to test and experiment with new models but allow for adjustments where needed. If every hire can never be revoked, then it is hard for entrepreneurs to change course.[11]

As you saw in chapters 6 and 7, human capital is the core input to building startups. A top priority for ecosystem players, therefore, should be funding primary, secondary, and university programs.

Governments and regulators who want to build their ecosystems should start by ensuring these basic table stakes. Not everything needs to be perfect, but, to thrive, an ecosystem needs to achieve a certain baseline. Brazil faces inflation, high interest rates, and a volatile political environment, and yet its fintech ecosystem is among the leaders globally. India has high poverty and high inflation but has created a global technology powerhouse in Bangalore. Each country was able to bring sufficient stability and adopt the right regulatory ecosystem to support innovation.

Of course, government regulators and other ecosystem players can do better than achieve a minimum baseline of stability or educational standards.

Help Entrepreneurs Think, and Be, Global

You have seen that entrepreneurs with international backgrounds working in globally connected environments are creating some of the most exciting companies in existence.

Ecosystem builders can encourage these born global trends in meaningful ways.

Foster Opportunities for Cross-Pollination

Fostering a cross-pollinating environment is an easy place to start.

It begins within the education system. Encouraging local students to pursue exchange programs, internships, or work opportunities abroad creates opportunities for students to build meaningful links with peers in other geographies and to be exposed to different cultures. Research has found a correlation between GDP growth and the rate of international education.[12] China had 9 percent GDP growth between 2001 and 2017, and during the same period a nearly 20 percent growth rate in undergraduate students studying in the United States. Similarly, Vietnam saw 6.5 percent GDP growth over the same period, with more than 15 percent growth in students studying abroad.[13]

The opposite is also true: a lack of cross-pollination may hamper innovation. Japan's GDP growth has continued to slow, these days hovering consistently at less than 1 percent annually, and the country has been losing its preeminence in technological innovation.[14] Perhaps not coincidentally (though there are a range of factors), student cross-pollination has also declined. In 2004, Japan sent more than eighty thousand students abroad. In 2018 this number declined by nearly 40 percent, at slightly more than fifty thousand.[15]

Governments can catalyze cross-pollination in the other direction by bringing in exchange students and entrepreneurs. Programs like Start-Up Chile and Start-Up Brazil look to institutionalize cross-pollination by encouraging entrepreneurs from around the world to start their businesses locally. Start-Up Chile offers startups as much as $100,000, free office space, and a number of other perks.[16]

Investors can support this as well. Two of the leading Latin American funds—Kaszek and Monashees—have institutionalized cross-pollination within their portfolios. Kaszek runs a proprietary one-week leadership and innovation program at the Graduate School of Business at Stanford (at Kaszek's expense), exposing its portfolio companies to professors and industry experts. Monashees organizes an annual trip to visit another ecosystem. So far, they have brought their entrepreneurs to visit China, Israel, and elsewhere.

Nonprofits are well placed to support these exchanges. Venture for America (VFA) is looking to bridge the divide between the United States' two coasts and the middle of the country. Borrowing the model of Teach for America, VFA places recent college graduates in innovative companies in fourteen cities, such as Pittsburgh, Birmingham, and St. Louis. The competitive program accepts only two hundred fellows out of a few thousand applications every year. More than 30 percent of VFA alumni have gone on to start their own startups, many of them in their newly adopted cities.[17] C100, a nonprofit membership-driven organization, links Canadian technology ecosystems with Silicon Valley by connecting leading entrepreneurs in Canada with mentorship, capital, and advice from Silicon Valley and beyond.[18]

Cross-pollination isn't solely about the transfer of international ideas. Cross-industry and cross-sector experience also helps. Corporate management rotational programs are great opportunities to give young graduates exposure to multiple roles and departments in companies. Similarly, government fellowships have the dual benefit of infusing the government with external thinking, and the students with new perspectives on how the government works.

Support Immigration

As you have seen, immigrants are a driving force of innovation and entrepreneurship globally. In the United States the majority of unicorns were started by at least one immigrant, and immigrants are responsible for a quarter of entrepreneurship.[19]

Unquestionably, the changing stance on immigration in the United States is shooting the country's innovation ecosystem in the foot. Enabling the hiring of qualified immigrant entrepreneurs or team members at fast-growing startups is critical if the virtuous cycle of innovation in Silicon Valley is to continue. Many qualified and trained executives from around the world consider moving to Silicon Valley to start their businesses. Often these ready-made entrepreneurs easily attract capital and create jobs. By making it difficult for them to come, the United States incentivizes them to choose a more accessible entrepreneur visa program elsewhere.

A look at open startup jobs on AngelList (a leading platform for startups in the United States) shows more than ten thousand unfilled startup jobs in the United States. Yet only about 10 percent of these companies are able to sponsor an immigrant.[20] By holding up immigration, the United States is holding up the growth of these companies, and in turn the creation of future jobs (and the creation of incremental tax dollars).

Governments should make it easier for entrepreneurs to move in and start businesses. The United States should reinstate the entrepreneur visa program—a program that allowed entrepreneurs who raised $100,000 in government grants or $250,000 in venture capital to stay in the United States for a renewable thirty-month term.[21] Similar programs are being successfully implemented in many markets, making it easy for entrepreneurs to come in and succeed. This policy in turn catalyzes sector development.[22]

Others can support immigration as well. A case in point is Unshackled Ventures. Founded in 2014, Unshackled is an early-stage venture capital firm that is designed specifically for foreign-born entrepreneurs. Its unique venture builder model invests in entrepreneurs from the get-go, offers them complete immigration and employment support, and facilitates access to a network of investors and customers.[23] To date, the fund has made more than thirty investments in founders from twenty different countries, from six different continents.[24]

The reality is that America's population is dwarfed by giants like India and China. In a few years, India will have more people working in technology in Bangalore than there are in Silicon Valley. China is already on par, depending on the metric. In 2018, China minted thirty-seven new unicorns, nipping at the heels of the fifty-five in the United States, and outpaced the United States in venture capital investment.[25] American exceptionalism—and Silicon Valley's dominance—are based on the foundation of immigration, and the country's competitiveness endures only by attracting the best minds around the world.

My recommendation for countries around the world is to consider immigrant entrepreneurs as a valuable and competitive asset. Do everything you can to attract them—or someone else will. Last year, on the 101 (the main highway in Silicon Valley), a billboard read, "Have H1B problems? Come to Canada!"[26] Perhaps they will.

Create Global Launching Pads

Neither born global startups nor decentralized startups scale in an ad hoc way. Instead, they strategically select well-connected hubs rich with talent as launching pads. In turn, strategic policy makers can make their markets more attractive as launching pads.

One of the reasons London became popular for fintech startups was that it served as an easy base to expand across Europe. With a central bank that was open to innovation and a regulatory match with Europe that would allow companies to "passport" across the continent, London developed an agglomeration of venture capital and startups. It also did not hurt that London had regional specialization in financial services (more on that later). Of course, as the United Kingdom potentially exits the European Union and thereby closes itself off from the region, these advantages and this specialization are disappearing.

Singapore, the hub for innovation in Southeast Asia, serves as another example. Despite representing less than 1 percent of the region's population of six hundred million, it is the launching pad for four of the ten Southeast Asia unicorns.[27] This is in part because of Singapore's connectivity links across the region. As one of the world's leading airlines, Singapore Airlines provides physical links. Singapore has a strong rule of law and a strong academic system, enabling local entrepreneurs. The country also has an accommodating immigration system that has managed to attract global talent. In Startup Genome's 2017 "Global Ecosystem Rankings Report," Singapore outranked Silicon Valley as the top place for startup talent.[28] Finally, the government is focused on cementing greater links with global entrepreneurs. It rolled out the Global Innovation Alliance (GIA), which helps entrepreneurs connect with hubs such as Bangkok, Beijing, Germany, Tokyo, Munich, Paris, and San Francisco.[29]

Similarly, in the Middle East, Dubai has positioned itself as the region's launching pad. The U.A.E. is the base for more than 40 percent of all startups in the Arab world, and among the sixty acquisitions in the region in the past five years, most were Dubai-based companies.[31]

Policy can help offer an attractive place for entrepreneurs in the creative class to live. Innovators can often choose to live anywhere. Elements that have been suggested as attractive to such entrepreneurs include liberal values, economical housing, and a concentration of other cultural elements.[32]

As distributed models take hold, ecosystem builders can support this phenomenon as well. Estonia's government has taken this practice to the extreme. Through its e-residency program, people from around the world can get an Estonian government ID and access the country's digital business environment. Benefits include allowing entrepreneurs to create an EU company while being location agnostic, starting from anywhere in the world, registering to accept online payments, and joining a global network of e-residents in 165 countries.[33]

Human Capital

Human capital is the lifeblood of startups. Access to this resource is also their greatest challenge. As you will see, this is a key area where ecosystem builders can help. Penny Pritzker, the former secretary of commerce under President Obama, and now the co-founder of P33, a technology ecosystem-building organization in Chicago, once told me that "to support an innovation ecosystem requires a deep focus on an inclusive, local talent pipeline. Deep collaboration across the spectrum of companies and sources of capital as well as a focus on training and apprenticeship policy are critical to success."[34]

In many emerging ecosystems, the first wave of entrepreneurs are often immigrants or repatriates. Over time, as they import their global learning and practices and as the ecosystem matures, it becomes easier for local entrepreneurs to enter the field. For this passing of the baton to succeed, local talent must be able to access training and educational opportunities—not only to find employment at a startup but also to start their own companies.

Ecosystem builders have a massive opportunity to support Frontier Innovators on this front. It starts with the baseline of supporting and properly funding local school and university programs and goes far beyond formal education.

Ecosystem participants can support specialized organizations like the African Leadership University or local coding boot camps. If the cost of tuition is a barrier, this is a great area in which to explore subsidization. Hotels.ng has a subsidized training program that identifies Nigeria's best hidden talent. There are opportunities to do more training for the general technological industry as a whole.

Mentorship programs like Endeavor help founders access the resources they need. Others, like Rippleworks (a foundation started by cryptocurrency startup Ripple, Chris Larsen, and Doug Galen), match global experts with the needs of particular global startups and social enterprises. For instance, the foundation matched Zola with experts on customer service when that became a pain point.[35] As Doug explained to me, "Many funders and organizations are working tirelessly to improve the quality and size of the talent pool, with innovative education and upskilling efforts, but these will take years. In the meantime, we need to help social entrepreneurs solve their most immediate challenges now. Capacity building fills this gap. This need is immediate, vast, and full of great organizations actually bridging this talent gap."[36]

Lack of diversity is an endemic problem in the technology industry, and it is uniquely thorny in many emerging markets. Frontier Innovators like Shopify and Hotels.ng have provided compelling ideas. Government, corporations, and the nonprofit sector have an opportunity and, I would argue, an obligation to support the talent pipeline more broadly and provide greater opportunities to women and other underrepresented communities.

Capital and Economics

Camels survive in challenging environments, operating for days without access to water and food. However, they eventually need sustenance to survive. Here, the entire ecosystem can help. However, the response should be considered and not excessive.

As you have seen, many ecosystems are starved for capital. Investors have an opportunity to support emerging ecosystems. For example, non-profit initiatives like the Rise of the Rest tour and the Comeback Cities tour, both led by investors, help raise awareness of the startup ecosystem and opportunity in the Midwest region of the United States.

Venture capitalists can focus strategies on capital-deprived ecosystems, as Drive Capital has done in the Midwest or Kaszek in Latin America. They should also continue to experiment with new investment structures and models (e.g., revenue shares, evergreen funds, etc.). Limited partners (investors in venture capital funds) should support these innovations.

Governments have a role to play as well. Indeed, many ecosystems trace the beginnings of their capital models to government support of venture capital. In Israel, the Yozma program was a big driver of the venture capital sector's early development. In Hebrew, *Yozma* translates to "initiative"— an apt description for what it achieved in Israel's venture capital industry. The government program provided $80 million for a 40 percent stake in ten new venture capital funds to help get Israeli companies off the ground and to market. The rest, as they say, is history. Venture capital investments soared sixty-fold, from $58 million in the 1990s to $3.3 billion now.[37] Similarly, in the United States, as early as 1958, the Small Business Investment Corporation (SBIC) provided debt and equity to high-risk small businesses that were unable to access capital from traditional sources.[38]

Foundations and multilaterals are an undertapped source of capital. Foundations should shift part of their endowments to supporting entrepreneurs or investors at the Frontier. Impact-focused investing is a particularly potent channel.

Corporations, similarly, have an ability to invest in and support start-ups globally, as companies like Tencent, Alibaba, and Naspers have demonstrated. In the United States, corporations have more than $1.9 trillion in cash on their balance sheets. Unlocking only a portion of this capital to reinvest in their local communities would be a game-changer.[39]

Of course, a Camel is not designed to live by the watering hole all the time. In the same way, in capital-starved environments, the temptation can often be to provide capital to alleviate this challenge entirely. Indeed, no startup entrepreneur will ever say there is too much available capital. Yet, as many people have convincingly argued, while a lack of capital can be a bottleneck it is rarely the key constraint.[40] Rather, the key challenge is often finding a sustainable business model. The advantage of the Camel model is its focus on sustainability and resilience. Drowning an ecosystem in capital risks undercutting a camel approach and the success it achieves. Therefore, ecosystem builders must carefully diagnose the problem, identify the gap by stage, sector, and geography, and craft targeted solutions.

Finally, interventions should be temporary rather than permanent subsidies. They should help start the virtuous cycle and then exit gracefully. Although support should be long term, it should not be eternal. The Yozma program in Israel, for instance, had a built-in exit timeline.

Provide the Right Infrastructure

Frontier Innovators are often engaged in creating markets. Market players can support them by providing appropriate regulation and infrastructure.

Offer Regulatory Flexibility

Ecosystem builders have an opportunity to create an attractive regulatory landscape for innovators. A regulator's instinct is often to analyze every eventuality and provide rules upfront. In innovation, one cannot predict how a business will evolve. Closing doors off is a recipe for curtailing creativity. A more balanced and tolerant regulatory approach serves as a strong accelerator.

In this vein, the sandbox efforts of the central banks in Singapore, Malaysia, and the United Kingdom are noteworthy. Fintech is a highly regulated industry where experimentation is often difficult. In a *sandbox*, a regulator allows startups to operate within a constrained environment and with a specific risk level accepted. Regulators in turn agree not to overregulate the idea. They just let it play out. Once the idea evolves over

an agreed amount of time, regulators and startups jointly look at the results and evaluate the risks, rather than regulate the idea ahead of time.[41]

Through policy, countries can make themselves attractive as innovation sandboxes. Rwanda, for instance, has made itself an easy place to do
business, with limited corruption and a focused approach to supporting
entrepreneurs. In doing so, it has attracted global startups to its ecosystem, many of whom, like Zipline, chose to first launch there to experiment. Similarly, Rwanda was Babylon Health's first African market.

Support Ecosystem Infrastructure

Creators are often building entirely new industries and have to create
multiple business models at once (e.g., Zola, with its R&D unit, financing arm, distribution platform, and manufacturing team, or Guiabolso
with its bank interconnections, credit score, PFM, and lending product).
Sometimes, this practice is strategic and serves as a point of differentia-
tion (e.g., Apple building its own stores to control the distribution experience). However, Frontier Innovators often need to build undifferentiated
horizontal infrastructure out of necessity.

Ecosystem players can build this needed horizontal infrastructure.
In India, a live experiment is taking place with Aadhaar, a government-
sponsored universal identification program. It was launched by Nandan
Nilekani—the co-founder of Infosys (a key older sibling himself in the
Bangalore ecosystem)—while he was serving in government. Aadhaar
provides 1.3 billion Indian residents with a digital identity based on bio-
metrics, along with a unified platform to access government benefits, open
bank accounts, subscribe to telephones, and demonstrate their identity.[42]

The Aadhaar platform provides valuable foundational infrastructure
for the ecosystem. As demonstrated in the Matrimony.com case study,
identification infrastructure is critical. At the time, founder Murugavel
Janakiraman had to build a costly custom solution. Through Aadhaar,
identity verification could be as easy as a plug-in. The government in
India, aided by technologists from the volunteer group iSPIRT, are building IndiaStack, a portfolio of application programming interfaces (APIs)

that leverage Aadhaar as a plug-in for identity, making it easier to launch new services in a digital, paperless, cashless way.[43] Nandan explained the vision:

> The objective is to create digital public goods. The first was Aadhaar, which provides a public, verifiable identity. Subsequently, the National Payments Corporation of India offers a successful interoperable payment network called UPI. The next stage is data empowerment, where data is put in the hands of users to use for their own benefit. Our vision is that, enabled with all this infrastructure, magic can happen. All kinds of products and services can be reimagined.[44]

Corporations, foundations, and governments can also support ecosystem infrastructure. With regard to human capital, regional governments and some corporations supported the inclusive application program efforts of Hotels.ng as a public good. It would be powerful to do this nationally to help startups discover the best talent around the country and spread equal opportunity.

Principles of Ecosystem Support

Many ecosystem builders approach me for tactical advice on supporting their particular ecosystems. Developing an entrepreneurial ecosystem strategy is no small feat, and it requires deep knowledge of the local strengths, dynamics, and relationships at play. That's why I'm reticent to provide a standard recipe of advice. Instead, I propose a few principles to guide the way.

Keep the Entrepreneur at the Center

Startup best practice places customers front and center. The same should be true of ecosystem development. In this case, the customer is the entrepreneur. Serving other "customers"—such as developing a particular industry, creating new jobs, or solving social goals—may of course see traction, but it will not be as powerful in unlocking the virtuous cycle of entrepreneurial ecosystems.

From interviews with ecosystem builders around the world, I have learned that one of the key drivers of success (and predictors of failure) is entrepreneurial centricity. If outside players, rather than entrepreneurs themselves, dictate what is required for the ecosystem, then perverse incentives creep in and generally lead to suboptimal outcomes. Endeavor's analysis of the Nairobi ecosystem reports heavy external funding by donors, development finance institutions (DFIs), and corporations.[45] It counted one donor-funded incubator for every thirty startups in Nairobi. As the report explains, "Donors began to fund tech-oriented entrepreneurship initiatives, which led local organizations offering personal microfinance loans and educational services to refashion themselves and launch entrepreneurship support programs."[46] This contributed to less-productive microbusinesses and startup strategies that optimized for what would serve donor objectives rather than what would create great businesses.

Despite the rocky start, Kenyan entrepreneurs have made great strides in building their ecosystem over time. Yet, comparing the Nairobi ecosystem to the Bangalore ecosystem, only 1 percent of Nairobi companies grew sufficiently to employ more than one hundred people—one-sixth the rate that Bangalore achieved.[47]

The same dynamic plays out in venture capital. In the late 1990s, the Canadian government supported labor-sponsored funds, a tax-subsidized investment fund. By regulatory decree, these funds were restricted in the types and ways in which the capital could be invested.[48] Unsurprisingly, as Harvard Business School professor Josh Lerner discovered, labor-sponsored funds underperformed compared with other asset classes and had much higher likelihood of failure than traditional venture capital investments. Labor-sponsored funds were simply trying to place capital where entrepreneurs were not seeking it.

Ultimately, innovation ecosystem development should be centered on and led by entrepreneurs. Brad Feld's Boulder thesis, explored earlier, supports this philosophy, as does empirical data from the Kauffman Foundation.[49]

Focus on Big Wins, Too

For many ecosystem builders, the temptation is to support entrepreneurs at the earliest stages, seeing success in the rising numbers of new startups or the number of patents filed. But these metrics are correlated only with successful startup *activity*. They are not signals that startups will scale—one of the key markers of success for an ecosystem.

The Kauffman Foundation published a report that helps measure entrepreneurial ecosystems using twelve metrics that inform four indicators. The first indicator is density, which measures new and young firms per one thousand people, the share of employment in new and young firms, and sector density, especially in high technology. The second indicator is fluidity, which measures population flux, labor market reallocation, and high-growth firms. The third indicator is connectivity, which measures program connectivity, spin-off rate, and dealmaker networks. The fourth is diversity, which measures multiple economic specializations, mobility, and immigrants.[50]

I suggest a fifth, focused on the older siblings from chapter 11: the number of later-stage entrepreneurs who have successfully scaled to exit. Research has demonstrated that in sectors having multiple companies, the top three companies will impact more than 60 percent of the ecosystem. In Buenos Aires the portion is greater than 80 percent.[51] As you have seen, successful, scaled startups can kick-start the virtuous cycle of ecosystem development.

Take a Long-Term View

Rome was not built in a day. Neither are startup ecosystems. Silicon Valley took more than forty years to become what it is now. Israel's success can be traced back twenty years to the Yozma program.

Ecosystem builders must take a long-term view. An ecosystem's development takes longer than electoral cycles or the tenure of most corporate or foundation CEOs. Success requires passing the baton across at least a few generations in order to succeed.

Collaborate

Ecosystem development should not be siloed. It requires a collaborative approach with the community at large. Solutions like Endeavor, FUN, and ALU require partnership with the broader entrepreneurial community, but also the corporate, private, and nonprofit sectors. ALU worked with its students' future employers to identify gaps, build the curriculum, and create opportunities for internship and training. It worked with philanthropists to subsidize its early projects and with a range of corporate and venture investors to scale. Similarly, part of the magic of Endeavor is its deep alignment with leaders of the local business community who fund the program and mentor the startups.

Be Creative and Take Risks

Unfortunately, there is no single ecosystem development recipe. Ecosystem development is necessarily experimental. It should involve taking risks and trying creative new approaches. Not everything should succeed or become large.

In fact, the opposite is often true: smaller, more organic activities are powerful. Some will succeed and others will fail. But rapid experimentation is critical to find models that will succeed.

This Above All: To Thine Own Self Be True

Scaling an ecosystem at the Frontier is a different journey than in Silicon Valley or anywhere else. Therefore, heed Shakespeare's words: "To thine own self be true."

Many ecosystems around the world have a moniker of "Silicon X." There's Silicon Alley in New York, Silicon Plains in Utah, and Silicon

Savannah in Kenya. It is often an incorrect and pejorative comparison. Silicon Savannah, which refers collectively to all Sub-Saharan African ecosystems, uses an originally Native American word to describe a natural ecosystem that is certainly not representative of an entire subcontinent.[52]

Building multiple reproductions of Silicon Valley is not a productive objective. Successful global ecosystems should and will look different, leveraging local strengths.

Historically, technology was seen as a vertical industry unto itself, almost wholly independent of others. There were domains such as financial services, health care, industrials, and technology. In that world, Silicon Valley could dominate the market, as New York dominates finance and Québec dominates maple syrup.

Today, technology is horizontal; every company and every industry has technology built in. Regional expertise must play a critical role in local ecosystem development. London has become a global leader in fintech (for now). Columbus, Ohio, has become a thriving innovation hub in the US Midwest, specializing in agriculture and manufacturing.

Innovation ecosystems around the world will foster various types of startups. Some will focus on health care (and likely specific subsegments of it) while others will focus on robotics for heavy industries. The strengths of local ecosystems will determine the emergence of specialized sectors.

As you contribute to your local ecosystem, understand that Frontier Innovators differ from one another. Each operates in a unique environment defined by a political economy, a macroeconomic reality, and an ecosystem of individuals in the sector. Any ecosystem also necessarily includes a broader industry environment and set of expertise.

So don't call it Silicon Savannah. Just call it Kenya.

Conclusion

The Future Is at the Frontier

On April 10, 2018, Mark Zuckerberg was called in for his second day of testimony in the US Senate. He was being asked a barrage of questions regarding the role of Facebook in the aftermath of the Cambridge Analytica scandal. His prepared answers were written on a piece of paper in front of him, and well rehearsed.

One answer concerned a potential Facebook breakup. He never received the corresponding question, but his canned statement underscores the current state of the world. "Break Up FB? U.S. tech companies key asset for America; break up strengthens Chinese companies," his notepad read.[1]

Facebook's chief worry wasn't its US competitors like Twitter, LinkedIn, and Snapchat. To Facebook, the real competition is international. Facebook has an enviable 2.3 billion active monthly users on its platform.[2] Yet WeChat is close behind, with 1.1 billion and growing rapidly.[3] Among the twenty largest global technology companies, eight are Chinese. That's up from three only ten years ago.[4]

Technology innovation has gone global.

Household names now come from everywhere: Spotify from Sweden, Waze from Israel, and Alibaba from China. Twenty years ago, at the height of the 1990s technology bubble, Silicon Valley was the top place for innovation. In many ways, it was the only place. But much has changed. In the 1990s, more than 95 percent of the world's venture capital was located the United States. But now the figure is more like 50 percent.[5] This shift will only continue. Increasingly, innovation will come from everywhere.

As the world shifts away from Silicon Valley and toward the Frontier, the conventional rules no longer apply. The best entrepreneurs are charting their own course, leading us toward a more creative, sustainable, global, impactful, and well-rounded vision of innovation.

I hope this book leaves you with five key takeaways.

1. Innovation Is Global

All of our best practices remain centered in a singular time and place—Silicon Valley, today—and for a particular type of business. For a long time, Silicon Valley's rule book for driving innovation and creating startup ecosystems has been the only one we have had. But Silicon Valley's rule book rarely translates to the rest of the world, and the rest of the world is no longer trying to fit the mold.

The rule book, in and of itself, is not wrong. To the contrary, it works extraordinarily well in Silicon Valley. But it is specific to the types of products being built in Silicon Valley (asset-light apps), the aspirations of the businesses (growth at any cost), and the available ecosystem and infrastructure (one that is rich and well developed).

In contrast, the rest of the world—what I have called the Frontier—is large, wide ranging, and varied. It stretches from ecosystems having little entrepreneurial activity and concentration, to markets having macroeconomic uncertainty and political risk. That's why building startups at the Frontier is different and why uncritically adopting Silicon Valley's approaches is a recipe for disaster. Models focused solely on growth will be starved by a limited capital market, ambushed by unexpected currency risk, or wiped out by any number of other challenges.

To copy and paste the Silicon Valley approach without deeply understanding its underlying assumptions is foolhardy and ignorant. Successful Frontier Innovators don't even try.

2. A New Model for Innovation Has Emerged

A new model for innovation, developed by and adapted to the Frontier, is rooted in lessons from entrepreneurs around the world.

Frontier Innovators have redefined innovation best practices in myriad and meaningful ways. Frontier Innovators create industries rather than disrupt them, focus on acute pain points in ecosystems, and build products that target the mass market. They solve systemic societal challenges using innovative technological and business approaches, from inventing street addresses to developing novel financial services and health care solutions.

Often, they must build the vertical stack and the horizontal stack. This task can add challenging complexity to building a successful business at the Frontier, but it can also offer competitive advantages. That said, Frontier Innovators don't just grow at any cost. They build "Camels" that are, first and foremost, sustainable and resilient when compared with their unicorn cousins. Facing riskier macroenvironments, Frontier Innovators focus on resilience.

Often immigrants or repatriates, Frontier Innovators take inspiration from various sources, including their own rich life experience. They often build companies that are global from the get-go, piecing together a large opportunity from fragmented regional markets. They tap the best talent from around the world and build A-teams.

Frontier Innovators prioritize the significant social and economic development impact of their companies. While not all social enterprises are startups, most Frontier startups have overlaps with social enterprises.

Frontier Innovators' companies often target more-impactful industries than their Silicon Valley counterparts. Perhaps because Frontier Innovators understand the impact that their products can have, they thoughtfully manage risk to their customers and to their companies rather than moving fast and breaking things.

Meanwhile, investors at the Frontier are beginning to innovate on the financing side. Key players are pioneering new models like evergreen funds, revenue share structures, computerized decision making, and investments by users.

Finally, Frontier Innovators are ecosystem builders. They actively shape culture, provide mentorship, build ecosystem infrastructure, and develop talent—all while developing their startups. Some exponentially accelerate ecosystem development and kick-start a virtuous cycle.

3. It's a Playbook, Not a Rule Book

Taken collectively, these lessons serve as a new playbook for entrepreneurs everywhere and not only at the Frontier. However, they should not be thought of as a formulaic recipe for success: do A, B, and C, and the result will be Z. Rather, the playbook is a collection of strategies from which aspiring entrepreneurs can draw to maximize their chances of success no matter what challenges they face. You should use your best judgment to choose which play makes sense for a particular situation, and disregard other elements.

Context is key. In places like Brazil, with a large local market and culturally distinct neighbors, it often makes sense to take a more focused national approach. In contrast, in neighboring Uruguay, startups need to think regionally or globally from the outset. Countries with rich venture capital ecosystems and local startups are less likely to rely on creative approaches to venture financing, leaving them free to follow the original Silicon Valley approach. Cities like Toronto or Shanghai have deep technical and management talent markets, meaning that the lessons on building A-teams remain important but are perhaps less urgent.

These strategies intersect and reinforce one another. Often, creating industries requires building the full stack, because more of the infrastructure and ecosystem is lacking at the outset. Creators are often Multi-Mission Athletes, who build businesses with an integral element of social impact. Camels can develop resilience by being born global and full stack, with multiple reinforcing business models. Occasionally, these trends pull in different directions. For instance, adopting a distributed strategy can obviate the need to build A-teams locally.

Silicon Valley approaches should also not be discarded entirely. Silicon Valley remains one of the best places to learn about customer-centric product development, creative design thinking, and product evolution.

Relativism is what innovating at the Frontier is all about. Some of the lessons from the playbook will be readily applicable in different ecosystems. Other ecosystems will feel uncomfortable and challenging for innovators trying to employ a particular approach. That's natural. Much as it would be difficult to understand the Impressionist art movement by looking at a single one of Monet's water lilies, it is important to take a step back and consider these trends holistically. Taken together, the principles in the Frontier Innovator's new playbook offer a more grounded, evolved, and flexible approach to building startups than you will find in the Silicon Valley canon.

4. Don't Copy Silicon Valley

To build vibrant Frontier startup ecosystems, all players—policy makers, regulators, foundations, investors, and large companies—have a role to play. To do so, they should not look to replicate Silicon Valley but instead support Frontier Innovators based in the Frontier playbook, choosing a course of action inspired by the strategies explored in this book.

For instance, supporting cross-pollination initiatives helps connect ecosystems. Improving local educational institutions, welcoming immigration, and investing in training programs can sustain and grow the local talent ecosystem. Fostering the appropriate legal and regulatory systems also will encourage innovation and startup creation. Offering horizontal infrastructure can provide enabling layers to decrease the cost and risk of startups. And kick-starting the capital ecosystem responsibly, and in partnership with innovators, can create a virtuous cycle.

5. Silicon Valley Needs a Refresh

Frontier Innovators are writing their own playbook out of necessity, so that their companies can survive and thrive in adverse conditions.

Classic Silicon Valley companies thrive in good times. But such times never last. In October 2008, leading venture capital firm Sequoia Capital shared a presentation with its portfolio companies titled "RIP Good Times," presaging the financial crisis. One of its conclusions was that CEOs should prioritize sustainability and resilience.[6]

The past decade has seen one of the longest bull markets in history, and capital and optimism are plentiful. Late-stage companies are seeing stratospheric valuations, staying private longer, and focusing on growth at all costs. At the same time, extreme economic inequality and homelessness are on the rise in the Bay Area, and tech companies are increasingly under fire for unethical behavior. And, quite simply, they are no longer pushing the limits of innovation the way they used to.

Many of the best startup companies are built in downturns—for example, Amazon and Netflix.[7] One theory for this is that people have less money to spend and entrepreneurs see an opportunity to create more-efficient companies (and some people who would otherwise be employed are forced into entrepreneurship).[8] In the current euphoria, Silicon Valley has forgotten this. To remember and learn, we can look to the Frontier and the playbook pioneered by its innovators. It offers Silicon Valley a chance to reflect on what's working and consider how it can evolve into the next, more sustainable version of itself—before it's too late.

Like all cycles, it is certain that one day venture funding will dry up again. Much as in the aftermath of 2001 and 2008, when only the most robust businesses survived, we may be reminded that the desert camel is a better long-term mascot than a unicorn after all.

The Future Is at the Frontier

There are now startup communities in nearly every country around the world. Although Silicon Valley will likely remain the leader in startups and innovation for years to come, it will no longer maintain a monopoly on best practices.

Ecosystems around the world are at different stages of development. In emerging markets, most are in their infancy. In former manufacturing towns in the United States, they may be in decline or experiencing a difficult rebirth. The best ecosystems will leverage lessons from across the world and will build in a way that reflects the local market's skills, assets, and needs.

In a few markets, the virtuous cycle is already in motion. Successful startups have yielded a trove of mentors, angel investors, and trained innovators. But for most Frontier ecosystems, waiting for the flywheel to kick in won't be sufficient.

Rudyard Kipling once wrote, "Oh, East is East, and West is West, and never the twain shall meet." To the contrary, innovation is shifting globally. East and West have much to learn from and with each other, and now is the moment to capitalize on the opportunity, for it is truly a vast one.

Although the United States still commands half of the world's venture capital, a wave of change is swelling, and it is reaching shores around the world.[9] Together, emerging and developing markets account for more than 6.4 billion people, some 85 percent of the world's population—and that doesn't even include those parts of the Frontier located in more-developed countries.[10]

Just look to China for a preview of what happens when innovation ecosystems kick into gear as they are now doing worldwide. In the span of a decade, China grew to be the second-largest tech ecosystem in the world, and it is arguably far more diversified than Silicon Valley in terms of technologies that span economic sectors like health care and transportation.[11]

Bangalore, Chicago, São Paolo, Singapore, and many other parts of the world are becoming innovation powerhouses. Around the globe, nearly five hundred ecosystems are producing startups. Just imagine what will happen as funding becomes more democratized and accessible to those outside the Bay Area.

A sea change is on the horizon as all of these outside-the-Valley entrepreneurs step to the fore of innovation. To succeed, they repeatedly subvert and reimagine Silicon Valley's rules, out-innovating everyone else as they write a new playbook for a new game. To keep up and remain a home for world-changing innovation, we should all consider taking a leaf from their book.

Notes

Introduction

1. "Off-Grid Solar Market Trends Report 2018" (Washington, DC: International Finance Corporation), January 2018.

2. Ilya A. Strebulaev and Will Gornall, "How Much Does Venture Capital Drive the U.S. Economy?" Stanford Graduate School of Business, October 21, 2015, https://www.gsb.stanford.edu/insights/how-much-does-venture-capital-drive-us-economy.

3. Tim Kane, "The Importance of Startups in Job Creation and Job Destruction," Kauffman Foundation Research Series, July 2010, https://www.kauffman.org/what-we-do/research/firm-formation-and-growth-series/the-importance-of-startups-in-job-creation-and-job-destruction.

4. Keith Collister, "Harvard's Josh Lerner Asks Why Bother with Venture Capital?" *Jamaica Observer*, September 12, 2014, http://www.jamaicaobserver.com/business/Harvard-s-Josh-Lerner-asks-why-bother-with-venture-capital-_17535881.

5. Enrique Dans, "Hey! We Live in the Age of Innovation: Who Needs Rules?" *Forbes*, December 6, 2017, https://www.forbes.com/sites/enriquedans/2017/12/06/hey-we-live-in-the-age-of-innovation-who-needs-rules/#2538c451246c.

6. George Avalos, "'Immense Growth' Makes the Bay Area the World's 19th-Largest Economy, If It Were a Nation," *Mercury News*, July 10, 2018, https://www.mercurynews.com/2018/07/10/immense-growth-makes-bay-area-worlds-19th-largest-economy-google-facebook-apple-adobe/.

7. "San Francisco Bay Area Startups," 2019, https://angel.co/san-francisco-bay-area; and Mark Muro and Jacob Whiton, "Tech Is (Still) Concentrating in the Bay Area: An Update on America's Winner-Take-Most Economic Phenomenon," Brookings Institution, December 17, 2018, https://www.brookings.edu/blog/the-avenue/2018/12/17/tech-is-still-concentrating-in-the-bay-area-an-update-on-americas-winner-take-most-economic-phenomenon/.

8. Adam Satariano, "The World's First Ambassador to the Tech Industry," *New York Times*, September 3, 2019, https://www.nytimes.com/2019/09/03/technology/denmark-tech-ambassador.html.

9. Leigh Buchanan, "Study: U.S. Businesses No Longer Dominate in Venture Capital Funding," *Inc.*, October 5, 2018, https://www.inc.com/leigh-buchanan/american-businesses-no-longer-dominate-venture-capital.html.

10. "Number of Mobile Subscribers Worldwide Hits 5 Billion," GMSA Newsroom, June 13, 2017, https://www.gsma.com/newsroom/press-release/number-mobile-subscribers-worldwide-hits-5-billion/.

11. "Number of Worldwide Social Network Users from 2010 to 2021 (in Billions)," Statista, 2019, https://www.statista.com/statistics/278414/number-of-worldwide-social-network-users/.

12. Richard Florida and Ian Hathaway, "Rise of the Global Startup City: Startup Revolution Report," Center for American Entrepreneurship, 2019, http://startupsusa.org/global-startup-cities/.

13. Lise He, "How Many Startups Are There in China?" *Quora*, November 27, 2018, https://www.quora.com/How-many-startups-are-there-in-China.

14. "Global Startup Ecosystem Report 2017," Startup Genome, April 2018, https://startupgenome.com/all-reports.

15. "How Many Startups Are There?" Get2Growth, http://get2growth.com/how-many-startups/.

16. "Global Startup Ecosystem Report 2017," Startup Genome, https://startupgenome.com/all-reports.

17. Anne S. Habiby and Deirdre M. Coyle Jr., "The High-Intensity Entrepreneur," *Harvard Business Review*, September 2010, https://hbr.org/2010/09/the-high-intensity-entrepreneur.

18. "The Global Unicorn Club: Current Private Companies Valued at $1B+," CB Insights, 2019, https://www.cbinsights.com/research-unicorn-companies.

19. Mansoor Iqbal, "Uber Revenue and Usage Statistics (2018) [2019]," *Business of Apps*, February 2019 [updated May 10, 2019], http://www.businessofapps.com/data/uber-statistics/; Trefis.com, "Number of Rides Uber Gave Worldwide from 2016 to 2019 (in Billions)," Statista, 2019, https://www.statista.com/statistics/946298/uber-ridership-worldwide/; Jane Zhang, "Didi by the Numbers: Ride-Hailing Firm Covered More Miles in 2018 Than 5 Earth-to-Neptune Round-Trips," *South China Morning Post*, January 23, 2019, https://www.scmp.com/tech/start-ups/article/2181542/didi-numbers-ride-hailing-firm-covered-more-miles-2018-5-earth; Xinhua, "DiDi completes 7.43b Rides in 2017," ChinaDaily.com, September 2018, http://www.chinadaily.com.cn/a/201801/09/WS5a541c98a31008cf16da5e76.html; Fanny Potkin, "Indonesia's Go-Jek Close to Profits in All Segments, Except Transport: CEO," Reuters, August 2018, https://www.reuters.com/article/us-indonesia-gojek-interview/indonesias-go-jek-close-to-profits-in-all-segments-except-transport-ceo-idUSKBN1L20SI; Marina Pasquali, "Key Figures on Taxi and Car Sharing App 99 in Brazil as of 2018," Statista, 2019, https://www.statista.com/statistics/882180/brazil-key-figures-taxi-car-sharing-app-99/; and Robin Wauters, "Cabify Hits 13 Million Customers Globally, Raises $160 Million from Rakuten and Others at $1.4 Billion Valuation," *techeu*, January 22, 2018, https://tech.eu/brief/cabify-hits-13-million-customers-globally-raises-160-million-rakuten-others-1-4-billion-valuation/.

20. J. Clement, "Number of PayPal's Total Active Registered User Accounts from 1st Quarter 2010 to 4th Quarter 2018 (in Millions)," Statista, July 26, 2019, https://www.statista.com/statistics/218493/paypals-total-active-registered-accounts-from-2010/; and Trefis, "Is Paytm Worth $20 Billion?" *Forbes*, December 2018, https://www.forbes.com/sites/greatspeculations/2018/12/03/is-paytm-worth-20-billion/#3327d9834439.

21. Olivia Solon, "Tech's Terrible Year: How the World Turned on Silicon Valley in 2017," *Observer*, December 23, 2017, https://www.theguardian.com/technology/2017/dec/22/tech-year-in-review-2017.

22. Susan Wu, "It's Time for Innovators to Take Responsibility for Their Creations," *Wired*, December 25, 2017, https://www.wired.com/story/its-time-for-innovators-to-take-responsibility-for-their-creations.

23. Daniel Weisfield, "Peter Thiel at Yale: We Wanted Flying Cars, Instead We Got 140 Characters," Yale School of Management, April 27, 2013, https://som.yale.edu/blog/peter-thiel-at-yale-we-wanted-flying-cars-instead-we-got-140-characters.

24. Biz Carson, "Silicon Valley Startups Are Obsessed with Developing Tech to Replace Their Moms" May 10, 2015, https://www.businessinsider.com/san-francisco-tech-startups-replacing-mom-2015-5; Ray Fisman and Tim Sullivan, "The Internet of 'Stuff Your Mom Won't Do for You Anymore,'" hbr.org, July 26, 2016, https://hbr.org/2016/07/

the-internet-of-stuff-your-mom-wont-do-for-you-anymore; Emily Chang, *Brotopia: Breaking Up the Boys' Club of Silicon Valley* (New York: Portfolio, 2018).

25. "List of Automobile Manufacturers in Michigan," Wikipedia, May 2019, https://en .wikipedia.org/wiki/List_of_automobile_manufacturers_of_Michigan.

26. Glenn Counts, Steve Ronson, and Kurt Spenser, "Detroit: The New Motor City," *Ethics of Development in a Global Environment* (EDGE), July 1999, https://web.stanford .edu/class/e297c/poverty_prejudice/citypoverty/hdetroit.htm.

27. General Motors, "General Motors Production By Plant," https://media.gm.com/ content/dam/Media/gmcom/investor/2012/Production-by-Plant-December-2012-NA.pdf.

28. Michelle Robertson, "So Many People Are Leaving the Bay Area, a U-Haul Shortage Is Jacking Up Prices," *SFGATE*, February 15, 2018, https://www.sfgate.com/expensive -san-francisco/article/U-Haul-San-Francisco-Bay-Area-prices-shortage-12617855.php.

29. "Off-Grid Solar Market Trends Report 2018"; James Chen, "What Are Frontier Markets?" *Investopedia*, March 26, 2018 [updated October 15, 2019], https://www .investopedia.com/terms/f/frontier-market.asp; and Early Growth Financial Services, "What Is Frontier Tech?" 2018, https://earlygrowthfinancialservices.com/what-is-frontier -tech/.

30. Brad Feld, *Startup Communities: Building an Entrepreneurial Ecosystem in Your City* (Hoboken, NJ: Wiley, 2012).

31. China has developed its own startup ecosystem. While it shares many similarities with Silicon Valley, it is also different in a variety of important ways. The Chinese government has mobilized a range of resources to kick-start the ecosystem, through investments in ecosystem, physical space, venture capital funding, and the like. Local regulations have made it harder, and in some cases impossible, for foreign technology companies to access the market, creating room for local players to thrive. The domestic market dwarfs that of every other country except the United States, giving room to scale large companies in a single market. This book covers parts of the Chinese ecosystem, although China's model is unique and often hard to replicate in other markets, and thus many parts will be out of scope.

32. Deal Sunny, "Entrepreneurship Infographic: 46 Facts Every Entrepreneur Needs To Know About," 2015, https://www.dealsunny.com/blog/entrepreneurship-infographic.

33. Rhett Morris and Lili Török, "Fostering Productive Entrepreneurship Communities," Endeavor Insight, October 2018, https://endeavor.org/content/uploads/2015/06/ Fostering-Productive-Entrepreneurship-Communities.pdf.

34. Fabio Sergio, "The Human Side of Inclusion," MasterCard Center for Inclusive Growth, January 20, 2015, https://mastercardcenter.org/insights/human-side-inclusion/.

35. American University, "New Study Reveals the Worldwide Reach of Social Entrepreneurship," Science X Network, June 1, 2016, https://phys.org/news/2016-06-reveals -worldwide-social-entrepreneurship.html; and Jay Boulkin, "Social Enterprise: Statistics from Around The World," Social Good Stuff, 2017, http://socialgoodstuff.com/2016/08/ statistics-from-around-the-world/.

36. "Startup Activity Swings Upward for Third Consecutive Year," Kauffman Foundation, May 8, 2017, https://www.kauffman.org/newsroom/2017/05/startup-activity-swings -upward-for-third-consecutive-year-annual-kauffman-index-reports.

Chapter 1

1. Author interview with Timbo Drayson, November 30, 2017.

2. Marissa Drouillard, "Addressing Voids: How Digital Start-Ups in Kenya Create Market Infrastructure," *Digital Kenya*, 2018, http://digitalkenyabook.com/.

3. Caitlin F. Dolkart, "Nairobi by Numbers: The Emergency Facts," Flare Emergency Services by Capsule, December 13, 2017, http://blog.capsule.co.ke/faqs/.

4. Interview, Drayson, 2017.

5. Marissa Drouillard, "Conversation #4: Finding the Right Problem to Solve," in *Bitange Ndemo* and Tim Weiss, eds., *Digital Kenya: An Entrepreneurial Revolution in the Making* (London: Palgrave Macmillan, 2017).

6. "OkHi Launches Mobile App for Businesses to Share Their Locations with Clients," *aptantech*, December 22, 2017, http://aptantech.com/2017/12/okhi-launches-mobile -app-for-businesses-to-share-their-locations-with-clients/.

7. Soylent is a popular meal replacement beverage, with a following among software engineers, to promote efficiency.

8. Bruce Broussard and John Sculley, "It's Time to Disrupt the $3 Trillion Healthcare Industry," *Forbes*, November 29, 2016, https://www.forbes.com/sites/sciencebiz/2016/11/16/ its-time-to-disrupt-the-3-trillion-healthcare-industry/#72d4fdd718b3; Meeri Kim, "Silicon Valley's Attempt to Disrupt Education," Learning & Development blog, November 11, 2016, http://bold.expert/silicon-valleys-attempt-to-disrupt-education/; Maya Kosoff, "The 'WTF' Plan to Disrupt Politics Is Everything That's Wrong with Silicon Valley," *Vanity Fair*, July 5, 2017, https://www.vanityfair.com/news/2017/07/the-wtf-plan-to-disrupt-politics -is-everything-thats-wrong-with-silicon-valley'; and Eric He, "How Silicon Valley Is Inventing the Future of Cars," July 28, 2017, https://www.paloaltoonline.com/news/2017/07/ 28/how-silicon-valley-is-inventing-the-future-of-cars.

9. Chance Barnett, "The Disruption of Venture Capital," startupgrind, June 27, 2016, https://medium.com/startup-grind/the-disruption-of-venture-capital-df32c8916f9b; Dan Primack, "A Disruptor Shakes Up Angel Investing," *Fortune*, November 13, 2014, http:// fortune.com/2014/11/13/angellist-ceo-naval-ravikant-disruptor/; and Jurica Dujmovic, "Startup Accelerators Are Aiming to Disrupt These Industries," MarketWatch, June 22, 2017, http://www.marketwatch.com/story/startup-accelerators-are-aiming-to-disrupt-these -industries-2017-06-22.

10.. "Proof of Concept," Season 1, Episode 7, *Silicon Valley*, directed by Mike Judge, written by Mike Judge, John Altschuler, Dave Krinsky, and Clay Tarver, June 2014, HBO.

11. Clayton M. Christensen, Michael E. Raynor, and Rory McDonald, "What Is Disruptive Innovation?" *Harvard Business Review*, December 2015, hbr.org/2015/12/what-is -disruptive-innovation.

12. Clayton M. Christensen, *The Innovator's Dilemma: When New Technologies Cause Great Firms to Fail* (Boston: Harvard Business Review Press, 2016).

13. Jill Lepore, "The Disruption Machine: What the Gospel of Innovation Gets Wrong," *New Yorker*, June 23, 2014, http://www.newyorker.com/magazine/2014/06/23/the -disruption-machine.

14. To analyze this, my colleagues and I identified the largest emerging market startups—those that have scaled the fastest or raised the most money according to industry sources and have partnered with leading investors. The Silicon Valley sample set was based on publicly available lists of unicorns.

15. For one thing, in Silicon Valley, the definition of disruption increasingly has been stretched, pulled, and fitted to represent any case in which an innovation is used or an incumbent has faltered. My definition of creators could also be stretched or defined alternatively. For our purposes here, I have focused on the creation of formal products or services to address acute pain points. This definition largely excludes the informal economy, which constitutes a huge segment of emerging-market economies. Moreover, I have focused on creation of new markets or formalization of informal markets and have excluded cases where current offerings are present even if highly dysfunctional. For example, Bridge International Academies is a startup that manages a network of low-cost private schools across East Africa; its product is better, cheaper, and in some cases life changing, but under my set of definitions it would not be categorized as a creator. Second, even after finalizing the aforementioned definitions, characterizing innovations as either creators or disruptors is still more art than science. One could argue that Fetchr (a startup you will meet later in the book that is creating a last-mile delivery supply chain

in the Middle East), which I deem a creator, is not creating a new industry but only disrupting a fragmented, informal, disaggregated industry that doesn't serve e-commerce needs. Conversely, one could argue that WeWork, excluded from the creators list, has built an entirely new category of commercial real estate (rather than disrupting existing managed space). And for some segments, companies can be creators in some markets and disruptors in others (e.g., Uber arguably created a new transportation segment in the United States with its shared taxis via UberPool and yet is disrupting taxis with UberX). See also Christensen, Raynor, and McDonald, "What Is Disruptive Innovation?"

16. Asli Demirgüç-Kunt, Leora Klapper, Dorothe Singer, Saniya Ansar, and Jake Hess, "The Global Findex Database World Bank," http://bit.ly/3a5TOzX.

17. Lisa Johnson, "Four Crucial Insights for the Future of Financial Inclusion," Accion, July 25, 2018, https://www.accion.org/4-crucial-insights-future-financial-inclusion.

18. James Manyika, Susan Lund, Marc Singer, Olivia White, and Chris Berry, "Digital Finance for All: Powering Inclusive Growth in Emerging Economies," McKinsey Global Institute, September 2016, https://mck.co/2TqAQOq.

19. Nick Hughes and Susie Lonie, "M-PESA: Mobile Money for the 'Unbanked' Turning Cellphones into 24-Hour Tellers in Kenya," *Innovations: Technology, Governance, Globalization* 2, no. 1-2 (2007), doi:10.1162/itgg.2007.2.1-2.63.

20. Safaricom Limited, "Celebrating 10 Years of Changing Lives," 2017, https://www.safaricom.co.ke/mpesa_timeline/.

21. Joshua Masinde, "Kenya's M-Pesa Platform Is So Successful Regulators Worry It Could Disrupt the Economy," Quartz Africa, December 28, 2016, https://qz.com/873525/safaricoms-m-pesa-has-kenyas-government-worried-what-happens-in-the-event-of-a-crash/.

22. Francesco Pasti, "State of the Industry Report of Mobile Money," GSMA, 2018, https://www.gsma.com/mobilefordevelopment/wp-content/uploads/2019/02/2018-State-of-the-Industry-Report-on-Mobile-Money.pdf; and Hughes and Lonie, "M-PESA: Mobile Money for the 'Unbanked.'"

23. Tavneet Suri and William Jack, "The Long-Run Poverty and Gender Impacts of Mobile Money," *Science*, December 9, 2016, science.sciencemag.org/content/354/6317/1288.full.

24. Hughes and Lonie, "M-PESA: Mobile Money for the 'Unbanked'"; and "State of the Industry Report on Mobile Money," GSMA, 2018, https://www.gsma.com/r/state-of-the-industry-report/.

25. Bitange Ndemo, "Inside a Policymaker's Mind: An Entrepreneurial Approach to Policy Development and Implementation," in *Digital Kenya: An Entrepreneurial Revolution in the Making*, eds. Bitange Ndemo and Tim Weiss (London: Palgrave Macmillan, 2017), 356.

26. William Boulding and Markus Christen, "First-Mover Disadvantage," *Harvard Business Review*, October 2001, https://hbr.org/2001/10/first-mover-disadvantage. The researchers conducted a survey of more than 350 consumer businesses and 850 industrial businesses. They determined pioneers often had sales advantages but faced longer-term cost disadvantages.

27. Fernando Suarez and Gianvito Lanzolla, "The Half-Truth of First-Mover Advantage," *Harvard Business Review*, August 2014, https://hbr.org/2005/04/the-half-truth-of-first-mover-advantage.

28. Hughes and Lonie, "M-PESA: Mobile Money for the 'Unbanked.'"

29. Ndemo, "Inside a Policymaker's Mind."

30. Peter Thiel and Blake Masters, *Zero to One: Notes on Startups, or How to Build the Future* (London: Virgin Books, 2015).

31. Ibid.

32. Peter Thiel, "Competition Is for Losers," *Wall Street Journal*, September 12, 2014, https://www.wsj.com/articles/peter-thiel-competition-is-for-losers-1410535536.

33. "Tanzania's Mobile Money Revolution," Consultative Group to Assist the Poor (CGAP), March 2015, http://www.cgap.org/research/infographic/tanzanias-mobile-money -revolution.

34. Ryan Craggs, "Where Uber Is Banned Around the World," *Condé Nast Traveler*, April 20, 2017, https://www.cntraveler.com/story/where-uber-is-banned-around-the -world.

35. "Safaricom Bets Future on Mobile Payments Mpesa," *Financial Times*, May 3, 2019, https://www.ft.com/content/5eba36aa-6d7b-11e9-80c7-60ee53e6681d?shareType=nongift.

36. Of course, data privacy and fair use of personal data are key considerations. This is a rapidly evolving conversation in the field, and standards are quickly being put in place. I believe that when done responsibly, these models are strong net positives to increasing access to affordable financial services to those who previously did not enjoy them.

37. "OkHi Launches Mobile App for Businesses to Share Their Locations with Clients," *aptantech*, December 22, 2017, http://aptantech.com/2017/12/okhi-launches-mobile -app-for-businesses-to-share-their-locations-with-clients/.

Chapter 2

1. These rates likely underestimate the cost of credit, given expensive overdraft fees. "Bank Lending Rate," *Trading Economics*, 2019, https://tradingeconomics.com/country-list/ bank-lending-rate.

2. Ibid.

3. Neil Patel, "How Mint Grew to 1.5 Million Users and Sold for $170 Million in Just 2 Years," Neil Patel Blog, https://neilpatel.com/blog/how-mint-grew/.

4. "Credit and Loan Reporting Systems in Brazil," Western Hemisphere Credit and Loan Reporting Initiative, Centre For Latin American Monetary Studies, March 2005, http://www.whcri.org/PDF/report_brazil.pdf.

5. Author interview with Ben Gleason, August 3, 2018.

6. Ibid.

7. Author interview with Inanc Balci, November 3, 2018.

8. "Our Achievements," Jumia Group, 2019, https://group.jumia.com/.

9. Author interview with David Vélez, July 24, 2018.

10. "Nubank Valuation Jumps to $10 Billion on $400 Million Mega Round," *Finextra*, July 29, 2019, https://www.finextra.com/newsarticle/34174/nubank-valuation-jumps-to-10 -billion-on-400-million-mega-round.

11. Author interview with Ben Gleason, August 3, 2018.

12. Author interview with Saed Nashef, September 26, 2018.

13. "List of Fetcher's 3 Funding Rounds from 8 Investors," Crunchbase, 2019, https:// www.crunchbase.com/search/funding_rounds/field/organizations/num_funding_rounds/ scout-technologies.

14. Marco Kusumawijaya, "Jakarta at 30 Million: My City Is Choking and Sinking—It Needs a New Plan B," *Guardian*, November 21, 2016, https://www.theguardian.com/cities/ 2016/nov/21/jakarta-indonesia-30-million-sinking-future; "Urban Expansion in East Asia—Indonesia," World Bank, January 26, 2015, http://www.worldbank.org/en/news/ feature/2015/01/26/urban-expansion-in-east-asia-indonesia; "Jakarta Population 2018," populationof2018.com, 2019, http://populationof2018.com/jakarta-population-2018.html; and Resty Woro Yuniar, "End of the Road for Southeast Asia's Bike Taxis?" *South China Morning Post*, October 1, 2017, http://www.scmp.com/week-asia/politics/article/2112922/ end-road-indonesias-motorbikes.

15. Safrin La Batu, "Police Want Brakes Put on Car Ownership," *Jakarta Post*, February 15, 2016, http://www.thejakartapost.com/news/2016/02/15/police-want-brakes-put-car -ownership.html.

16. Nick Van Mead, "The World's Worst Traffic: Can Jakarta Find an Alternative to the Car?" *Guardian*, November 26, 2017, https://www.theguardian.com/cities/2016/nov/23/world-worst-traffic-jakarta-alternative.

17. Author interview with Nadiem Makarim, August 5, 2018.

18. "Nadiem Makarim on 'High Flyers,'" Bloomberg, December 20, 2017, https://www.bloomberg.com/news/videos/2017-12-20/full-show-nadiem-makarim-on-high-flyers-10-14-video; and Ambika Chopra, "From Call Centre to the Country's First Unicorn: How Go-Jek Is Becoming a Way of Living in Indonesia," *Inc42 Media*, December 03, 2016, https://inc42.com/indonesia/indonesian-startup-ecosystem-go-jek/.

19. "Nadiem Makarim on 'High Flyers,'" Bloomberg.

20. Avantika Chilkoti, "Opening the Throttle in Indonesia," *Financial Times*, December 22, 2015, https://www.ft.com/content/d774419c-8a0f-11e5-9f8c-a8d619fa707c.

21. Author interview with Nadiem Makarim, August 5, 2018.

22. Madeleine Karlsson, Gaia Penteriani, Helen Croxson, Alexandra Stanek, Robin Miller, Darshana Pema, and Fadzai Chitiyo, "Accelerating Affordable Smartphone Ownership in Emerging Markets," GSMA, July 2017, p. 17, https://www.gsma.com/mobilefordevelopment/wp-content/uploads/2017/07/accelerating-affordable-smartphone-ownership-emerging-markets-2017.pdf.

23. Adding payments as a product or service could be considered a vertical stack integration. However, as Nadiem Makarim built the platform, the financial services offering was much broader than payments, with the ambition of offering savings and lending products as well. Therefore, it can more appropriately be considered part of the horizontal stack.

24. "Number of Monthly Active WeChat Users from 4th Quarter 2011 to 2nd Quarter 2019 (in Millions)," Statista, 2019, https://www.statista.com/statistics/255778/number-of-active-wechat-messenger-accounts/; and Xinhua, "China's Alipay Now Has over 900m Users Worldwide," *China Daily*, November 2018, http://www.chinadaily.com.cn/a/201811/30/WS5c00a1d3a310eff30328c073.html.

25. Judith Balea, "Go-Jek Buys 3 Fintech Firms to Conquer Indonesia Payments," *Tech in Asia*, December 14, 2017, https://www.techinasia.com/go-jek-acquisition-kartuku-mapan-midtrans.

26. Author interview with Nadiem Makarim, 2018.

27. "Go-Jek Acquires Three Indonesian Fintech Startups," *Digital News Asia*, December 15, 2017, https://www.digitalnewsasia.com/business/indonesia's-go-jek-acquires-three-local-fintech-startups.

28. "Gojek," Crunchbase, 2019, https://www.crunchbase.com/organization/go-jek#section-overview.

29. Author interview with Nadiem Makarim, 2018.

30. Author interview with Vijay Shekhar Sharma, September 17, 2019; and "Paytm Valuation Rose 25% to $15 Billion in Latest Round, Says Vijay Shekhar Sharma," *Business Today*, August 22, 2019, https://www.businesstoday.in/current/corporate/paytm-valuation-rose-25-pc-to-usd-15-billion/story/374415.html.

31. Mohit Mittal, "WeChat—The One App That Rules Them All," Harvard Business School Digital Initiative, October 18, 2019, https://digital.hbs.edu/innovation-disruption/wechat%E2%80%8A-%E2%80%8Athe-one-app-rules/.

32. Dennis Schaal, "Oral History of Online Travel: Ctrip's Different Path to China's Consumers," *Skift*, June 6, 2016, https://skift.com/2016/06/06/oral-history-of-online-travel-ctrips-different-path-to-chinas-consumers/.

33. "Ctrip.com International, Ltd. (CTRP)," Yahoo Finance, 2019, https://finance.yahoo.com/quote/CTRP/; and "Most Innovative Companies: Ctrip," *Fast Company*, 2019, https://www.fastcompany.com/company/ctrip.

34. Marc Andreessen, "Why Software Is Eating the World," *Wall Street Journal*, August 20, 2011, https://on.wsj.com/3aa0ZHm.

Chapter 3

1. Friday Phiri, "Zoona—Innovative Mobile Finance," CTA, June 9, 2017, http://spore .cta.int/en/dossiers/article/zoona-innovative-mobile-finance.html (accessed March 1, 2018).

2. Graham Van der Made, "Zoona Raises $15-million in Series B Funding Round, 4Di Capital On-Board," Ventureburn, August 18, 2016, http://ventureburn.com/2016/08/ zoona-raises-15-million-series-b-funding-round-4di-capital-board/.

3. "The Causes and Consequences of China's Market Crash," *Economist*, August 24, 2015, https://www.economist.com/news/business-and-finance/21662092-china-sneezing -rest-world-rightly-nervous-causes-and-consequences-chinas.

4. Grieve Chelwa, "The Charts behind Zambia's Struggling Economy and a Controversial IMF Loan," Quartz Africa, November 23, 2015, https://qz.com/557335/the-charts -behind-zambias-flailing-economy-and-a-controversial-imf-loan/.

5. "XE Currency Charts: USD to ZMW," XE, nd [updated frequently], http://www.xe .com/currencycharts/?from=USD&to=ZMW&view=5Y.

6. Cromwell Schubarth, "These 500 Startups' Pitches Stood Out on Day Dave McClure Dressed as a Unicorn," *Silicon Valley Tech Flash*, August 12, 2015, http://bit .ly/35V9CSu.

7. Aileen Lee, "Welcome to the Unicorn Club: Learning from Billion-Dollar Startups," TechCrunch, November 2, 2013, https://techcrunch.com/2013/11/02/welcome-to-the -unicorn-club/.

8. Ibid.

9. Lora Kolodny, "One of Tech's Most Successful Investors Says Silicon Valley's Unicorns Need to 'Grow Up,'" CNBC, November 17, 2017, https://www.cnbc.com/2017/11/17/ bill-gurley-unicorns-need-to-grow-up.html.

10. Sarah Frier and Eric Newcomer, "The Fuzzy, Insane Math That's Creating So Many Billion-Dollar Tech Companies," Bloomberg, March 17, 2015, https://www .bloomberg.com/news/articles/2015-03-17/the-fuzzy-insane-math-that-s-creating-so-many -billion-dollar-tech-companies; and "$1B+ Market Map: The World's 326 Unicorn Companies in One Infographic," CB Insights, March 14, 2019 [updated periodically], https:// www.cbinsights.com/research/unicorn-startup-market-map/.

11. "The Haka is a traditional war cry and dance that is seen as a challenge from the Maori people, and describes the ancestors and events from the history of the tribe. Performed by the national side before every kick-off, the dance involves the stamping of feet, slapping of hands on the body and several facial contortions involving the tongue and eyes. It generally begins with the words: 'Ka mate! Ka mate! Ka ora! Ka ora!', which means: 'I die! I die! I live! I live!'. . . The Haka is also performed across the country at funerals, weddings and in certain school presentations and celebrations," from Jordan Davies and Sam Street, "Who Leads the Haka, Is It Always the Same Song, and Why Do New Zealand Rugby Perform It Before Every Match?" *Sun*, August18, 2018 [updated October 19, 2019], https://www.thesun.co.uk/sport/3816859/haka-new-zealand-all-blacks -australia-bledisloe-cup/.

12. Paul Graham, "Startup = Growth," Paulgraham.com, September 2012, http:// www.paulgraham.com/growth.html.

13. Paul Graham, "Wealth," Paulgraham.com, May 2014, http://paulgraham.com/ wealth.html.

14. Reid Hoffman and Chris Yeh, *Blitzscaling: The Lightning-Fast Path to Building Massively Valuable Companies* (New York: Currency, 2018), p. 27.

15. Kevin Muldoon, "The Top Ten Resilient Animals on Earth," Kevinmuldoon.com, May 9, 2013, https://www.kevinmuldoon.com/resilient-animals-earth/.

16. "Magic Leap: Funding Rounds," Crunchbase, https://www.crunchbase.com/ search/funding_rounds/field/organizations/funding_total/magic-leap; and Jonathan Shieber, "Magic Leap Is Real and It's a Janky Marvel," October 9, 2018, https:// techcrunch.com/2018/10/09/magic-leap-is-real-and-its-a-janky-marvel/.

17. Joshua Franklin and Diptendu Lahiri, "Ride-Hailing Firm Lyft Launches IPO Road Show in Uber's Shadow," Reuters, March 18, 2019, https://reut.rs/2NncUrm; Lyft, Inc., Form S-1 Registration Statement, nd, http://bit.ly/36Vuz0W; and Faiz Siddiqui, "Uber Reports a $1 Billion Loss in First Quarterly Earnings after IPO," *Washington Post*, May 30, 2019, https://wapo.st/2FPnvqX.

18. Erin Griffith, "More Start-Ups Have an Unfamiliar Message for Venture Capitalists: Get Lost," *New York Times*, January 11, 2019, https://www.nytimes.com/2019/01/11/technology/start-ups-rejecting-venture-capital.html.

19. The Midas list is the industry ranking, led by *Forbes* and TrueBridge Capital Partners, ranking the industry's top deal makers (see https://www.forbes.com/midas/); and "King Midas and His Touch," Greeka, accessed November 9, 2019 https://www.greeka.com/greece-myths/king-midas/.

20. Alexandra Ludka, "Meet the New Facebook Millionaires," ABC News, May 16, 2012, https://abcnews.go.com/Technology/facebook-millionaires/story?id=15499090.

21. Julie Bort, "Twitter's IPO Created 1,600 New Millionaires and a $2.2 Billion Tax Bill, Analyst Says," *Business Insider*, November 11, 2013, http://www.businessinsider.com/twitter-ipo-created-1600-millionaires-2013-11.

22. Eric Kutcher, Olivia Nottebohm, and Kara Sprague, "Grow Fast or Die Slow," McKinsey & Company, April 2014, https://www.mckinsey.com/industries/high-tech/our-insights/grow-fast-or-die-slow.

23. Griffith, "More Start-Ups Have an Unfamiliar Message for Venture Capitalists: Get Lost."

24. Yoree Koh and Rolfe Winkler, "Venture Capitalist Sounds Alarm on Startup Investing," *Wall Street Journal*, September 15, 2014, https://www.wsj.com/articles/venture-capitalist-sounds-alarm-on-silicon-valley-risk-1410740054.

25. "Venture Pulse Q417," KPMG Enterprise, January 16, 2018, https://assets.kpmg.com/content/dam/kpmg/xx/pdf/2018/01/venture-pulse-report-q4-17.pdf.

26. Brazil's population is estimated to be about 209 million for 2017: $575 million/209 million = $2.75/per capita; and $8.5 billion/4.7 million Silicon Valley area residents = $1,809.

27. "PitchBook—NVCA Venture Monitor," pitchbook.com, April 9, 2018, https://pitchbook.com/news/reports/1q-2018-pitchbook-nvca-venture-monitor.

28. Edward J. Egan, Anne Dayton, and Diana Carranza, "The Top 100 U.S. Startup Cities in 2016," James A. Baker Institute for Public Policy of Rice University, December 2017, https://www.bakerinstitute.org/media/files/files/38132e23/mcnair-pub-rankinguscities-122117.pdf.

29. "Startup Burn Accelerates After Series A Funding," CB Insights, November 7, 2014, https://www.cbinsights.com/research/days-between-funding-rounds/.

30. "PitchBook—NVCA Venture Monitor." The US West Coast represents 60 percent of deal value (investments) and 40 percent of deal amount. The rest of the United States is the opposite. A similar dynamic is playing out in emerging markets.

31. Endeavor, Endeavor OPEN survey results, 2018.

32. "Global Restructuring & Insolvency Guide 2016," Baker McKenzie, 2016, p. 236, http://bit.ly/3a5Ug17.

33. James B. Stewart, "A Fearless Culture Fuels U.S. Tech Giants," *New York Times*, June 18, 2015, https://www.nytimes.com/2015/06/19/business/the-american-way-of-tech-and-europes.html.

34. Author interview with Mike Evans, February 21, 2019.

35. Connie Loizos, "A Quick Look at How Series A and Seed Rounds Have Ballooned in Recent Years, Fueled by Top Investors," April 25, 2019, https://techcrunch.com/2019/04/25/a-quick-look-at-how-fast-series-a-and-seed-rounds-have-ballooned-in-recent-years-fueled-by-top-investors/.

36. "Overview: Door Dash," Crunchbase, 2019, https://www.crunchbase.com/organization/doordash.

37. Author interview with Mike Evans, 2019.

38. "Grubhub Reports Record Fourth-Quarter Results," Grubhub, February 8, 2018, https://investors.grubhub.com/investors/press-releases/press-release-details/2018/Grubhub-Reports-Record-Fourth-Quarter-Results/default.aspx.

39. "Grubhub Stock Profile," Google Finance, as of August 9, 2019, http://bit.ly/3adaB3R.

40. Author interview with Mike Evans, 2019.

41. Author interview with Monica Brand Engel, May 9, 2019, in-person.

42. "2018 Chicago VC Ecosystem," Chicago Venture Summit, 2018, https://files.pitchbook.com/website/files/pdf/2018_Chicago_Venture_Ecosystem_AHH.pdf.

43. Neil Patel, "90% of Startups Fail: Here's What You Need to Know About the 10%," *Forbes*, January 16, 2015, https://www.forbes.com/sites/neilpatel/2015/01/16/90-of-startups-will-fail-heres-what-you-need-to-know-about-the-10/#60caed7b6679; and Erin Griffith, "Why Startups Fail, According to Their Founders," *Fortune*, September 25, 2014, http://fortune.com/2014/09/25/why-startups-fail-according-to-their-founders/.

44. Anne S. Habiby and Deirdre M. Coyle Jr., "The High-Intensity Entrepreneur," *Harvard Business Review*, September 2010, https://hbr.org/2010/09/the-high-intensity-entrepreneur.

45. Author interview with Troy Henikoff, March 12, 2019.

46. Author interview with Jason Fried, April 10, 2019.

47. "State of Salaries Report," *Hired*, 2018, https://hired.com/state-of-salaries-2018; and "Compensation Research," PayScale, nd, https://www.payscale.com/data.

48. Maya Kosoff, "The Era of Silicon Valley Giving Away Free Stuff Is Coming to an End," *Vanity Fair*, May 18, 2016, https://www.vanityfair.com/news/2016/05/the-era-of-silicon-valley-giving-away-free-stuff-is-coming-to-an-end.

49. Sarah Kessler, "Meal-Kit Customers Dine and Dash," *Fast Company*, October 20, 2016, https://www.fastcompany.com/3064792/meal-kit-customers-dine-and-dash.

50. Kosoff, "The Era of Silicon Valley Giving Away Free Stuff Is Coming to an End."

51. David Mehegan, "Dan Ariely: Learning to Ward Off Those Bad Decisions," *New York Times*, March 2018, https://www.nytimes.com/2008/03/19/health/19iht-ariel.1.11252785.html.

52. Author interview with Mike Evans, 2019.

53. Author interview with Keith Davies, October 25, 2018.

54. Author interview with Ryan Smith, March 27, 2019.

55. "Overview of Qualtrics," Crunchbase, 2019, https://www.crunchbase.com/organization/qualtrics#section-overview.

56. Tim O'Reilly, "The Fundamental Problem with Silicon Valley's Favorite Growth Strategy," Quartz, February 5, 2019, https://qz.com/1540608/the-problem-with-silicon-valleys-obsession-with-blitzscaling-growth/.

57. Hiten Shah, "How an Anti-Growth Mentality Helped Basecamp Grow to Over 2 Million Customers," FYI, 2019, https://usefyi.com/basecamp-history/.

58. Author interview with Keith Davies, 2018.

59. Omidyar Network [Arjuna Costa], "This Investor Shares How to Weather a Crisis and Come Out Stronger," Omidyar Network Blog, October 14, 2016, https://www.omidyar.com/blog/investor-shares-how-weather-crisis-and-come-out-stronger.

60. Author interview with Sujay Tyle, December 10, 2018.

61. James de Villiers, "Meet the 24-Year-Old American Prodigy Set to Disrupt SA's Used Car Industry—Within the Next Two Years," *Business Insider South Africa*, July 1, 2018, https://www.businessinsider.co.za/24-year-old-sujay-tyle-largest-second-hand-car-dealer-south-africa-naspers-frontier-car-group-2018-6.

62. "Frontier Car Group," Crunchbase, https://www.crunchbase.com/organization/frontier-cars-group#section-overview.

63. Author interview with Ella Gudwin, December 19, 2018.

64. Tarun Khanna and Krishna G. Palepu, "Why Focused Strategies May Be Wrong for Emerging Markets," *Harvard Business Review*, July–August 1997, https://hbr.org/1997/07/why-focused-strategies-may-be-wrong-for-emerging-markets.

65. Ibid.

66. Eskor John, "Developing Strategies to Harness the Power of Parallel Entrepreneurship in Africa," in Bitange Ndemo and Tim Weiss, eds., *Digital Kenya: An Entrepreneurial Revolution in the Making* (London: Palgrave Macmillan, 2017).

67. Internal analysis of leading startups across Sub-Saharan Africa, India, Latin America, and Silicon Valley.

68. Dana Olsen, "US Venture Capital Activity So Far This Year in 15 Charts," Pitch-Book, July 18, 2018, https://pitchbook.com/news/articles/us-venture-capital-activity-so-far-this-year-in-15-charts.

69. Author interview with Ryan Smith, 2019.

70. Author interview with Achmad Zaky, June 18, 2019.

71. Author interview with Mike Evans, 2019.

72. Paul Martino "It's Not You, It's the Post-Seed Gap," TechCrunch, December 13, 2016, https://techcrunch.com/2016/12/13/its-not-you-its-the-post-seed-gap/.

73. https://www.zebrasunite.com/.

Chapter 4

1. "Steve Jobs: Biography," Biography.com, April 27, 2017 [updated August 21, 2019], https://www.biography.com/business-figure/steve-jobs; Darren Marble, "Jeff Bezos Quit His Job at 30 to Launch Amazon—Here Are the 3 Simple Strategies He Used to Do It," *Inc.*, March 27, 2018, https://www.inc.com/darren-marble/jeff-bezos-quit-his-job-at-30-to-launch-amazon-heres-how-to-know-if-its-right-time-for-your-big-move.html; Tom Huddleston Jr., "What Microsoft Billionaire Bill Gates Was Doing at 20 Years Old," CNBC, March 29, 2018 [updated April 9, 2018], https://www.cnbc.com/2018/03/29/what-microsoft-billionaire-bill-gates-was-doing-at-20-years-old.html; and Evan Tarver, "Mark Zuckerberg Success Story: Net Worth, Education and Influence," Investopedia, July 30, 2018, https://www.investopedia.com/articles/personal-finance/081315/mark-zuckerberg-success-story-net-worth-education-top-quotes.asp.

2. The data points in this chapter on the number of founders who attended undergraduate and graduate universities outside their home countries; gained strategy consulting, investment banking, and management and technical expertise at global companies; worked at well-known tech startups; founded companies at a given age; participated in startup accelerators; are members of global entrepreneurship organizations; and have returned to their home countries after spending time in Silicon Valley and other influential startup centers, was gathered from public sources including LinkedIn, Crunchbase, Bloomberg, and news articles. In cases where the founder's exact birthdate was not available, I made an educated guess based on undergraduate and graduate school graduation dates. In the case of Latin America's founders, data on age or graduation dates was available for forty-seven of the forty-nine founders.

3. Alice Haine, "Generation Start-up: Funding Was 'Petrifying' in the Early Days, Says Fetchr Founder," *National*, September 4, 2017, https://www.thenational.ae/business/economy/generation-start-up-funding-was-petrifying-in-the-early-days-says-fetchr-founder-1.625104.

4. "Accelerating Status in Emerging Markets: Insights from 43 Programs," Global Accelerator Learning Initiative, May 2017, http://bit.ly/2TpERCW.

5. Analysis via publicly available data.

6. I refer to the founders of Grab, Garena, Lazada, Gojek, Tokopedia, Traveloka, and Bukalapak. The statistic was derived by finding the total number of co-founders for

whom information about education or previous work experience was publicly available. For the purposes of the data, international experience was defined by our team as five or more years of studying or working outside one's home country. According to our data on Latin America, thirty-three of the forty-seven co-founders had international experience.

7. This statistic was derived by finding the number of selected startups across the five frontier markets for which information about joining an accelerator was publicly available. The global accelerators used in the calculation include 1,776 ventures, Fabrica de Startups, Girl Affect Accelerator, Google Launchpad, GSMA Ecosystem Accelerator, New Economy Accelerator, Rocket Internet, Runway Incubator, Spring Accelerator, and USAID. Of the sample, fourteen of the sixty-four startups participated in a global accelerator program.

8. Alex Lazarow, "The Innovation Supply Chain: How Ideas Traverse Continents and Transform Economies," TechCrunch, November 27, 2018, https://techcrunch.com/2018/11/27/the-innovation-supply-chain-how-ideas-traverse-continents-and-transform-economies/.

9. Alexandre Lazarow and Nicolas du Cray, "Where East Meets West: Consumer Fintech at a Crossroads," LinkedIn Publishing, December 18, 2018, https://www.linkedin.com/pulse/where-east-meets-west-consumer-fintech-crossroads-lazarow-cfa/.

10. "Get more Uber When You Use Uber," accessed November 6, 2019, https://www.uber.com/c/uber-credit-card/.

11. Dara Khosrowshahi, "An Operating System for Everyday Life," Uber Newsroom, September 27, 2019, https://www.uber.com/newsroom/everyday-life-os/?from=timeline&isappinstalled=0.

12. Author interview with JF Gauthier, August 28, 2018.

13. Rhett Morris and Lili Török, "Fostering Productive Entrepreneurship Communities," Endeavor Insight, October 2018, https://endeavor.org/content/uploads/2015/06/Fostering-Productive-Entrepreneurship-Communities.pdf.

14. T. E. Narasimhan and Swati Garg, "Booming Biz of Online Marriages," *Business Standard*, January 20, 2013, https://www.business-standard.com/article/companies/booming-biz-of-online-marriages-111122200022_1.html.

15. "India's BharatMatrimony Ushers in New Era of Arranged Marriages," BBC News, May 4, 2011, https://www.bbc.com/news/business-13144028.

16. Author interview with Murugavel Janakiraman, December 13, 2018.

17. Narasimhan and Garg, "Booming Biz of Online Marriages."

18. Anisha Baghudana, "From Bharatmatrimony to Bharatmatrimon(e)y!" The HBS Case Method, March 09, 2015, https://hbs.me/2FLJ7EG; "Overview: Matrimony.com," Crunchbase, 2019, https://www.crunchbase.com/organization/matrimony-com#section-ipo-stock-price; and author interview with Murugavel Janakiraman, December 13, 2018.

19. Author nterview with Mudassir Sheikha, December 17, 2018.

20. Ainsley Harris, "Bros Dominate VC, Where 91% of Decision-Makers Are Male," *Fast Company*, March 7, 2018, https://www.fastcompany.com/40540948/91-of-decision-makers-at-u-s-venture-capital-firms-are-men.

21. Gené Teare, "In 2017, Only 17% of Startups Have a Female Founder," TechCrunch, April 19, 2017, https://techcrunch.com/2017/04/19/in-2017-only-17-of-startups-have-a-female-founder/.

22. Mary Ann Azevedo, "Untapped Opportunity: Minority Founders Still Being Overlooked," February 27, 2019, https://news.crunchbase.com/news/untapped-opportunity-minority-founders-still-being-overlooked/.

23. Collin West and Gopinath Sundaramurthy, "Startups With At Least 1 Female Founder Hire 2.5x More Women," October 17, 2019, https://www.kauffmanfellows.org/journal_posts/female_founders_hire_more_women.

24. Christopher M. Schroeder, "A Different Story from the Middle East: Entrepreneurs Building an Arab Tech Economy," *MIT Technology Review*, August 3, 2017, https://www.technologyreview.com/s/608468/a-different-story-from-the-middle-east-entrepreneurs-building-an-arab-tech-economy/.

25. Ibid.

26. Iain Thomas, "The Next Hemingway Is Flipping Burgers," *Huffington Post*, August 13, 2015, https://www.huffingtonpost.com/iain-s-thomas/the-next-hemingway-is-fli_b_7982800.html.

27. Lin-Manuel Miranda, "Yorktown (The World Upside Down)," from the musical *Hamilton*, Original Broadway Cast Recording, July 8, 2016.

28. Dinah Wisenberg Brin, "Immigrants Form 25% of New U.S. Businesses, Driving Entrepreneurship in 'Gateway' States," July 31, 2018, https://www.forbes.com/sites/dinahwisenberg/2018/07/31/immigrant-entrepreneurs-form-25-of-new-u-s-business-researchers/#4cf713ac713b.

29. Morris and Török, "Fostering Productive Entrepreneurship Communities."

30. Vivek Wadhwa, "Silicon Valley Can't Be Copied," *MIT Technology Review*, July 3, 2013, https://www.technologyreview.com/s/516506/silicon-valley-cant-be-copied/; and Wisenberg Brin, "Immigrants Form 25% of New U.S. Businesses."

31. Stuart Anderson, "Immigrants and Billion-Dollar Companies," National Foundation for American Policy, October 2018, http://bit.ly/2tjqchF.

32. Author interview with Jeremy Johnson, September 5, 2018.

33. Hannah Kuchler, "Silicon Valley Ageism: 'They Were, Like, Wow, You Use Twitter?'" *Financial Times*, July 30, 2017, https://on.ft.com/2None2w; and Karen Wickre, "Surviving as an Old in the Tech World," *Wired*, August 2, 2017, https://www.wired.com/story/surviving-as-an-old-in-the-tech-world/.

34. In this dataset, the age of venture capital–backed founders skewed younger, but at thirty-nine years, it is still meaningfully older than the stereotype. Pierre Azoulay, Benjamin Jones, J. Daniel Kim, and Javier Miranda, "Age and High-Growth Entrepreneurship," NBER Working Paper No. 24489, April 2018, https://www.nber.org/papers/w24489.

35. Morris and Török, "Fostering Productive Entrepreneurship Communities."

36. Pierre Azoulay, Benjamin Jones, J. Daniel Kim, and Javier Miranda, "Research: The Average Age of a Successful Startup Founder Is 45," hbr.org, July 11, 2018, https://hbr.org/2018/07/research-the-average-age-of-a-successful-startup-founder-is-45; and Azoulay et al., "Age and High-Growth Entrepreneurship."

Chapter 5

1. "Gross Domestic Product, 3rd Quarter 2018 (Advance Estimate)," Bureau of Economic Analysis, press release, October 26, 2018, https://www.bea.gov/news/2018/gross-domestic-product-3rd-quarter-2018-advance-estimate.

2. Analysis based on public data.

3. Catherine Shu, "Garena Rebrands to Sea and Raises $550 Million More to Focus on Indonesian E-commerce," TechCrunch, May 7, 2017, https://techcrunch.com/2017/05/07/sea-change/.

4. Analysis based on publicly available data.

5. Sample of top startups in SSA identified based on interviews with ten Africa-focused investors. Sample includes Interswitch, OGE/Zola, Jumia Group, Fundamo, Takealot.com, Andela, AgriProtein, Twiga Foods, M-KOPA, Konga.com, Bridge International Academies, Zoona, and African Leadership University.

6. Georgeta Gheorghe, "The Story of UiPath—How Did It Become Romania's First Unicorn?" *Business Review*, September 4, 2018, http://business-review.eu/news/the-story-of-uipath-how-it-became-romanias-first-unicorn-164248.

7. As the global client roster grew larger, UiPath eventually moved the sales headquarters to New York to be more proximate to its clientele, although it kept the product and technology development centered in Bucharest. Author interview with Daniel Dines, March 14, 2019.

8. "Romanian Tech Startup UiPath Raises USD 30 Mln to Develop Intelligent Software Robots," *Romania Insider*, April 27, 2017, https://www.romania-insider.com/romanian-tech-startup-uipath-raises-usd-30-mln-develop-intelligent-software-robots/; and "UiPath: Our Investors," UiPath, https://www.uipath.com/company/investors.

9. "UiPath Raises $225 Million Series C Led by CapitalG and Sequoia," UiPath, September 18, 2018, http://bit.ly/2ToGf8Q.

10. Author interview with Daniel Dines, March 14, 2019.

11. Michael Rennie, "Born Global," *McKinsey Quarterly*, No. 4, Autumn 1993, https://www.questia.com/library/journal/1G1-15424561/born-global.

12. This was referred to as the Uppsala model. Gary Knight and S. Cavusgil, "The Born Global Firm: A Challenge to Traditional Internationalization Theory," *Advances in International Marketing* 8 (1996): 11–26.

13. Ibid. Referred to as "psychic distance."

14. Erind Hoti, "An Overview of Success Factors of Born-Global SMEs in an Emerging Market Context," *Macrotheme Review*, Winter 2015, http://bit.ly/2NGpjHh.

15. Author interview with Daniel Dines, UiPathForward 2018, interviewed by Dave Vellante and Stu Miniman, theCube, YouTube, October 4, 2018, https://www.youtube.com/watch?v=R_JDK68TQ0g.

16. Author interview with Divyank Turakhia, December 9, 2018.

17. Ibid.

18. Nicolas Colin, "The Digital World Is Not a Flat Circle: The Family Papers #001," *Salon*, October 23, 2015, https://salon.thefamily.co/the-digital-world-is-not-a-flat-circle-e5a6a27bbe8.

19. Victoria Ho, "Uber Comes to Asia, Starts Trials in Singapore," TechCrunch, January 30, 2013, https://techcrunch.com/2013/01/30/uber-starts-trials-in-singapore/; and Avery Hartmans and Paige Leskin, "The History of How Uber Became the Most Feared Startup in the World to Its Massive IPO," *Business Insider*, May 18, 2019, https://www.businessinsider.com/ubers-history.

20. Alex Hern, "Uber Reverses Out of China with $7bn Sale to Didi Chuxing," *Guardian*, August 2016, https://www.theguardian.com/technology/2016/aug/01/uber-china-didi-chuxing.

21. "Cloud Growth Rate Increased Again in Q1; Amazon Maintains Market Share Dominance," Synergy Research Group, April 27, 2018, https://www.srgresearch.com/articles/cloud-growth-rate-increased-again-q1-amazon-maintains-market-share-dominance.

22. Alex Lazarow, "Fintech Used to Be a Local Game: Today It Can Be Global," *Forbes*, May 29, 2019, https://www.forbes.com/sites/alexlazarow/2019/05/29/fintech-used-to-be-a-local-game-today-it-can-be-global/#30ccc4d04756.

23. Author interview with Alejandro Cantú, August 1, 2018.

24. Author interview with Fadi Ghandour, January 3, 2019.

25. Author interview with Fadi Ghandour, August 8, 2018.

26. The 2017 GDP per capita was US$936 in Tanzania, and US$750 in Rwanda, whereas it was US$1,662 in Cote d'Ivoire and US$1,641 in Ghana, per the World Bank, https://data.worldbank.org/country. In 2016, the percentage of population with access to electricity grew to around 30% in Tanzania and Rwanda, while the figure was 64% in Cote d'Ivoire and 79% in Ghana.

27. "Kiva by the Numbers," 2019, https://www.kiva.org/about.

28. Author interview with Matt Flannery, September 4, 2018.

29. Louis Pasteur, Forbes Quotes, https://www.forbes.com/quotes/6145/.

Chapter 6

1. Isis Gaddis, Jacques Morisset, and Waly Wane, "Only 14% of Tanzanians Have Electricity: What Can Be Done?" World Bank Blogs, October 31, 2012, http://blogs.worldbank.org/africacan/only-14-of-tanzanians-have-electricity-what-can-be-done.

2. Financial Post, "'A Giant Leap Backward': Yahoo Boss Marissa Mayer Under Fire for Banning Employees from Working from Home," February 26, 2013, https://business.financialpost.com/productive-conversations/a-giant-leap-backward-marissa-mayer-under-fire-for-banning-employees-from-working-from-home.

3. Many authors have explored the subject of distributed team models. For example, Anupam Rastogi, "Are Distributed Teams the New Cloud for Startups?" Medium, December 11, 2018, https://medium.com/@anupamr/distributed-teams-are-the-new-cloud-for-startups-14240a9822d7; and Gerry Claps, "The Difference Between Remote and Distributed Teams in Startups," https://www.blossom.co/blog/remote-versus-distributed-teams.

4. Rastogi, "Are Distributed Teams the New Cloud for Startups?"

5. Ibid.

6. Author interview with Ruzwana Bashir, May 8, 2019.

7. Author interview with Dalton Wright, January 22, 2019.

8. Author interview with Wade Foster, April 30, 2019.

9. Patrick Gorman, "Zapier CEO Wade Foster on Managing a 100% Remote Workforce," *Chief Executive*, October 31, 2018, https://chiefexecutive.net/zapier-ceo-wade-foster-on-managing-a-100-remote-workforce/.

10. Brie Reynolds, "Remote Companies Have More Women Leaders, and These Are Hiring," Remote.co, November 6, 2017, https://remote.co/remote-companies-have-more-women-leaders-these-are-hiring/.

11. Ibid.

12. Zachary Crockett, "Life in the Silicon Prairie: Tech's Great Migration to the Midwest," *Hustle*, June 9, 2018, https://thehustle.co/life-in-the-silicon-prairie-techs-great-migration-to-the-midwest/.

13. Ibid.

14. "Good Design Is Good for Business," https://www.invisionapp.com/about.

15. Rachel Starnes, "Building InVision Studio with a Fully Remote Team," InVision Design, December 11, 2017, https://www.invisionapp.com/inside-design/studio-remote-design-team/.

16. "About InVisionApp," Crunchbase, 2019, https://www.crunchbase.com/organization/invisionapp#section-overview.

17. Author interview with Jasper Malcolmson, March 26, 2019.

18. Ibid.

19. Author interview with Kevin Fishner, September 6, 2019. See also Ron Miller, "HashiCorp Scores $100m Investment on a $1.9 Billion Valuation," TechCrunch, November 1, 2018, https://techcrunch.com/2018/11/01/hashicorp-scores-100m-investment-on-1-9-billion-valuation/.

20. Author interview with Wade Foster, 2019.

21. Author interview with Jason Fried, April 10, 2019.

22. Author interview with Matt Flannery, September 4, 2018.

23. Author interview with Jason Fried, 2019.

24. Author interview with Mark Frein, November 1, 2019.

25. Globant 10-K, via SEC. Market capitalization via Google Finance, http://bit.ly/3aMAacs.

26. Author interview with Martin Migoya, May 6, 2019.

27. Ibid.

28. Ibid.

29. Starnes, "Building InVision Studio with a Fully Remote Team."

30. Author interview with Kevin Fishner, 2019.

31. Author interview with Mark Frein, November 1, 2019.

32. Gorman, "Zapier CEO Wade Foster on Managing a 100% Remote Workforce."

33. "The 8 Reasons That Video Conferencing Is Better Than In-Person Conferencing," IPRO, October 2, 2017, https://www.ipromedia.us/8-reasons-video-conferencing -better-person-conferencing/.

34. Examples include Zoom for videoconferencing, Slack for asynchronous chat, Trello for task management, GitHub for software development, LastPass for password management, and DocuSign for signatures, among many others.

35. Alison Griswold, "A Nearly Complete List of the 238 Places That Bid for Amazon's Next Headquarters," Quartz, November 4, 2017, https://qz.com/1119945/a-nearly -complete-list-of-the-238-places-that-bid-for-amazons-next-headquarters/; and "Amazon Selects New York City and Northern Virginia for New Headquarters," Day One, Amazon Press Release, November 13, 2018, https://blog.aboutamazon.com/company-news/amazon -selects-new-york-city-and-northern-virginia-for-new-headquarters.

36. Mark Niesse, "City of Amazon Proposed to Attract Company's HQ2 to Georgia," *Atlanta Journal Constitution*, October 3, 2017, http://bit.ly/2u0XSk8.

37. Shirin Ghaffary, "Even Tech Workers Can't Afford to Buy Homes in San Francisco," Vox, March 19, 2019, https://www.vox.com/2019/3/19/18256378/tech-worker-afford -buy-homes-san-francisco-facebook-google-uber-lyft-housing-crisis-programmers.

38. Marc Emmer, "Technology Companies Are Leaving Silicon Valley in Droves: Here's Where They're Going," *Inc.*, September 25, 2018, https://www.inc.com/marc -emmer/technology-companies-are-leaving-silicon-valley-in-droves-heres-where-theyre -going.html.

39. "Remote Work by the Numbers," Simple Texting, March 30, 2018, https:// simpletexting.com/remote-work-statistics/.

40. Hailley Griffis, "State of Remote Work 2018 Report: What It's Like to Be a Remote Worker in 2018," Buffer, 2019, https://open.buffer.com/state-remote-work-2018/ #companies.

41. Mary Meeker, "Internet Trends Report 2019," June 11, 2019, https://www.bondcap .com/pdf/Internet_Trends_2019.pdf.

42. Rastogi, "Are Distributed Teams the New Cloud for Startups?"

43. Boris Wertz, "Changing the Narrative on Distributed Teams in Silicon Valley," Medium, August 7, 2018, https://medium.com/@bwertz/changing-the-narrative-on -distributed-teams-in-silicon-valley-bc55c5e619b1.

44. INSEAD, "Innovating Without Fear," *INSEAD Alumni Magazine*, July 10, 2017, https://alumnimagazine.insead.edu/innovating-without-fear/; and Sramana Mitra, "From Startup to 500 Million Dollars: VistaPrint CEO Robert Keane (Part 2)," One Million by One Million Blog, June 25, 2009, https://www.sramanamitra.com/2009/06/25/wwfrom -startup-to-500-million-vistaprint-ceo-robert-keane-part-2/.

45. Author interview with Robert Keane, March 8, 2019.

46. Ibid.

47. http://bit.ly/2Rfxifg; TV Mahalingam, "How Nilesh Parwani Leveraged Internet and Lured Vistaprint into India," *Economic Times*, January 20, 2013, https:// economictimes.indiatimes.com/news/company/corporate-trends/how-nilesh-parwani -leveraged-internet-and-lured-vistaprint-into-india/articleshow/18092814.cms; and Jason Keith and Jeff Esposito, "Vistaprint Expands Global Presence into Australia," CNN Money, August 5, 2010, https://money.cnn.com/news/newsfeeds/articles/marketwire/ 0648420.htm.

48. Sara Castellanos, "Cimpress, Formerly Vistaprint, to Leave Lexington HQ This Year," *Boston Business Journal*, July 22, 2015, https://www.bizjournals.com/boston/blog/techflash/2015/07/cimpress-formerly-vistaprint-to-leave-lexington-hq.html.

49. Author interview with Robert Keane, March 8, 2019.

Chapter 7

1. *The Social Network*, Box Office Mojo (synopsis and statistics), https://www.boxoffice mojo.com/movies/?id=socialnetwork.htm.

2. Apple, https://www.apple.com/job-creation/; "Number of Tesla Employees from July 2010 to December 2018," Statista, 2019, https://www.statista.com/statistics/314768/number -of-tesla-employees/; SpaceX, http://www.spacex.com/about; and "Number of Full-Time Facebook Employees from 2004 to 2018," Statista, https://www.statista.com/statistics/273563/number-of-facebook-employees/.

3. Stanford University, "Facts 2018," http://facts.stanford.edu/academics/graduate -profile; "Facts and Figures," Berkeley Engineering, 2019, https://engineering.berkeley .edu/about/facts-and-figures; "Occupational Employment and Wages, May 2018: 15-1111 Computer and Information Research Scientists," Bureau of Labor Statistics, 2019, https:// www.bls.gov/oes/current/oes151111.htm#(1); and "Occupational Employment and Wages, May 2018: 15-1132 Software Developers, Applications," Bureau of Labor Statistics, 2019, https://www.bls.gov/oes/current/oes151132.htm#st.

4. "Stanford Entrepreneurship Management Courses," Stanford Graduate School of Business, https://www.gsb.stanford.edu/stanford-community/entrepreneurship/management-courses.

5. Suhas Motwani, "The 15 Best Associate and Rotational Product Manager Programs," Medium, August 27, 2018, https://medium.com/pminsider/product-management -digest-apm-3c2631683139._

6. Silicon Valley Product Management Association, https://svpma.org/about/.

7. Michael Booz, "These 3 Industries Have the Highest Talent Turnover Rates," LinkedIn Talent Blog, March 2018, https://business.linkedin.com/talent-solutions/blog/trends-and-research/2018/the-3-industries-with-the-highest-turnover-rates.

8. Katie Hafner, "Google Options Make Masseuse a Multimillionaire," *New York Times*, November 12, 2007, https://www.nytimes.com/2007/11/12/technology/12google.html.

9. *The Alliance* outlines different types of alliances. "Tours of duty" refers to shorter-term "single deployments," focused on completing specific finite missions. Some are "rotational" for entry-level employees and are two to four years. "Foundational" tours are for those whose lives are more closely linked to the success of the company and thus longer term. "Transformational" tours are negotiated one-on-one with the employer, and both the employee and the employer are "transformed" through the project. Reid Hoffman, Chris Yeh, and Ben Casnocha, *The Alliance: Managing Talent in the Networked Age* (Boston: Harvard Business Review Press, 2014).

10. Author interview with Josh Simair, October 26, 2018.

11. Ibid.

12. Survey administered to readers of *[99%Tech]*, my personal newsletter, and to students in the Stanford Graduate School of Business, Harvard Business School, Haas School of Business, and Wharton School of Business entrepreneurship groups, as well as individual outreach to operators and investors in emerging markets.

13. "The Human Capital Crisis: How Social Enterprises Can Find the Talent to Scale," Rippleworks report, 2016, http://bit.ly/2uME8RL; author interview with Doug Galen, January 24, 2019; and Will Gaybrick, "Tech's Ultimate Success: Software Developers Are Now More Valuable to Companies Than Money," CNBC, September 6, 2018, https://www.cnbc.com/2018/09/06/companies-worry-more-about-access-to-software -developers-than-capital.html.

14. "Future Undergraduate Students: Department Overview," University of Manitoba, 2019, http://umanitoba.ca/faculties/engineering/departments/ece/pros_students/undergrad/index.html.

15. "The Human Capital Crisis: How Social Enterprises Can Find the Talent to Scale."

16. Ian Duncan, "Research Reveals University Degree Holders Can Take Five Years to Get a Job," UReport, July 7, 2017, https://www.standardmedia.co.ke/ureport/story/2001246480/reserach-reveals-university-degree-holders-can-take-five-years-to-get-a-job.

17. Author interview with Amanda Lannert, April 15, 2019.

18. Tristin Hopper, "Mars and the North Pole Are Warmer Than Winnipeg: A Guide to How Damned Cold It Is," *National Post*, December 27, 2017, https://nationalpost.com/news/canada/mars-and-the-north-pole-are-warmer-than-winnipeg-a-guide-to-how-damned-cold-it-is.

19. Author interview with Josh Simair, October 26, 2018.

20. Author interview with Josh Simair, 2018; and Sean Silkoff, "Winnipeg Startup SkipTheDishes Gobbled Up by Britain's Just Eat," *Globe and Mail*, December 15, 2016, https://www.theglobeandmail.com/technology/winnipeg-startup-skipthedishes-purchased-by-britains-just-eat/article33341734/.

21. Michael Lewis, *Moneyball: The Art of Winning an Unfair Game* (New York: W. W. Norton, 2003).

22. Author interview with Josh Simair, 2008.

23. "Seed Round—Shortlist—2017-09-19," Crunchbase, https://www.crunchbase.com/funding_round/shortlist-5-seed--3837ea6c#section-lead-investors; and author interview with Paul Breloff, June 6, 2019.

24. Jean-Michel Lemieux, "Dev Degree—A Big Bet on Software Education," Shopify, September 24, 2018, https://engineering.shopify.com/blogs/engineering/dev-degree-a-big-bet-on-software-education.

25. "Dev Degree: Overview," Dev Degree, https://www.devdegree.ca/dev-degree-model.

26. Author interview with Jean-Michel Lemieux, May 10, 2019.

27. Lemieux, "Dev Degree—A Big Bet on Software Education."

28. Author interview with Jean-Michel Lemieux, 2019.

29. "Shopify's Dev Degree Expands to York University," Shopify, September 24, 2018, https://news.shopify.com/shopifys-dev-degree-expands-to-york-university.

30. V. Kasturi Rangan and Katharine Lee, "Bridge International Academies: A School in a Box," Harvard Business School Case 511-064, October 2010 (revised April 2013), https://www.hbs.edu/faculty/Pages/item.aspx?num=39462.

31. Author interview with Brittany Forsyth, April 24, 2019.

32. Jing Cao, "IBM Paid $1.3 Billion to Acquire Cleversafe in Hybrid-Cloud Push," Bloomberg, February 23, 2016, https://www.bloomberg.com/news/articles/2016-02-24/ibm-paid-1-3-billion-to-acquire-cleversafe-in-hybrid-cloud-push.

33. Author interview with Chris Gladwin, April 12, 2019.

34. William Craig, "The Importance of Having a Mission-Driven Company," *Forbes*, May 15, 2018, https://www.forbes.com/sites/williamcraig/2018/05/15/the-importance-of-having-a-mission-driven-company/#1ed687983a9c.

35. Zameena Mejia, "Nearly 9 out of 10 Millennials Would Consider Taking a Pay Cut to Get This," CNBC, June 28, 2018, https://www.cnbc.com/2018/06/27/nearly-9-out-of-10-millennials-would-consider-a-pay-cut-to-get-this.html.

36. Author interview with David Levine, February 15, 2019.

37. Ibid.

38. Author interview with Josh Simair, 2018.

39. Of course, there are multiple dynamics at play here. Employees are less likely to demand stock options, but at the same time management is less likely to offer them. Dominic Jacquesson, "Introducing Our Guide to Stock Options for European Entre-

preneurs," Index Ventures, December 4, 2018, https://www.indexventures.com/blog/introducing-our-guide-to-stock-options-for-european-entrepreneurs.

40. Author interview with Lyndsay Handler, November 11, 2018.

41. Ibid.

Chapter 8

1. "Mixed Martial Arts," *Encyclopedia Britannica*, 2019, https://www.britannica.com/sports/mixed-martial-arts.

2. Jenny Flinn, "The Rise and Rise of Ultimate Fighting (and Why Boxing Is Now So Passé)," *Conversation*, March 9, 2016, https://theconversation.com/the-rise-and-rise-of-ultimate-fighting-and-why-boxing-is-now-so-passe-55910.

3. Charlotte Edwardes, "Ali Parsa: The Former Refugee Bringing Algorithms to Healthcare," *Evening Standard*, July 12, 2018, https://www.standard.co.uk/futurelondon/health/ali-parsa-the-former-refugee-bringing-algorithms-to-healthcare-a3885941.html.

4. Ibid.

5. NHS Support Federation, "Circle Health," nd, https://www.nhsforsale.info/private-providers/circle-new/.

6. Edwardes, "Ali Parsa: The Former Refugee Bringing Algorithms to Healthcare."

7. "Babylon Health Services," Babylon, https://www.babylonhealth.com/product.

8. Aliya Ram, "Babylon Signs Tencent Deal to Deploy Health Technology on WeChat," *Financial Times*, April 05, 2018, https://www.ft.com/content/40fae194-381d-11e8-8eee-e06bde01c544.

9. "Babylon Health: Rwanda Case Study," Babylon Health, 2019, https://marketing-assets.babylonhealth.com/business/Rwanda-Case-Study.pdf.

10. Ingrid Lunden, "Babylon Health Confirms $550m Raise at $2+ Billion Valuation to Expand Its AI-Based Health Services," TechCrunch, August 2, 2019, https://techcrunch.com/2019/08/02/babylon-health-confirms-550m-raise-to-expand-its-ai-based-health-services-to-the-us-and-asia.

11. A. H. Maslow, "A Theory of Human Motivation," *Psychological Review* 50, no. 4 (1943), 370–396.

12. Ibid.

13. "Accelerating Status in Emerging Markets: Insights from 43 Programs," Global Accelerator Learning Initiative, May 2017, http://bit.ly/38hmWT9.

14. "Capital Evolving: Alternative Investment Strategies to Drive Inclusive Innovation," Village Capital, 2018. The report states, "This number was derived from the CB Insights dataset and is current as of 10.12.18." See also "The Global Unicorn Club," CB Insights, 2019, https://www.cbinsights.com/research-unicorn-companies. The methodology includes adding up the number of companies in industries (companies in industries listed as biotechnology, edtech, energy, fintech, food, healthcare) by the total number of companies. The total dollar amount of these companies was added up as well and amounted to only 13 percent of total companies.

15. Identified sample of the fastest-growing startups, valued at more than $100m, in Africa, Latin America, and Southeast Asia. Startup list sourced from interviews with venture capitalists in each region.

16. Soumya Gupta, "Rivigo Is Changing the Way Women Look at Trucking Business, Says Gazal Kalra," *BW Businessworld*, May 9, 2017, http://www.businessworld.in/article/Rivigo-Is-Changing-The-Way-Women-Look-At-Trucking-Business-Says-Gazal-Kalra/09-05-2017-117861/.

17. Rajat Gupta, Sriram Jambunathan, and Thomas Netzer, "Building India: Transforming the Nation's Logistic Infrastructure," McKinsey & Company, September 2010, https://mck.co/3acf1rF; and "India Aiming to Reduce Logistics Cost to Less than 10% of GDP by 2022," *Business Standard*, August 24, 2018, https://www.business-standard.com/

article/news-cm/india-aiming-to-reduce-logistics-cost-to-less-than-10-of-gdp-by-2022
-118082400367_1.html.

18. Neha Mittal et al., "The Endemic Issue of Truck Driver Shortage—A Comparative Study between India and the United States," *Research in Transportation Economics*, 2018, https://www.researchgate.net/publication/325985103_The_endemic_issue_of_truck
_driver_shortage_-_A_comparative_study_between_India_and_the_United_States.

19. "High-Impact Entrepreneurs Create the Most Jobs: Endeavor and GEM Release New Report," Endeavor, September 16, 2011, https://endeavor.org/blog/research/endeavor
-gem-report-2011/.

20. Ibid.

21. "A Unified Logistics Platform Facilitating One-Stop Solution for All Needs," Rivigo, https://rivigo.com/products#freight-marketplace.

22. Author interview with Deepak Garg, August 9, 2018, by phone.

23. Mihir Dalal, "Logistics Start-Up Rivigo Services in Talks to Raise up to $400 Million," LiveMint, September 07, 2018, https://www.livemint.com/Companies/
1RbFAMBoyebXFj7dhcoNGM/Logistics-startup-Rivigo-Services-in-talks-to-raise-up-to
.html.

24. Marshall Ganz, Tamara Kay, and Jason Spicer, "Social Enterprise Is Not Social Change," *Stanford Social Innovation Review*, Spring 2018, https://ssir.org/articles/entry/
social_enterprise_is_not_social_change.

25. Leo Mirani, "What Google Really Means by 'Don't Be Evil,'" Quartz, October 21, 2014, https://qz.com/284548/what-google-really-means-by-dont-be-evil/.

26. "Why Pledge 1% Is One of the Most Innovative Companies of 2017," *Fast Company*, February 13, 2017, https://www.fastcompany.com/3067480/why-pledge-1-is-one-of-the
-most-innovative-companies-of-2017.

27. Mike Montgomery, "What Entrepreneurs Can Learn from the Philanthropic Struggles of Toms Shoes," *Forbes*, April 28, 2015, https://www.forbes.com/sites/mikemontgomery/
2015/04/28/how-entrepreneurs-can-avoid-the-philanthropy-pitfalls/#371280b71c38.

28. Ross Baird, *The Innovation Blind Spot: Why We Back the Wrong Ideas—And What to Do about It* (Dallas: BenBella Books, 2017), chapter 4.

29. Author interview with Deepak Garg, August 8, 2018.

30. Sumanth Raj Urs, "200 Engineers, 261 Million People: GO-JEK's Impact in Indonesia," Medium, January 23, 2018, https://blog.gojekengineering.com/200-engineers-261
-million-people-go-jeks-impact-in-indonesia-b8f87934e6c1.

31. Erica Glasener, "The Magic of Banyan Trees," *Tribune Business News*, January 23, 2012, https://search.proquest.com/abicomplete/docview/917252674/
AF487DE8677A488BPQ/15?accountid=14437.

32. Author interview with Deepak Garg, August 8, 2018.

33. "Mobile Money Metrics," GSMA, 2019, https://www.gsma.com/
mobilemoneymetrics/#global?y=2017?v=overview?g=global.

34. John Delaney, "A New Consumer Protection Agenda for Working Families," *Huffington Post*, September 9, 2017, https://www.huffingtonpost.com/john-k-delaney/a-new
-consumer-protection_b_11910482.html.

35. "State of Homelessness," National Alliance to End Homelessness, 2019, https://endhomelessness.org/homelessness-in-america/homelessness-statistics/state-of
-homelessness-report/.

36. Zack Friedman, "Student Loan Debt Statistics in 2018: A $1.5 Trillion Crisis," *Forbes*, June 13, 2018, https://www.forbes.com/sites/zackfriedman/2018/06/13/student-loan
-debt-statistics-2018/#4cdd86cb7310.

37. Larry Fink, "A Sense of Purpose," BlackRock, 2019, https://www.blackrock.com/
corporate/investor-relations/larry-fink-ceo-letter.

38. "Business Roundtable Redefines the Purpose of a Corporation to Promote 'An Economy That Serves All Americans,'" Press Release, August 19, 2019, https://www

.businessroundtable.org/business-roundtable-redefines-the-purpose-of-a-corporation-to
-promote-an-economy-that-serves-all-americans.

39. William Dowling, "The Business Case for Caring—A Helio Analysis of Certified
B Corps," The UpRound by CircleUp, June 1, 2018, https://circleup.com/blog/2018/06/01/
the-business-case-for-caring-a-helio-analysis-of-certified-b-corps/.

40. Mozaffar Khan, George Serafeim, and Aaron Yoon, "Corporate Sustainability: First Evidence on Materiality", November 9, 2016, The Accounting Review 91, no. 6,
pp. 1697–1724, https://papers.ssrn.com/sol3/papers.cfm?abstract_id=2575912; and George
Serafeim, "Public Sentiment and the Price of Corporate Sustainability," October 12, 2018,
https://papers.ssrn.com/sol3/papers.cfm?abstract_id=3265502.

41. Jesus Godoy Bejarano and Diego Téllez, "Mission Power and Firm Financial
Performance," Center for Research in Economics and Finance (CIEF), Working Paper
No. 17-04, February 23, 2017, http://dx.doi.org/10.2139/ssrn.2929832.

Chapter 9

1. Carmel Lobello, "The Stories Behind 3 Great Business Mantras," The Week, June 24,
2013, https://theweek.com/articles/462863/stories-behind-3-great-business-mantras.

2. Morgan Brown, "Uber—What's Fueling Uber's Growth Engine?" GrowthHackers,
nd, https://growthhackers.com/growth-studies/uber.

3. Ian Frazier, "The Vertical Farm," New Yorker, January 1, 2017, https://www
.newyorker.com/magazine/2017/01/09/the-vertical-farm.

4. Ibid.

5. https://www.crunchbase.com/organization/aerofarms#section-overview; and author
interview with David Rosenberg, August 20, 2018.

6. Author interview with Chris Folayan, August 2, 2018.

7. Author interview with Thomaz Srougi, August 3, 2018.

8. Lydia Ramsey, "US Investors Are Pouring Millions into a Healthcare Company
That Doesn't Take Insurance and Lists Its Prices like a 'McDonald's Menu,'" Business Insider, August 14, 2018, https://www.businessinsider.com/how-dr-consulta-is-changing-the
-brazilian-healthcare-system-2018-8?IR=T.

9. Danny Crichton, "Using Tech and $100M, Dr Consulta Transforms Healthcare for
the Poorest," TechCrunch, June 19, 2018, https://techcrunch.com/2018/06/19/dr-consulta
-transforms-healthcare-for-the-poorest/.

10. Ibid.

11. Author interview with Ella Gudwin, December 19, 2018.

12. Author interview with David Rosenberg, August 20, 2018.

13. Ibid.

14. Ibid.

15. Ibid.

16. Charles Duhigg, The Power of Habit: Why We Do What We Do in Life and Business
(New York: Random House, 2012).

17. "A Guide to Anticipating the Future Impact of Today's Technology," Ethical OS,
2018, https://ethicalos.org/.

18. Author interview with Achmad Zaky, June 18, 2019.

19. Alex Hern, "Uber and Lyft Pull Out of Austin After Locals Vote Against Self-
Regulation," Guardian, May 9, 2016, https://www.theguardian.com/technology/2016/may/
09/uber-lyft-austin-vote-against-self-regulation; Jillian Jorgensen and Will Bredderman,
"Bill de Blasio's Quest to Cap Uber Ends with a Whimper," Observer, January 15, 2016,
http://observer.com/2016/01/bill-de-blasios-quest-to-cap-uber-ends-with-a-whimper/; and
Josie Cox, "Uber's Appeal Against TfL's Licence Ban Will Not Be Heard until Spring
2018," Independent, December 11, 2017, http://www.independent.co.uk/news/business/
news/uber-london-ban-appeal-tfl-licence-taxi-app-spring-2018-heard-court-ride-hailing

-a8103666.html. London decided not to renew Uber's operation license in the fall of 2017. Uber has appealed the decision and continues to operate in the city.

20. Itika Sharma Punit, "Panic Buttons Won't Fix Ola and Uber's Sexual-Assault Problem," Quartz India, June 7, 2018, https://qz.com/india/1298182/why-ola-and-ubers -measures-for-womens-safety-is-just-not-working/.

21. Austin Carr, "Why Jack Dorsey Killed the Square Credit Card," Fast Company, August 12, 2014, https://www.fastcompany.com/3032811/why-jack-dorsey-killed-the -square-credit-card.

22. Author interview with Yousef Hammad, July 30, 2018.

23. Author interview with David Rosenberg, 2018.

24. Bitange Ndemo and Tim Weiss, eds., Digital Kenya: An Entrepreneurial Revolution in the Making (London: Palgrave Macmillan, 2017).

25. Jorge Gaxiola Moraila, Alexis Leon Trueba, and Gabriel Franco Fernández, "The New Mexican FinTech Law—Balancing Innovation, Security and Stability," Financier Worldwide, August 2018, https://www.financierworldwide.com/the-new-mexican-fintech -law-balancing-innovation-security-and-stability.

26. Samantha Murphy, "Facebook Changes Its 'Move Fast and Break Things' Motto," Mashable, April 30, 2014, https://mashable.com/2014/04/30/facebooks-new-mantra-move -fast-with-stability/#3f4wKHt.zPqV.

27. Ibid.

28. Analysis of Facebook market capitalization, via Google Finance, for the last six months of 2018, https://www.google.com/search?q=facebook&tbm=fin.

Chapter 10

1. Josh Lerner, a Harvard Business School professor, accurately characterized the dynamic that creates this bond: "Venture Capital exists when entrepreneurs have an idea and no capital, and investors have capital but no good ideas." Josh Lerner and Paul Gompers, "The Venture Capital Revolution," Journal of Economic Perspectives 15 (2001): 145–168. doi: 10.1257/jep.15.2.145.

2. Author interview with Carlos Antequera, September 25, 2018.

3. Ibid.

4. A typical venture capital fund has a "2 & 20" structure. This consists of a 2 percent annual management fee on the capital investors have pledged, and a 20 percent share in the profits generated.

5. "Fin-Tech," Economist, December 2015, https://www.economist.com/news/finance -and-economics/21684805-there-were-tech-startups-there-was-whaling-fin-tech.

6. Ibid.

7. Ibid.

8. "Venture Capital Funnel Shows Odds of Becoming a Unicorn Are About 1%," CB Insights, September 6, 2018, https://www.cbinsights.com/research/venture-capital-funnel -2/; and Paul Gompers et al., "How Do Venture Capitalists Make Decisions?" National Bureau of Economic Research, NBER working paper number 22587, September 2016, doi:10.3386/w22587.

9. Pui-Wing Tam and Shayndi Raice, "A $9 Billion Jackpot for Facebook Investor," Wall Street Journal, January 28, 2012, https://on.wsj.com/2QRBtio.

10. William Alden and David Gelles, "In WhatsApp Deal, Sequoia Capital May Make 50 Times Its Money," New York Times, February 20, 2014, https://dealbook.nytimes.com/ 2014/02/20/in-whatsapp-deal-sequoia-capital-may-make-50-times-its-money/.

11. Cambridge Associates, "US Venture Capital Index and Selected Benchmark Statistics," March 31, 2018, https://www.cambridgeassociates.com/wp-content/uploads/2018/ 07/WEB-2018-Q1-USVC-Benchmark-Book.pdf.

12. "2019 AVCA Members," African Private Equity and Venture Capital Association, 2019, https://www.avca-africa.org/members/avca-members/. Count of "General Partner" venture capital and private equity funds listed.

13. Ibid. Count of "Full Member" venture capital and private equity funds listed for Private Capital Investment in Latin America.

14. "Venture Monitor 1Q18," PitchBook, 2018, https://files.pitchbook.com/website/files/pdf/1Q_2018_PitchBook_NVCA_Venture_Monitor.pdf.

15. For instance, Google purchased fifteen companies in 2017 alone. "The Google Acquisition Tracker," CB Insights, nd, https://www.cbinsights.com/research-google-acquisitions.

16. "Ex-U.S. Private Equity & Venture Capital Index and Selected Benchmark Statistics," Cambridge Associates, December 31, 2015, http://bit.ly/3a6u5XY. 15-year average across all geographies. Reflects 565 funds globally.

17. Prequin, "Venture Capital in Emerging Markets," ValueWalk, May 10, 2018, https://www.valuewalk.com/2018/05/venture-capital-in-emerging-markets/.

18. Paul Gompers et al., "How Do Venture Capitalists Make Decisions?"; and Tomer Dean, "The Meeting That Showed Me the Truth about VCs," TechCrunch, June 1, 2017, https://techcrunch.com/2017/06/01/the-meeting-that-showed-me-the-truth-about-vcs/.

19. Anne S. Habiby and Deirdre M. Coyle Jr., "The High-Intensity Entrepreneur," *Harvard Business Review*, September 2010, https://hbr.org/2010/09/the-high-intensity-entrepreneur.

20. "The Crunchbase Exited Unicorn Leaderboard," accessed January 26, 2020, https://techcrunch.com/unicorn-leaderboard/exited/.

21. Asia Partners analysis of Sharpe ratios of industries, internal analysis, August 2018. This covers the 2002–2017 time period and looks at Southeast Asia technology stocks as proxy for technology as industry.

22. Of course, the suggestion is not to get a collection of investors to support innovators for the sake of it. "Party rounds"—the pejorative term used for seed rounds with five or more funds—are not what I am talking about. In party rounds, funds approach the investment as a passing-of-the-hat type of opportunity—a small bet to have a look for the next round, akin to buying an option. While, in theory, a party round means that many people are available to help or share strategic advice, unfortunately it often indicates that no one is invested sufficiently to offer assistance. Ultimately, small seed bets are not meaningful allocations of the VC funds and are thus deprioritized.

23. Francesco Corea, "Artificial Intelligence and Venture Capital," Medium, July 18, 2018, https://medium.com/@Francesco_AI/artificial-intelligence-and-venture-capital-af5ada4003b1; and Xuan Tian, "The Role of Venture Capital Syndication in Value Creation for Entrepreneurial Firms," *Review of Finance*, forthcoming (available at SSRN: https://ssrn.com/abstract=954188).

24. Eliot Brown, "In Silicon Valley, the Big Venture Funds Keep Getting Bigger," *Wall Street Journal*, July 25, 2017, https://www.wsj.com/articles/in-silicon-valley-the-big-venture-funds-keep-getting-bigger-1501002000.

25. "Something Ventured," documentary film, directed by Dan Geller and Dayna Goldfine (April 24, 2011).

26. Jason Rowley, "Where and Why Venture Capitalists Invest Close to Home," TechCrunch, November 16, 2017, https://techcrunch.com/2017/11/16/where-and-why-venture-capitalists-invest-close-to-home/.

27. Serena Saitto, "The Biggest Tech Investor Silicon Valley Ignores," *The Information*, February 21, 2018, https://www.theinformation.com/articles/the-biggest-tech-investor-silicon-valley-ignores.

28. Staff Writer 3, "The Greatest Venture Capital Investment Ever? Naspers Cashes in $10bn Tencent Stake for Whopping 55,000% Return," African Business Central, March 30,

2018, https://www.africanbusinesscentral.com/2018/03/30/the-greatest-venture-capital -investment-ever-naspers-cashes-in-10bn-tencent-stake-for-whopping-55000-return/.

29. Saitto, "The Biggest Tech Investor Silicon Valley Ignores."

30. "Vostok Emerging Finance," 2017, http://www.vostokemergingfinance.com/.

31. "Series D—GuiaBolso—2017-10-18," Crunchbase, https://www.crunchbase.com/ funding_round/guiabolso-series-d--c5330480#section-locked-charts.

32. Alex Graham, "Exploring Evergreen Funds with a VC Investor Who Raised One," TopTal Finance, nd, https://www.toptal.com/finance/venture-capital-consultants/ evergreen-funds.

33. For its newest global fund, Carlyle, the global private equity firm, launched a long-dated fund. This is one of the most well-documented examples in the space; see "The Carlyle Group Raises $3.6 Billion for First Long-Dated Private Equity Fund, "Car- lyle Group, press release, October 19, 2016, https://www.carlyle.com/media-room/news -release-archive/carlyle-group-raises-36-billion-first-long-dated-private-equity.

34. "Baidu, Alibaba and Tencent: BAT Companies Dominate Chinese VC," PitchBook blog, April 29, 2019, https://pitchbook.com/blog/baidu-alibaba-and-tencent-bat-companies -dominate-chinese-vc.

35. Jon Russell, "Alibaba's Ant Financial Is Raising $3B in Debt to Finance a Global M&A Spree," TechCrunch, February 8, 2017, https://techcrunch.com/2017/02/08/alibabas -ant-financial-is-raising-3b-in-debt-to-finance-a-global-ma-spree/.

36. Josh Horwitz, "The 'SoftBank of China' Has Quietly Invested Tens of Billions Globally Since 2015," Quartz, May 17, 2018, https://qz.com/1279190/tencent-the-softbank -of-china-has-invested-tens-of-billions-globally-since-2015/.

37. Crunchbase company profiles, "Grab" and "Go-Jek," https://www.crunchbase.com/ organization/go-jek, https://www.crunchbase.com/organization/grabtaxi.

38. Fred Imbert, "SoftBank Launches $5 Billion Latin America Tech Fund," CNBC, March 7, 2019, https://www.cnbc.com/2019/03/07/softbank-launches-5-billion-latin -america-tech-fund.html.

39. "The 2018 Global CVC Report," CB Insights, 2019, https://www.cbinsights.com/ research/report/corporate-venture-capital-trends-2018/.

40. Jean-François Caillard, "Why Is the Corporate Venture Growing So Fast? What Are the Keys?" October 27, 2017, https://medium.com/@jfcaillard/why-is-the-corporate -venture-growing-so-fast-what-are-the-keys-b7cab8156b5e; and Teddy Himler, "Corpo- rate VC Is on the Rise: Here's What to Know," *Forbes*, February 14, 2017, https://www .forbes.com/sites/valleyvoices/2017/02/14/corporate-vc-on-the-rise/#178efe5abbf2.

41. "The 2018 Global CVC Report," CB Insights.

42. Melissa Mittelman, "TPG Seals Record $2 Billion for Fund Co-Led by Bono," Bloomberg, October 3, 2017, https://www.bloomberg.com/news/articles/2017-10-03/tpg -seals-record-2-billion-for-rise-impact-fund-co-led-by-bono.

43. "What Is Impact Investing and How Did It Begin?" The Case Foundation, Sep- tember 2014, http://www.gih.org/Examples/EXDetail.cfm?ItemNumber=6907, accessed August 12, 2018; and Abby Schultz, "Impact Investors Hold US$228 Billion in Assets," *Barrons*, June 6, 2018, https://www.barrons.com/articles/impact-investors-hold-us-228 -billion-in-assets-1528294454.

44. Author interview with Keith Harrington, June 27, 2018.

45. Ibid.

46. These funds include firms like Lighter Capital (an early pioneer of the model) in Seattle, Cypress Growth Capital in Dallas, and Decathlon Capital Partners in Park City, Utah.

47. Bartosz Trocha, "How 83 Venture Capital Firms Use Data, AI & Proprietary Soft- ware to Drive Alpha Returns," Medium, July 1, 2018, https://hackernoon.com/winning -by-eating-their-own-dogs-food-83-venture-capital-firms-using-data-ai-proprietary -da92b81b85ef; and Eze Vidra, "How Venture Capital Funds Leverage AI and Big Data,"

VC Cafe, November 28, 2018, https://www.vccafe.com/2018/11/28/how-venture-capital-funds-leverage-ai-and-big-data/.

48. Kate Clark, "Clearbanc Plans to Disrupt Venture Capital with 'The 20-Min Term Sheet,'" TechCrunch, April 4, 2019, https://techcrunch.com/2019/04/03/clearbanc-plans-to-disrupt-venture-capital-with-the-20-min-term-sheet/.

49. Connie Loizos, "Social Capital Has Started Investing in Startups, Sight Unseen," TechCrunch, October 25, 2017, https://techcrunch.com/2017/10/25/social-capital-has-started-investing-in-startups-sight-unseen/.

50. Eze Vidra, "Turns Out Venture Capital Is a People Business, or Is It?" VC Cafe, June 12, 2018, https://www.vccafe.com/2018/06/12/turns-out-venture-capital-is-a-people-business-or-is-it/.

51. Katy Steinmetz, "How Chamath Palihapitiya Wants to Disrupt Silicon Valley," *Time*, July 19, 2018, http://time.com/5342756/chamath-palihapitiya/; and Ashley Carroll, "From Experiment to Product: Capital-as-a-Service One Year Later," Medium, June 18, 2018, https://medium.com/social-capital/from-experiment-to-product-capital-as-a-service-one-year-later-6d8b4b9c038b.

52. The average time to exit at the Frontier, as discussed in chapter 3, can exceed ten years. The average American marriage is 8.2 years; see Matthew Schimkowitz, "How Long Does an Average Marriage Last around the World?" Hopes&Fears, 2019, http://www.hopesandfears.com/hopes/city/city_index/214133-city-index-marriage-lengths.

53. James Chen, "Accredited Investor," Investopedia, February 23, 2019, https://www.investopedia.com/terms/a/accreditedinvestor.asp.

54. Ramana Nanda, Robert F. White, and Alexey Tuzikov, "Initial Coin Offerings," Harvard Business School Technical Note 818-067, November 2017 (Revised December 2017), https://www.hbs.edu/faculty/Pages/item.aspx?num=53510.

55. David Floyd, "Billion: 2018 ICO Funding Has Passed 2017's Total," Coin Desk, April 19, 2018, https://www.coindesk.com/6-3-billion-2018-ico-funding-already-outpaced-2017/$6.3.

56. Shobhit Seth, "80% of ICOs Are Scams: Report," Investopedia, April 2, 2018, https://www.investopedia.com/news/80-icos-are-scams-report/.

57. Many ICOs are raised by the companies outlining their business plans in a white paper (an explanation outlining what the coin will be for and how the money will be used). In venture capital, to raise similar amounts of capital would traditionally require meaningfully more business traction.

58. Lupercal Capital, "ICOs: A Changing Regulatory Environment," February 7, 2018, https://hackernoon.com/icos-a-changing-regulatory-environment-77119ffff26b.

59. M. Szmigiera, "Crowdfunding—Statistics & Facts," Statista, November 29, 2018, https://www.statista.com/topics/1283/crowdfunding/.

60. "Crowdfunding," Statista, nd, https://www.statista.com/outlook/335/100/crowdfunding/worldwide#market-globalRevenue.

61. Author interview with Erik Hersman, May 17, 2018, via WhatsApp.

Chapter 11

1. Author interview with Hernan Kazah, June 7, 2018.

2. "E-commerce in Latin America—Statistics & Facts," Statista, July 13, 2018, https://www.statista.com/topics/2453/e-commerce-in-latin-america/.

3. "Mercado Libre (MELI): IPO Details," Crunchbase, 2019, https://www.crunchbase.com/ipo/mercadolibre-ipo--51d436e2#section-details; and "MercadoLibre, Inc. (MELI)," Yahoo Finance, 2019, https://finance.yahoo.com/quote/MELI?p=MELI.

4. Author interview with Hernan Kazah, 2018.

5. Kaszek Ventures, 2019, https://www.kaszek.com/portfolio.

6. "The Multiplier Effect," Endeavor, https://readymag.com/endeavor/multipliereffect/.

7. Ibid.

8. "Global Network of Failure Researchers," Failure Institute, September 7, 2017, https://thefailureinstitute.com/researchers-network/.

9. Author interview with Pepe Villatoro, June 20, 2018.

10. "Stories About Failure," Fuckup, 2019, https://fuckupnights.com/; and author interview with Pepe Villatoro, June 20, 2018.

11. Sophus A. Reinert, Dawn H. Lau, and Amy MacBeath, "Going Rogue: Choson Exchange in North Korea," Harvard Business School Case 717-015, October 2016 (Revised October 2017), https://www.hbs.edu/faculty/Pages/item.aspx?num=51812.

12. Ibid.

13. Author interview with Geoffrey See, August 19, 2018.

14. "Learn, Network, Startup," Startup Weekend, 2019, https://startupweekend.org/.

15. Author interview with Yasser Bashir, October 25, 2018.

16. Mehreen Omer, "Breaking: Careem Acquires Savaree," Pakwired, March 30, 2016, https://pakwired.com/careem-acquires-savaree/._

17. Author interview with Fred Swaniker, July 12, 2018.

18. Fred Swaniker, "The Leaders Who Ruined Africa, and the Generation Who Can Fix It," TED talk, transcript, October 2014, https://www.ted.com/talks/fred_swaniker_the_leaders_who_ruined_africa_and_the_generation_who_can_fix_it/transcript.

19. David Fine et al., "Africa at Work: Job Creation and Inclusive Growth," McKinsey & Company, August 2012, https://www.mckinsey.com/featured-insights/middle-east-and-africa/africa-at-work.

20. Fred Swaniker, "4 Lessons Learned About What It Takes to Be an Entrepreneur," video, YouTube, July 29, 2016, https://www.youtube.com/watch?v=wa5Dt2busNA.

21. Nate Berg, "How the African Leadership Academy Is Fighting the Continent's Education Exodus," *Fast Company*, December 20, 2010, https://www.fastcompany.com/1702244/how-african-leadership-academy-fighting-continents-education-exodus.

22. "Founders' Story," African Leadership Academy, 2019, http://www.africanleadershipacademy.org/about/founders-story/.

23. "Success after ALA," African Leadership Academy, 2019, http://www.africanleadershipacademy.org/about/our-impact/university-placements/; "Reekworth Highlights 2017," Reekworth Junior (Mabelreign Campus), December 12, 2017, https://www.reekworthjuniorschool.com/single-post/2017/12/12/Reekworth-Highlights-2017; and "Mapping Change in Africa: Meet 5 Enterprising ALA Alumni," African Leadership Academy, March 28, 2018, http://www.africanleadershipacademy.org/ala-alumni-enterprise/.

24. "AAE," African Leadership Network (ALN), October 6, 2017, http://africanleadershipnetwork.com/.

25. "Our Meta Skills," ALU, December 16, 2016, https://www.alueducation.com/about/our-meta-skills/.

26. "Are You Ready for the Opportunity Presented by Africa's Growing Insurance Industry?" ALU School of Insurance, nd, https://www.alueducation.com/soi/.

27. "Computer Science," ALU, 2017, https://www.alueducation.com/programmes/undergraduate/degree-programmes/computer-science/.

28. Yinka Adegoke, "African Leadership University Has Raised $30 Million to Help Reinvent Graduate Education," Quartz Africa, January 4, 2019, https://qz.com/africa/1515015/african-leadership-university-raises-30-million-series-b/.

29. "Hello, We Are iHub," iHub Nairobi, 2019, https://ihub.co.ke/.

30. Toby Shapshak, "Kenya's iHub Enters a New Chapter," *Forbes*, March 11, 2016, https://www.forbes.com/sites/tobyshapshak/2016/03/11/kenyas-ihub-enters-a-new-chapter/#535dca644f6a.

31. Irene Hau, "[4TH GEN #5] Case Study: iHub," The Sound of the City Blog, WordPress, May 12, 2015, https://thesoundofthecity.wordpress.com/2015/05/12/4th-gen-5-case-study-ihub/. iHub was recently acquired by the Nigerian innovation center and

seed-fund CcHub; see https://techcrunch.com/2019/09/26/nigerias-cchub-acquires-kenyas
-ihub-to-create-mega-africa-incubator/.

32. Author interview with Matt Clifford, October 23, 2018.

33. Entrepreneur First, https://www.joinef.com/.

34. Rhett Morris and Lili Török, "Fostering Productive Entrepreneurship Communities: Key Lessons on Generating Jobs, Economic Growth, and Innovation," Endeavor Insight, October 2018, https://endeavor.org/content/uploads/2015/06/Fostering-Productive
-Entrepreneurship-Communities.pdf.

35. Endeavor, "The Multiplier Effect," Endeavor Insight, https://readymag.com/
endeavor/multipliereffect/.

36. Endeavor, "The Power of Entrepreneur Networks: How New York City Became the Role Model for Other Urban Tech Hubs," Endeavor Insight Report, November 2014, http://www.nyctechmap.com/nycTechReport.pdf.

37. "Endeavor 2018/2019 Impact Report," November 2019; and "Endeavor Board: Linda Rottenberg," Endeavor, 2019, https://endeavor.org/global-board/linda-rottenberg/.

38. Global Off-Grid Lighting Association, "About Us," https://www.gogla.org/about-us.

39. "Aramex: Delivery Unlimited," Aramex, 2019, http://bit.ly/3a34nUa; and "Investor Presentation, Q2, 2019 Results," June 30, 2019, https://www.aramex.com/docs/default
-source/resources/inverstor_presentation_q2_2019.pdf.

40. Sami Mahroum, *Black Swan Start-ups: Understanding the Rise of Successful Technology Business in Unlikely Places* (London: Palgrave Macmillan, 2016).

41. "Overview: Maktoob," Crunchbase, 2019, https://www.crunchbase.com/
organization/maktoob#section-overview; and "Entrepreneur to Entrepreneur: Meet the Ron Conway of the Middle East (TCTV)," TechCrunch, September 16, 2010, https://
techcrunch.com/2010/09/16/middle-east-ron-conway-fadi-ghandour-shervin-pishevar/.

42. Elizabeth MacBride, "The Middle East's First Unicorn: Souq.com's CEO on Leadership, Timing and Coping with Rejection," *Forbes*, March 25, 2016, https://www.forbes
.com/sites/elizabethmacbride/2016/03/25/e-commerce-gold-in-the-middle-east-behind
-souqs-success-story/#58610b4c1ee0.

43. Jon Russell, "Amazon Completes Its Acquisition of Middle Eastern E-commerce Firm Souq," TechCrunch, July 3, 2017, https://techcrunch.com/2017/07/03/amazon-souq
-com-completed/; and Ronaldo Mouchawar, "Souq's CEO on Building an E-Commerce Powerhouse in the Middle East," *Harvard Business Review*, September–October 2017, https://hbr.org/2017/09/souq-coms-ceo-on-building-an-e-commerce-powerhouse-in-the
-middle-east.

44. Heather Somerville, Alexander Cornwell, and Saeed Azhar, "Uber Buys Rival Careem in $3.1 Billion Deal to Dominate Ride-Hailing in Middle East," Reuters, March 25, 2019, https://www.reuters.com/article/us-careem-m-a-uber/uber-buys-rival
-careem-in-3-1-billion-deal-to-dominate-ride-hailing-in-middle-east-idUSKCN1R70IM.

45. Christopher T. Rogers and Peter Weed, "What Careem's $3.1 Billion Acquisition Means for the Middle East," *Forbes*, April 17, 2019, https://www.forbes.com/sites/
valleyvoices/2019/04/17/what-careems-3-1-billion-acquisition-means-for-the-middle-east/
#2fba3c887fa2.

46. Noor Shawwa, "The Success and Multiplier Effects That Careem's Acquisition by Uber Will Have on the Middle East's Startup Ecosystem," *Entrepreneur*, April 2, 2019, https://www.entrepreneur.com/article/331568._

47. Morris and Török, "Fostering Productive Entrepreneurship Communities."

48. Ibid.

49. "100 Flipkart Employees to Turn Millionaires Post Walmart Deal, but Here's the Catch," News Minute, May 11, 2018, https://www.thenewsminute.com/article/100-flipkart
-employees-turn-millionaires-post-walmart-deal-here-s-catch-81087.

50. Anne S. Habiby and Deirdre M. Coyle Jr., "The High-Intensity Entrepreneur," *Harvard Business Review*, September 2010, https://hbr.org/2010/09/the-high-intensity
-entrepreneur.

51. Ibid.

52. Tom Huddleston Jr., "This 36-Year-Old Self-Made Billionaire Started His First Business at 16 with a $500 Loan from His Dad—Here's His Best Advice," CNBC, July 2018, https://www.cnbc.com/2018/07/30/how-div-turakhia-became-indias-youngest-self -made-billionaire.html.

53. Author interview with André Street, August 20, 2018.

54. The seminal story of the "Traitorous Eight" illustrates the power of older siblings in kick-starting the ecosystem flywheel. In the 1950s, Silicon Valley was only one of many hubs building transistors (computer processors), and certainly not the leader. But things quickly changed in the West's favor. William Shockley, who coinvented the transistor while at Bell Labs, founded his own company, Shockley Semiconductor Labs, in 1956 in Mountain View, California. It was the first company to make transistors out of silicon. Shockley attracted a number of top computer scientists from the East Coast, which was still the hub of computer science development. In 1957, eight of Shockley's employees left to launch their own firm, Fairchild Semiconductor. Now dubbed the Traitorous Eight, they partnered with Sherman Fairchild and helped scale the company to become a leading manufacturer of transistors. In the early 1960s, Fairchild helped make computer components for the Apollo program. Over the next decade, many of the Traitorous Eight and their employees left Fairchild and founded their own companies. Gordon Moore (of Moore's law) and Robert Noyce founded Intel in 1968. Eugene Kleiner co-founded the storied venture capital firm Kleiner Perkins. Other employees went on to start the chip companies AMD and Nvidia, and Don Valentine founded Sequoia, arguably the most successful venture capital firm in history.

55. Rhett Morris, "The First Trillion-Dollar Startup," TechCrunch, July 26, 2014, https://techcrunch.com/2014/07/26/the-first-trillion-dollar-startup/.

56. Charlie Parrish, "Meet the PayPal Mafia, the Richest Group of Men in Silicon Valley," *Business Insider*, September 20, 2014, https://www.businessinsider.com/meet-the -paypal-mafia-the-richest-group-of-men-in-silicon-valley-2014-9.

57. Analysis summing market caps of PayPal Mafia–founded businesses, based on public data.

58. "The Multiplier Effect," 2019, https://readymag.com/endeavor/multipliereffect/.

59. The acceleration graphs come from publicly available data from CB Insights by market. For each year, the total number of unicorns is represented by the number of unicorns from previous years plus the number of new unicorns that year.

60. Analysis could be further refined by exploring exits at a range of valuation sizes (not just unicorns), concentration in time, and geographic proximity, among other factors. The idea came from a discussion with Nick Nash, co-founder of Asia Partners, and a trend the company had observed in China and India.

61. Figure 11-2 cuts off China unicorn acceleration, today over 100. Latin America has many years with low unicorn count before acceleration.

62. Author interview with Amanda Lannert, April 15, 2019.

Chapter 12

1. "Entrepreneurial Ecosystem Diagnostic Toolkit," Aspen Network of Development Entrepreneurs, December 2013, https://assets.aspeninstitute.org/content/uploads/files/ content/docs/pubs/FINAL%20Ecosystem%20Toolkit%20Draft_print%20version.pdf.

2. Originally proposed by Alfred Marshall in his book *Principles of Economics, Great Mind Series*, first published in 1890. It was pushed forward by other thinkers, including Michael Porter through his theories of economic clusters. See Michael Porter, "Clusters and the New Economics of Competition," *Harvard Business Review*, November–December 1998, https://hbr.org/1998/11/clusters-and-the-new-economics-of-competition.

3. Author interview with Chris Heivly, February 15, 2019.

4. AnnaLee Saxenian, *Regional Advantage: Culture and Competition in Silicon Valley and Route 128* (Cambridge, MA: Harvard University Press, 1996), http://www.hup.harvard .edu/catalog.php?isbn=9780674753402&content=reviews.

5. Vivek Wadhwa, "Silicon Valley Can't Be Copied," *MIT Technology Review*, July 3, 2013, https://www.technologyreview.com/s/516506/silicon-valley-cant-be-copied/.

6. Saxenian, *Regional Advantage*.

7. Richard Florida, *The Rise of the Creative Class: And How It's Transforming Work, Leisure, Community, and Everyday Life* (New York: Basic Books, 2002); and Brad Feld, *Startup Communities: Building an Entrepreneurial Ecosystem in Your City* (Hoboken, NJ: Wiley, 2012), https://www.wiley.com/en-us/Startup+Communities%3A+Building+an+Entrepreneurial +Ecosystem+in+Your+City-p-9781118483312. Feld's excellent book succinctly summarizes the different ecosystem-building approaches and helped shape my own thinking on the subject.

8. Victor Hwang and Greg Horowitt, *The Rainforest: The Secret to Building the Next Silicon Valley* (Los Altos Hills, CA: Regenwald, 2012), http://therainforestbook.com/.

9. Feld, *Startup Communities*.

10. "Doing Business 2019: Training for Reform," International Bank for Reconstruction & Reform / World Bank Group, 2019, http://bit.ly/38aK8Cp.

11. Ana Maria Zárate Moreno, "Regulation, Innovation, and Entrepreneurship," Regulatory Studies Center, The George Washington University, December 8, 2015, https:// regulatorystudies.columbian.gwu.edu/sites/g/files/zaxdzs1866/f/downloads/RegInsight _AMZM-regulation-and-Innv%26entrep-literature-review120815.pdf.

12. Of course, this is a correlation and not causation. There are a range of factors that drive this, and GDP growth also influences the rate of international study, because it increases disposable dollars for investment.

13. Asia Partners Research, January 2018, https://www.asiapartners.com/; Rachel T. Barclay, Mandie Weinandt, and Allen C. Barclay, "The Economic Impact of Study Abroad on Chinese Students and China's Gross Domestic Product," *Journal of Applied Business and Economics* 19, no. 4 (2017), http://www.na-businesspress.com/JABE/BarclayRT _Web19_4_.pdf; Yukiko Shimmi, "The Problematic Decline of Japanese International Students," *International Higher Education* 64 (Summer): 9–10, https://ejournals.bc.edu/ index.php/ihe/article/download/8558/7691/; Annette Bradford, "Changing Trends in Japanese Students Studying Abroad" *International Higher Education* 83, Special Issue (2015), https://ejournals.bc.edu/index.php/ihe/article/download/9086/8193/; and Mantong Guo, "The Economic Impact of International Students on Their Countries of Origin," April 5, 2017, Georgetown University Master's Thesis, https://repository.library.georgetown.edu/ handle/10822/1043914.

14. Ibid; "GDP Growth (Annual %): Japan," The World Bank, 2019, https://bit.ly/ 38MNtrD.

15. Ibid; James McCrostie, "More Japanese Students May Be Studying Abroad, but Not for Long," *Japan Times*, August 9, 2017, https://www.japantimes.co.jp/community/2017/ 08/09/issues/japanese-may-studying-abroad-not-long/#.XGnuo5NKgnV.

16. While the results of the companies have been mixed (many have left the country after the program, and few have scaled), the organizers largely consider the initiative successful on the qualitative, cross-pollination front.

17. Author interview with Amy Nelson, November 2018.

18. "About Us," C100, https://www.thec100.org/.

19. Stuart Anderson, "Immigrants and Billion-Dollar Companies," Near Policy Brief, National Foundation for American Policy, October 2018, http://bit.ly/2thz2g0; and Dinah Wisenberg Brin, "Immigrants Form 25% of New U.S. Businesses, Driving Entrepreneurship in 'Gateway' States," *Forbes*, July 31, 2018, https://www.forbes.com/ sites/dinahwisenberg/2018/07/31/immigrant-entrepreneurs-form-25-of-new-u-s-business -researchers/#4cf713ac713b.

20. From a search of the AngelList job board, looking at all open roles in the United States and a comparative list willing to sponsor immigrants, as of February 25, 2019: www .Angel.co/jobs.

21. Justin Sink, "Trump Administration Blocks 'Startup Visas' That Tech Leaders Backed," Bloomberg, July 10, 2017, https://www.bloomberg.com/news/articles/2017-07-10/ trump-administration-blocks-startup-visas-tech-leaders-back.

22. Olivia Carville, "Trump Booted Foreign Startup Founders. Other Countries Embraced Them," Bloomberg, October 1, 2018, https://www.bloomberg.com/news/ articles/2018-10-01/trump-booted-foreign-startup-founders-other-countries-embraced -them; and "Attracting Foreign Entrepreneurs," Business Roundtable, 2019, https://www .businessroundtable.org/policy-perspectives/immigration/state-of-immigration/attracting -foreign-entrepreneurs.

23. Jordan Crook, "Unshackled Is a New $3.5m Early Stage Fund That Looks a Lot Like an Accelerator," TechCrunch, November 13, 2014, https://techcrunch.com/2014/11/ 13/unshackled-is-a-new-3-5m-early-stage-fund-that-looks-a-lot-like-an-accelerator/.

24. "Overview: Unshackled Ventures," Crunchbase, 2019, https://www.crunchbase .com/organization/unshackled-ventures#section-overview; and Kate Clark, "Unshackled Ventures Has $20m to Invest Exclusively in Immigrant Founders," May 2, 2019, https://techcrunch.com/2019/05/02/unshackled-ventures-has-20m-to-invest-exclusively-in -immigrant-founders/.

25. "37 Chinese Companies That Became Unicorns in 2018," CB Insights, March 6, 2019, https://www.cbinsights.com/research/china-unicorns-2018/; "55 US Companies That Became Unicorns in 2018," CB Insights, March 13, 2019, https://www.cbinsights.com/ research/us-unicorns-2018/; and Jason Rowley, "Chinese Startups Lead US Rivals in 2018 Venture Race," Crunchbase, October 17, 2018, https://news.crunchbase.com/news/chinese -startups-lead-us-rivals-in-2018-venture-race/.

26. An H-1B visa allows companies in the United States to temporarily employ foreign nationals for particular occupations. It falls under the Immigration and Nationality Act.

27. Suvir Varma and Alex Boulton, "Southeast Asia Churns Out Billion-Dollar Start-Ups," Bain & Company, December 20, 2018, https://www.bain.com/insights/southeast-asia -churns-out-billion-dollar-start-ups-snap-chart/.

28. "Global Ecosystem Ranking Report," Startup Genome, 2017 report, https://startup genome.com/reports.

29. Pooja Singh, "Why Singapore Is a Startup Paradise," *Entrepreneur Asia Pacific*, December 13, 2018, https://www.entrepreneur.com/article/324589.

30. Christopher M. Schroeder, "A Different Story from the Middle East: Entrepreneurs Building an Arab Tech Economy," *MIT Technology Review*, August 3, 2017, https://www.technologyreview.com/s/608468/a-different-story-from-the-middle-east -entrepreneurs-building-an-arab-tech-economy/.

31. Florida, *The Rise of the Creative Class*.

32. "Become an e-Resident," Republic of Estonia, https://e-resident.gov.ee/become-an -e-resident/.

33. Author interview with Penny Pritzker, April 19, 2019.

34. "Our Portfolio," Rippleworks, 2019, http://www.rippleworks.org/portfolio/.

35. Author interview with Doug Galen, January 24, 2019.

36. David Yin, "What Makes Israel's Innovation Ecosystem So Successful," *Forbes*, January 9, 2017, https://www.forbes.com/sites/davidyin/2017/01/09/what-makes-israels -innovation-ecosystem-so-successful/#1e1bb2b270e4.

37. John Paglia and David Robinson, "Measuring the Role of the SBIC Program in Small Business Job Creation," Library of Congress, January 2017, https://www.sba.gov/ sites/default/files/articles/SBA_SBIC_Jobs_Report.pdf.

38. James Manzi et al., "U.S. Corporate Cash Reaches $1.9 Trillion but Rising Debt and Tax Reform Pose Risk," S&P Global, May 25, 2017, https://www.spglobal.com/en/

research-insights/articles/us-corporate-cash-reaches-19-trillion-but-rising-debt-and-tax
-reform-pose-risk.

39. Eric Paley, "Toxic VC and the Marginal-Dollar Problem," TechCrunch, October 26, 2017, https://techcrunch.com/2017/10/26/toxic-vc-and-the-marginal-dollar-problem/.

40. "What Is a Regulatory Sandbox?" November 20, 2017, https://www.bbva.com/en/what-is-regulatory-sandbox/.

41. "Welcome to the Aadhaar Dashboard," Unique Identification Authority of India, https://uidai.gov.in/aadhaar_dashboard/index.php; and author interview with Nandan Nilekani, May 16, 2019, via phone.

42. "India Stack—The Bedrock of a Digital India," IndiaStack, December 7, 2017, https://indiastack.org/india-stack-the-bedrock-of-a-digital-india/.

43. Author interview with Nandan Nilekani, 2019.

44. "The Landscape for Impact Investing in East Africa: Kenya," Open Capital and Global Impact Investing Network, August 2015, https://bit.ly/2U2uQLV.

45. Ibid.

46. Rhett Morris and Lili Török, "Fostering Productive Entrepreneurship Communities: Key Lessons On Generating Jobs, Economic Growth, and Innovation," Endeavor Insight, October 2018, https://endeavor.org/content/uploads/2015/06/Fostering-Productive-Entrepreneurship-Communities.pdf.

47. James A. Brander, Edward Egan, and Thomas F. Hellmann, "Government Sponsored Versus Private Venture Capital: Canadian Evidence," National Bureau of Economic Research, May 2010, pp. 275–320, https://www.nber.org/chapters/c8226.pdf.

48. Yasuyuki Motoyama, Jared Konczal, Jordan Bell-Masterson, and Arnobio Morelix, "Think Locally, Act Locally: Building a Robust Entrepreneurial Ecosystem," Kauffman Foundation, April 2014, https://papers.ssrn.com/sol3/papers.cfm?abstract_id=2425675.

49. Dane Strangler and Jordan Bell-Masterson, "Measuring an Entrepreneurial Ecosystem," Kauffman Foundation, 2015, https://www.kauffman.org/-/media/kauffman_org/research-reports-and-covers/2015/03/measuring_an_entrepreneurial_ecosystem.pdf.

50. Endeavor, "The Multiplier Effect," Endeavor, 2019, https://readymag.com/endeavor/multipliereffect/.

51. Bitange Ndemo and Tim Weiss, eds., *Digital Kenya: An Entrepreneurial Revolution in the Making* (London: Palgrave Macmillan, 2017), http://digitalkenyabook.com/.

Conclusion

1. Alistair Barr, "Facebook's China Argument Revealed in Zuckerberg's Hearing Notes," Bloomberg, April 10, 2018, https://www.bloomberg.com/news/articles/2018-04-11/facebook-antitrust-rebuttal-revealed-in-zuckerberg-hearing-notes.

2. "Number of Monthly Active Facebook Users Worldwide as of 4th Quarter 2018 (in Millions)," Statista, 2019, https://www.statista.com/statistics/264810/number-of-monthly-active-facebook-users-worldwide/.

3. "Number of Monthly Active WeChat Users from 4th Quarter 2011 to 4th Quarter 2018 (in Millions)," Statista, 2019, https://www.statista.com/statistics/255778/number-of-active-wechat-messenger-accounts/.

4. Jeff Desjardins, "These Are the World's Largest Tech Giants," World Economic Forum, July 16, 2018, https://www.weforum.org/agenda/2018/07/visualizing-the-world-s-20-largest-tech-giants._

5. Richard Florida and Ian Hathaway, "Rise of the Global Startup City," Center for American Entrepreneurship, nd, http://startupsusa.org/global-startup-cities/.

6. "RIP Good Times," Sequoia Capital, 2008, https://www.sequoiacap.com/article/rip-good-times.

7. Jayson DeMers, "You Can Beat the Next Recession: Here Are 5 Companies That Did Just That," *Entrepreneur*, November 9, 2017, https://www.entrepreneur.com/article/304099.

8. "Downturn, Start Up," *Economist*, January 7, 2012, https://www.economist.com/node/21542390.

9. Anna Hensel, "U.S. Share of Global Venture Capital Fell More Than 20% in 5 Years," *VentureBeat*, October 5, 2018, https://venturebeat.com/2018/10/05/u-s-share-of-global-venture-capital-fell-more-than-20-in-5-years/.

10. Sim Sim Wissgott, "World Population in 2018: Facts and Numbers," CTGN, July 11, 2018, http://bit.ly/388ObyO.

11. Rebecca Fannin, "A New Era Unfolds from Silicon Dragon to Tech Titans of China," *Forbes*, September 8, 2019, http://bit.ly/36U0a3j.

Index

Acknowledgments

As the saying goes, "If you want to run fast, run alone. If you want to run far, run together." This book was made possible by the steadfast support of those running alongside me, and sometimes ahead of me, who helped propel me across the finish line.

First and foremost, thank you to my wife, Shea Loewen Lazarow. She is the reason I began this book, and the reason I finished it. Over the arduous marathon of the writing process, Shea was my constant companion, cheerleader, advocate, thought partner, and editor. Quite simply, this project would not have been possible without her.

Thank you to my family for their strong and enduring support. First to my mother, who taught me as a young child how to structure my thinking, and to whom I credit my proclivity for answering every question in three parts. Thank you to my brother and my father for supporting this project and all my other endeavors. The rest of my family was incredibly supportive, including my uncle Paul who provided invaluable feedback throughout. Special mention also goes to my family-in-law, who have adopted me and my family into their own—and to Wayne Loewen for being the first reviewer to read the manuscript.

My research team was critical to completing this book. Maya Lorey was a fabulous thought partner and pushed my thinking on a number of critical topics, including the impact of highly successful startups and the power of diversity. Nihar Neelakanti was a valued partner on distribution and marketing strategy. I also want to thank Maxwell Harrison, Julia Turnbull, Rushil Prakash, Julie Fukunaga, Paige Preston, and Sandy Lin for their invaluable research assistance.

Carol Franco, my agent, took a chance on me and worked tirelessly to find *Out-Innovate* a great home with Harvard Business Review Press. Carol, along with her husband, Kent Lineback, has been a consistent sounding board for the project, and for that I am endlessly appreciative.

The entire HBR Press team has been fabulous to work with. Thank you first and foremost to my editor, Jeff Kehoe, whose counsel I regularly sought and highly valued on the conception of the book, the framing of the issues I explore, and the book's positioning in the market. I am grateful to Alicyn Zall for her editorial support, Stephani Finks for the beautiful cover, Erika Heilman for leading the marketing of the book, Melinda Merino for her advice on the launch strategy, Allison Peter for shepherding me through production, Betsy Hardinger and Karen Palmer for their copyediting work, and the rest of the Press team for their invaluable support.

Countless friends and colleagues helped shape the critical ideas that propel *Out-Innovate*. Some of the earliest theories germinated with Yuwei Shi, my thoughtful coprofessor at the Middlebury Institute for International Studies, as we dealt with the dearth of material on global entrepreneurship during preparations for our class. Nick Nash, with whom I have collaborated on a number of projects, including the Kauffman Stewardship Pledge (a code of conduct for the venture capital industry), was a superb intellectual sparring partner, and his firm Asia Partners shared valuable research insights. Thank you to Chris Schroder, an early global entrepreneur and storytelling pioneer, for providing regular advice on the book and the publication process and for taking one of the first plunges into the manuscript. Thanks also to Brad Feld and the entire Endeavor team for their thought leadership on startup ecosystem development. Finally, hats off to Austin Arensberg, Emmanuel Smadja, and Mark Meras, consistent discussion partners, brainstormers, and strategists.

Many people took the time to read full and partial manuscripts of the book, and each provided a valuable perspective. Special thanks to Jay Harris, Keith Davies, Tom Barry, Chris Bishko, Mark Palmer, Sanjay Wagle, and Alex Bakir.

A number of people shared ideas or introduced me to people whose stories I could learn from and perhaps tell. This includes Ali Hashmi, Beau Seil, Bill Draper, Catherine Cheney, Chris Sheehan, Chris Yeh, Courtney Guertin, Dan Ariely, Ettore Leale, Jasper Malcolmson, Kate Connally, Rob Lalka, Ed Simnett, David del Ser, Maelis Carraro, Niko Klein, Patrick McKenna, Sangu Delle, Sheel Mohnot, Russ Siegelman, and Zheng Huang. Thank you as well to my entire Kauffman Fellows class, especially Sid Mofya, Dalthon Wright, Jeremy Yap, and Dan Abelon.

It is essential to acknowledge the formative impact of my colleagues at Omidyar Network, particularly Arjuna Costa, who invited me to join his team of one and immersed me in a world of global innovation, for which I will forever be grateful. Other colleagues at Omidyar Network provided key advice along this journey, including Tilman Ehrbeck, Jenny Johnston, Anamitra Deb, Peter Rabley, and many others. My colleagues at Cathay Innovation helped open my eyes to the European and Chinese ecosystems, and I would be remiss not to thank Denis Barrier, Mingpo Cai, and Simon Wu.

Thank you as well to the Bracken Bower Prize and the teams at McKinsey & Company and the *Financial Times*, notably Dominic Barton and Andrew Hill. Your prize was the catalyst for this project, which otherwise might have proved too daunting to start. The wider Bracken Bower community has provided critical support along the entire life cycle of this project, notably my friends Scott Hartley, Irene Sun, and Mehran Gul.

Over 250 entrepreneurs, investors, and ecosystem builders granted interviews for this book, and I was unfortunately only able to feature a small minority in the text. Thank you to each and every one of you for your time and invaluable insights. You are the backbone of *Out-Innovate*.

Lastly, thank you to all Frontier Innovators—the men and women in the arena. Thank you for what you do, for helping to change the world one venture at a time, and for inspiring the rest of us to dream bigger.

About the Author

ALEXANDRE LAZAROW has spent his career working at the intersection of investing, innovation, and economic development in the private, public, and social sectors. He is a venture capitalist with Cathay Innovation, a global firm that invests across Africa, Asia, Europe, and North America. Previously, Alex worked with Omidyar Network, a philanthropic investment firm that has invested over a billion dollars in hundreds of startups around the world. He has served as a strategy consultant with McKinsey & Company, a financial regulator with the Bank of Canada, and an M&A investment banker with the Royal Bank of Canada.

Alex is an adjunct professor specializing in impact investment and entrepreneurship at the Middlebury Institute of International Studies at Monterey. He is a Kauffman Fellow, CFA Charterholder, and a Stephen M. Kellen Term Member at the Council on Foreign Relations. He earned an MBA from Harvard Business School and a B.Comm from the University of Manitoba.

Alex is a regular columnist with *Forbes*, and his writing has been featured in the *Financial Times*, *Harvard Business Review*, *McKinsey Quarterly*, *TechCrunch*, *VentureBeat*, *Business Insider*, and *Insurance CIO Outlook* magazine, among others. He speaks regularly on global innovation trends and has presented at Collision, Endeavor, InsureTech Connect, Harvard Business School, the Social Innovation Summit, SOCAP, and the Corporate Venture Capital Summit.

He lives with his family in the San Francisco Bay area.